Moriarty

THE LAZARUS TREE

Writer: **Daniel Corey**

Artist: **Anthony Diecidue** (pages 5-55, 76-126)
Color (pages 55-76, 103-126)

Artist: **Mike Vosburg** (pages 56-75)
Layouts (pages 31-52)

Colors: **Perry Freeze**
(pages 5-52, 79-100)

Letters and Design: **Dave Lanphear**

Based on characters created by
Sir Arthur Conan Doyle

www.professorjamesmoriarty.com
www.twitter.com/dangerkatt
info@dangerkatt.com

DANGERKATT
CREATIVE STUDIO

IMAGE COMICS, INC.

Robert Kirkman - chief operating officer
Erik Larsen - chief financial officer
Todd McFarlane - president
Marc Silvestri - chief executive officer
Jim Valentino - vice-president

Eric Stephenson - publisher
Todd Martinez - sales & licensing coordinator
Jennifer de Guzman - pr & marketing director
Branwyn Bigglestone - accounts manager
Emily Miller - administrative assistant
Jamie Parreno - marketing assistant
Sarah deLaine - events coodinator
Kevin Yuen - digital rights coordinator
Tyler Shainline - production manager
Drew Gill - art director
Jonathan Chan - senior production artist
Monica Garcia - production artist
Vincent Kukua - production artist
Jana Cook - production artist
www.imagecomics.com

MORIARTY Volume 2.
ISBN: 978-1-60706-490-9

International Rights Representative: Christine Meyer (christine@gfloystudio.com)

THE STRAND MAGAZINE.
Vol. 2 September, 1914 No. 1

Our Time in Burma.

How we found a couple of guys that are completely obsessed with

PROFESSOR JAMES MORIARTY.

By Tim Powers and Sax Carr.

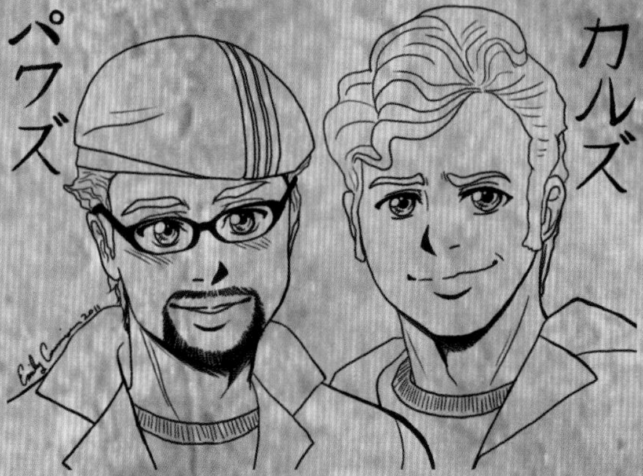
パフズ
カルズ

We were lucky. It was a fortunate set of coincidences that put us in contact with these two unknown comic creators, but we are glad it happened.

As critics, we are bombarded by books from big publishers, small publishers, self publishers and no publishers asking us to "mention" their book on our podcast "Fandom Planet." When we started the show, we agreed that we would only review the books we (or at least one of us) liked. There are several books that we have quietly ignored or never mentioned.

Tim's wife, Kelley, introduced us to her friend Daniel Corey, who was promoting his book "The Prophet." Kelley is not a comics fan and, at the time, didn't know a Ditko from a DeCarlo, but she knew Daniel was "a sweet guy" and suggested we take a look at the book.

Daniel sent us digital copies of "The Prophet" and what would eventually become the first arc of "Moriarty" and we fell in love with their work. With "Moriarty," Tim was especially enchanted by the spectacular artwork of ANTHONY DIECIDUE. Sax got more into Daniel's writing. We both loved the story arc and had to get these guys on the show as soon as possible. Within a couple days, Anthony and Daniel were in the studio nervously hoping someone would take an interest in their work.

"Moriarty: The Dark Chamber #1" hit the stands not long after we published our audio interview with Daniel and Anthony and we watched the issue sell out all over Los Angeles. The Wednesday it was released, Tim walked into Hi-De-Ho Comics in Santa Monica and the issue was sold out by 3PM and there was already a list for back-orders. Other comic shops around town reported similar news.

Then the reviews started coming in. The usual suspects had wonderful things to say about the book. Mainstream press, however, got in touch with Daniel and in a USA TODAY article, readers were treated to a combination of the very powerful talent combination in the book and Daniel Corey's personal charm, which opened the book to a whole new audience.

Subsequent issues had the same amount of heat. Increasingly large orders from every store in the greater Hollywood area weren't capable of preventing sell-out after sell-out.

"Moriarty: The Dark Chamber" was a hit. We felt like we had discovered, maybe not The Beatles, but maybe the Dave Clark Five, and we knew that the DangerKatt boys had a hit and the potential for more.

You are holding in your hands a collection of the second arc of the story, "Moriarty: The Lazurus Tree," which features not only the exceptional writing and characterization of Daniel Corey and the eye popping, dynamic art of Anthony Diecidue, but also an amazing "flashback" scene featuring the artwork of Mike Vosburg. Daniel, being a big fan of the spaghetti Western film genre, understands the concept of a proper flashback and Vosburg's art is a wonderful compliment (icing on an already sweet cake, if you will) to Anthony's.

We at Fandom Planet don't claim to have discovered the DangerKatt boys. Their collective and individual talents speaks for themselves and their storytelling is among the best crop of 21st century comics on the racks. We are, however, proud to be among the first to publicize this amazing work and honored that Daniel asked us to write the foreword for this, the second collection of stories.

We will always have a deep connection to this book, as it was really our first big "find" on Fandom Planet. We were so impressed, we called on Anthony to create our logo, which we must say, we are proud to display as much as we can. Still, we will always have a subtle smile of pride as we see Moriarty issues in our local brick and mortar comic shop. It's wonderful to have found something so embryonic and watch it grown into something even greater. It may not be too late for you to grab a piece of that feeling yourselves. After all, this is just the 2nd trade.

If this is your first time reading these stories, enjoy them. You are in for a treat. If you are re-reading, welcome back, old friend.

Oh... and if you are interested in what we may find next, you can always listen to our show at TheFandomPlanet.com. It's more than worth your time, if we do say so ourselves. Be assured that you can trust our opinions, after all, we LOVED this book. That has to count for something. Further, you can hear actual interviews with Daniel and Anthony discussing their books, their influences, their styles, even their friendship on more than one great episode of Fandom Planet where the boys were guests.

Los Angeles stand-up comedians, writers and podcast hosts **Tim Powers** and **Sax Carr** are the hosting team for the podcast "Fandom Planet" available on iTunes and at **www.TheFandomPlanet.com**. They can be reached on Twitter **@FandomPlanet** and by email at fandomplanet@yahoo.com.

✿ ✿ ✿

Tim and Sax portrait by Emily Cammisa. EmilyCammisa.com

Fandom Planet logo by Anthony Diecidue. artofant.com

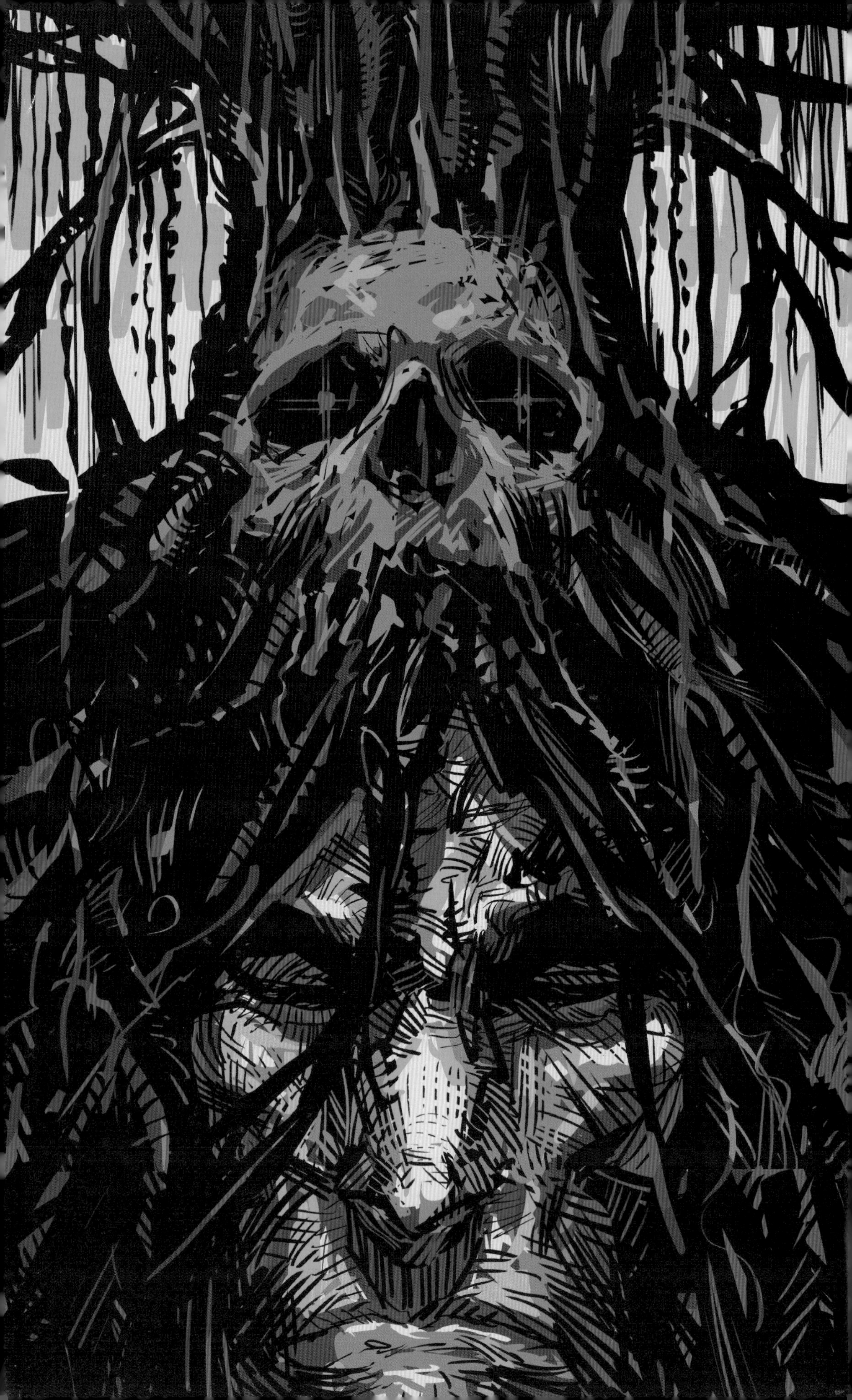

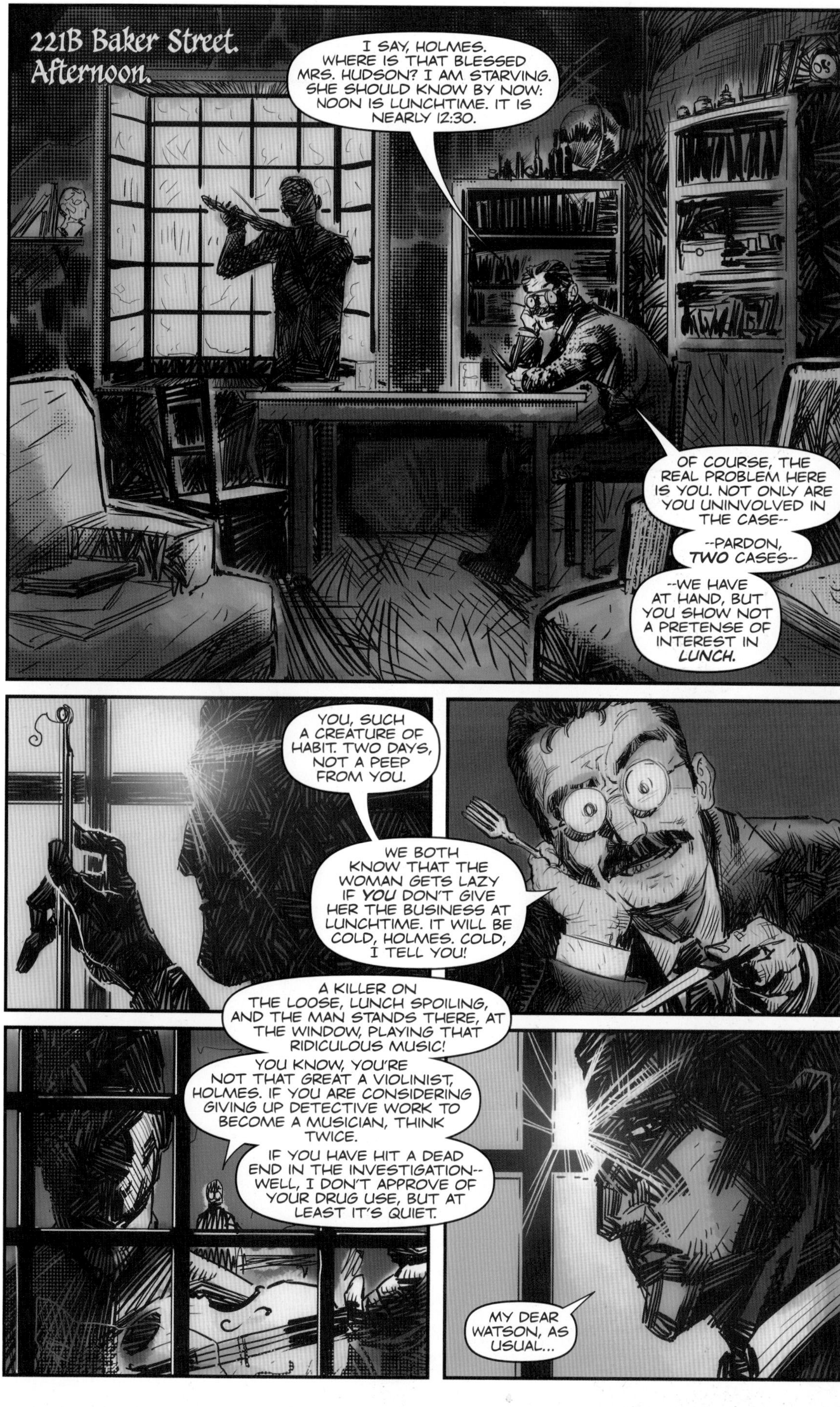
221B Baker Street. Afternoon.
I SAY, HOLMES. WHERE IS THAT BLESSED MRS. HUDSON? I AM STARVING. SHE SHOULD KNOW BY NOW: NOON IS LUNCHTIME. IT IS NEARLY 12:30.
OF COURSE, THE REAL PROBLEM HERE IS YOU. NOT ONLY ARE YOU UNINVOLVED IN THE CASE--
--PARDON, TWO CASES--
--WE HAVE AT HAND, BUT YOU SHOW NOT A PRETENSE OF INTEREST IN LUNCH.
YOU, SUCH A CREATURE OF HABIT. TWO DAYS, NOT A PEEP FROM YOU.
WE BOTH KNOW THAT THE WOMAN GETS LAZY IF YOU DON'T GIVE HER THE BUSINESS AT LUNCHTIME. IT WILL BE COLD, HOLMES. COLD, I TELL YOU!
A KILLER ON THE LOOSE, LUNCH SPOILING, AND THE MAN STANDS THERE, AT THE WINDOW, PLAYING THAT RIDICULOUS MUSIC!
YOU KNOW, YOU'RE NOT THAT GREAT A VIOLINIST, HOLMES. IF YOU ARE CONSIDERING GIVING UP DETECTIVE WORK TO BECOME A MUSICIAN, THINK TWICE.
IF YOU HAVE HIT A DEAD END IN THE INVESTIGATION-- WELL, I DON'T APPROVE OF YOUR DRUG USE, BUT AT LEAST IT'S QUIET.
MY DEAR WATSON, AS USUAL...

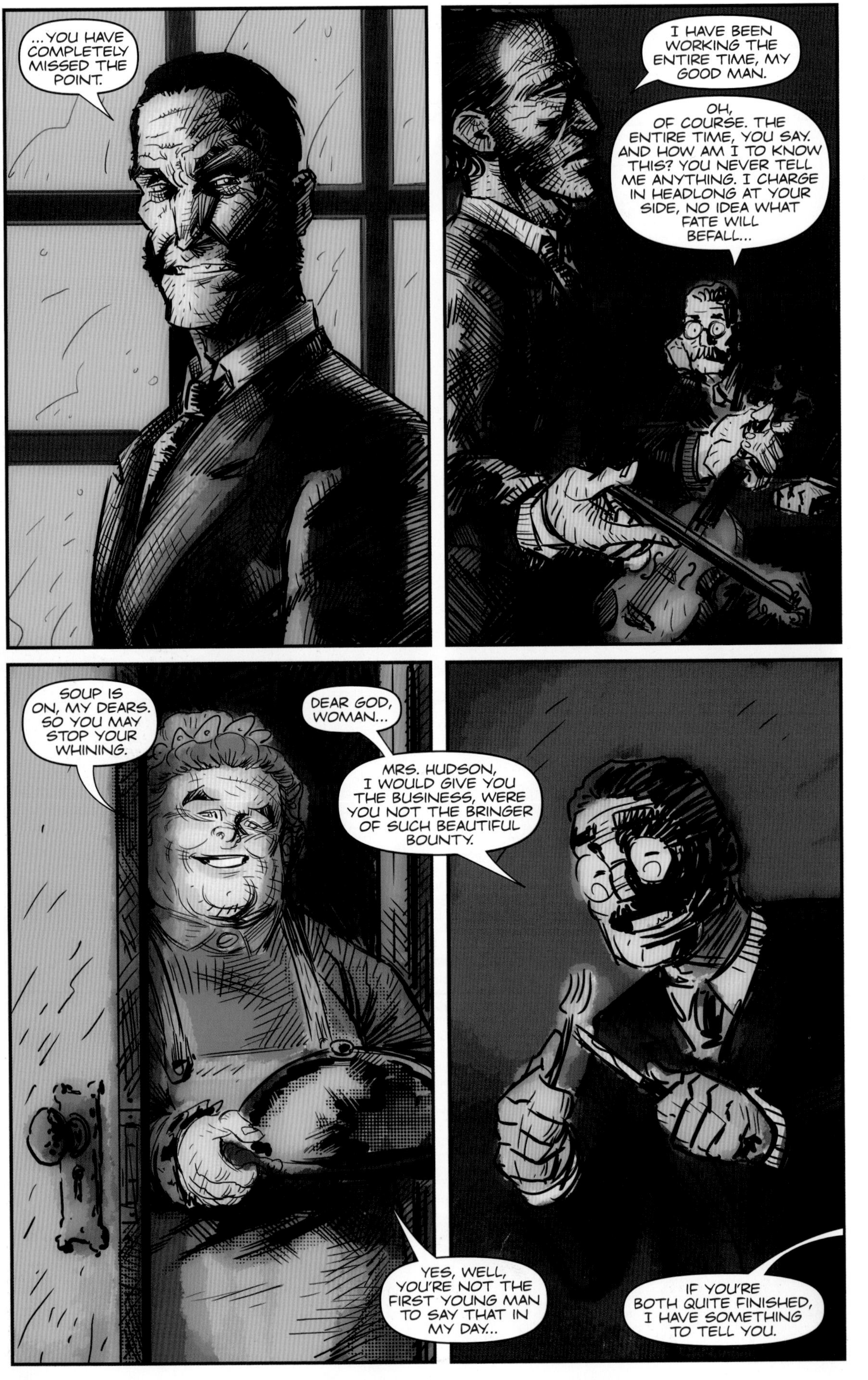
...YOU HAVE COMPLETELY MISSED THE POINT.
I HAVE BEEN WORKING THE ENTIRE TIME, MY GOOD MAN.
OH, OF COURSE. THE ENTIRE TIME, YOU SAY. AND HOW AM I TO KNOW THIS? YOU NEVER TELL ME ANYTHING. I CHARGE IN HEADLONG AT YOUR SIDE, NO IDEA WHAT FATE WILL BEFALL...
SOUP IS ON, MY DEARS. SO YOU MAY STOP YOUR WHINING.
DEAR GOD, WOMAN...
MRS. HUDSON, I WOULD GIVE YOU THE BUSINESS, WERE YOU NOT THE BRINGER OF SUCH BEAUTIFUL BOUNTY.
YES, WELL, YOU'RE NOT THE FIRST YOUNG MAN TO SAY THAT IN MY DAY...
IF YOU'RE BOTH QUITE FINISHED, I HAVE SOMETHING TO TELL YOU.

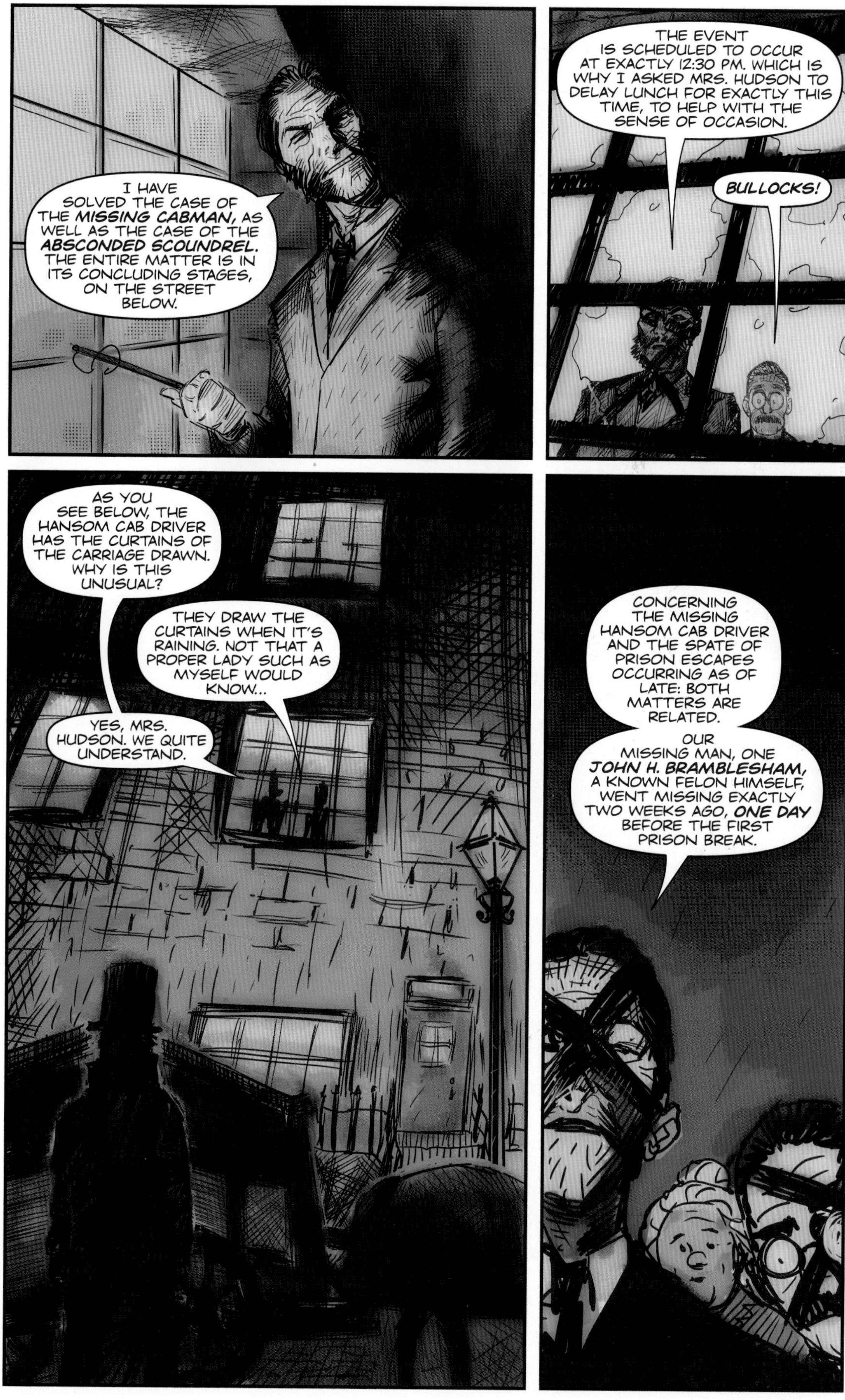
I HAVE SOLVED THE CASE OF THE **MISSING CABMAN,** AS WELL AS THE CASE OF THE **ABSCONDED SCOUNDREL.** THE ENTIRE MATTER IS IN ITS CONCLUDING STAGES, ON THE STREET BELOW.
THE EVENT IS SCHEDULED TO OCCUR AT EXACTLY 12:30 PM. WHICH IS WHY I ASKED MRS. HUDSON TO DELAY LUNCH FOR EXACTLY THIS TIME, TO HELP WITH THE SENSE OF OCCASION.
BULLOCKS!
AS YOU SEE BELOW, THE HANSOM CAB DRIVER HAS THE CURTAINS OF THE CARRIAGE DRAWN. WHY IS THIS UNUSUAL?
THEY DRAW THE CURTAINS WHEN IT'S RAINING. NOT THAT A PROPER LADY SUCH AS MYSELF WOULD KNOW...
YES, MRS. HUDSON. WE QUITE UNDERSTAND.
CONCERNING THE MISSING HANSOM CAB DRIVER AND THE SPATE OF PRISON ESCAPES OCCURRING AS OF LATE: BOTH MATTERS ARE RELATED.
OUR MISSING MAN, ONE **JOHN H. BRAMBLESHAM,** A KNOWN FELON HIMSELF, WENT MISSING EXACTLY TWO WEEKS AGO, **ONE DAY** BEFORE THE FIRST PRISON BREAK.

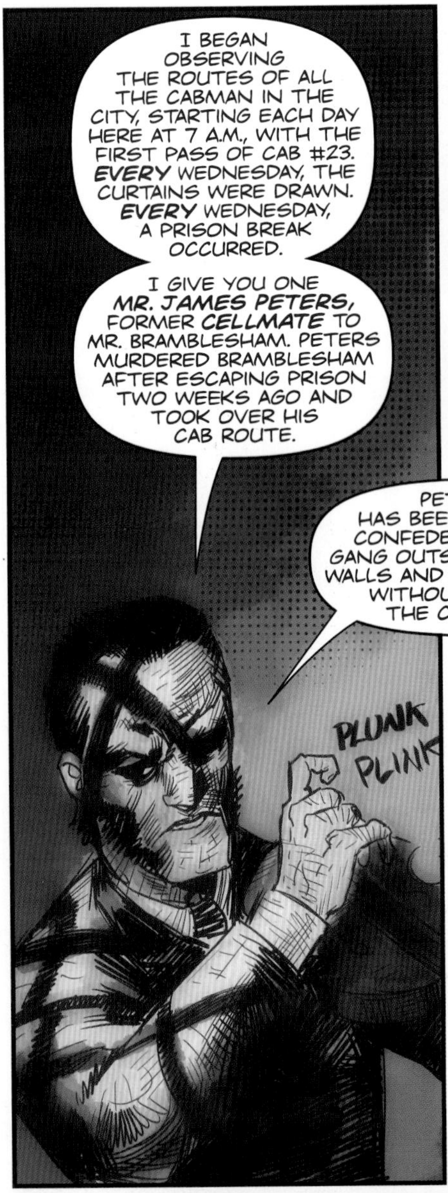
I BEGAN OBSERVING THE ROUTES OF ALL THE CABMAN IN THE CITY, STARTING EACH DAY HERE AT 7 A.M., WITH THE FIRST PASS OF CAB #23. EVERY WEDNESDAY, THE CURTAINS WERE DRAWN. EVERY WEDNESDAY, A PRISON BREAK OCCURRED.
I GIVE YOU ONE MR. JAMES PETERS, FORMER CELLMATE TO MR. BRAMBLESHAM. PETERS MURDERED BRAMBLESHAM AFTER ESCAPING PRISON TWO WEEKS AGO AND TOOK OVER HIS CAB ROUTE.
PETERSON HAS BEEN RETRIEVING CONFEDERATES OF HIS GANG OUTSIDE THE PRISON WALLS AND CARRYING THEM, WITHOUT EVENT, TO THE CITY'S LIMIT.
PLUNK
PLINK

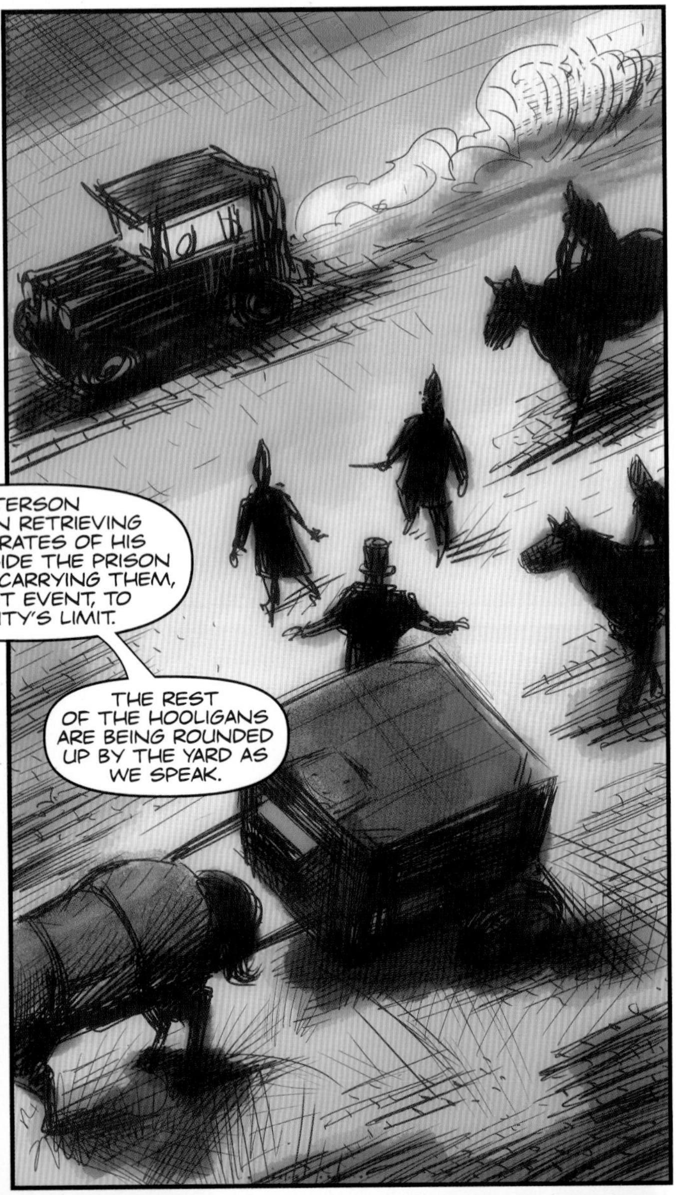
THE REST OF THE HOOLIGANS ARE BEING ROUNDED UP BY THE YARD AS WE SPEAK.

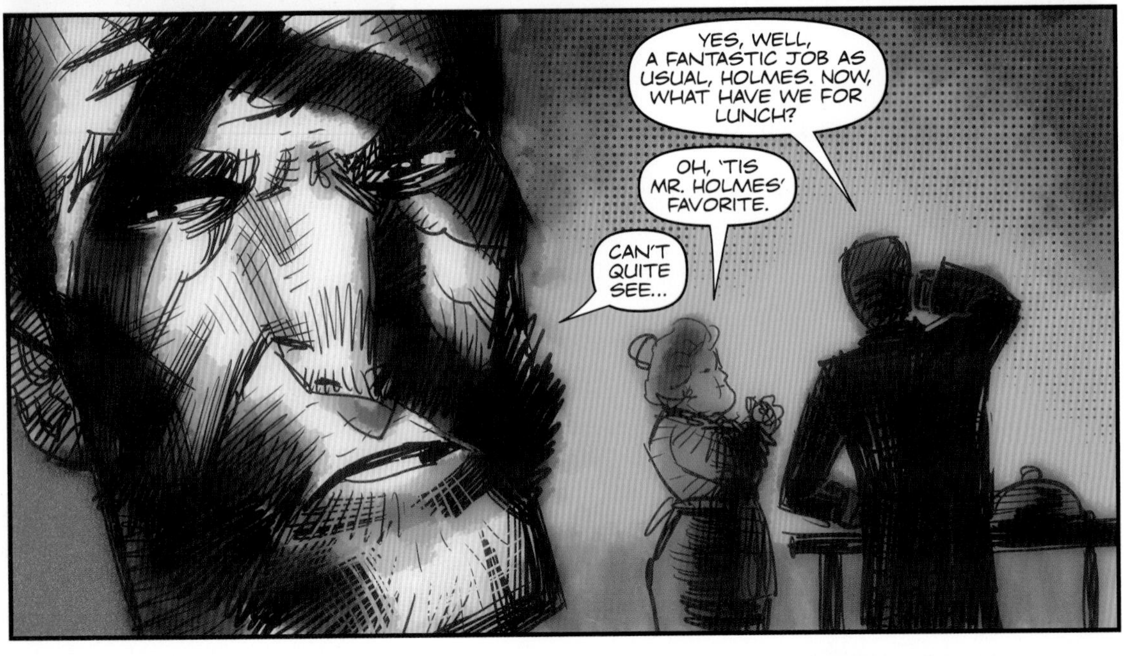
YES, WELL, A FANTASTIC JOB AS USUAL, HOLMES. NOW, WHAT HAVE WE FOR LUNCH?
OH, 'TIS MR. HOLMES' FAVORITE.
CAN'T QUITE SEE...

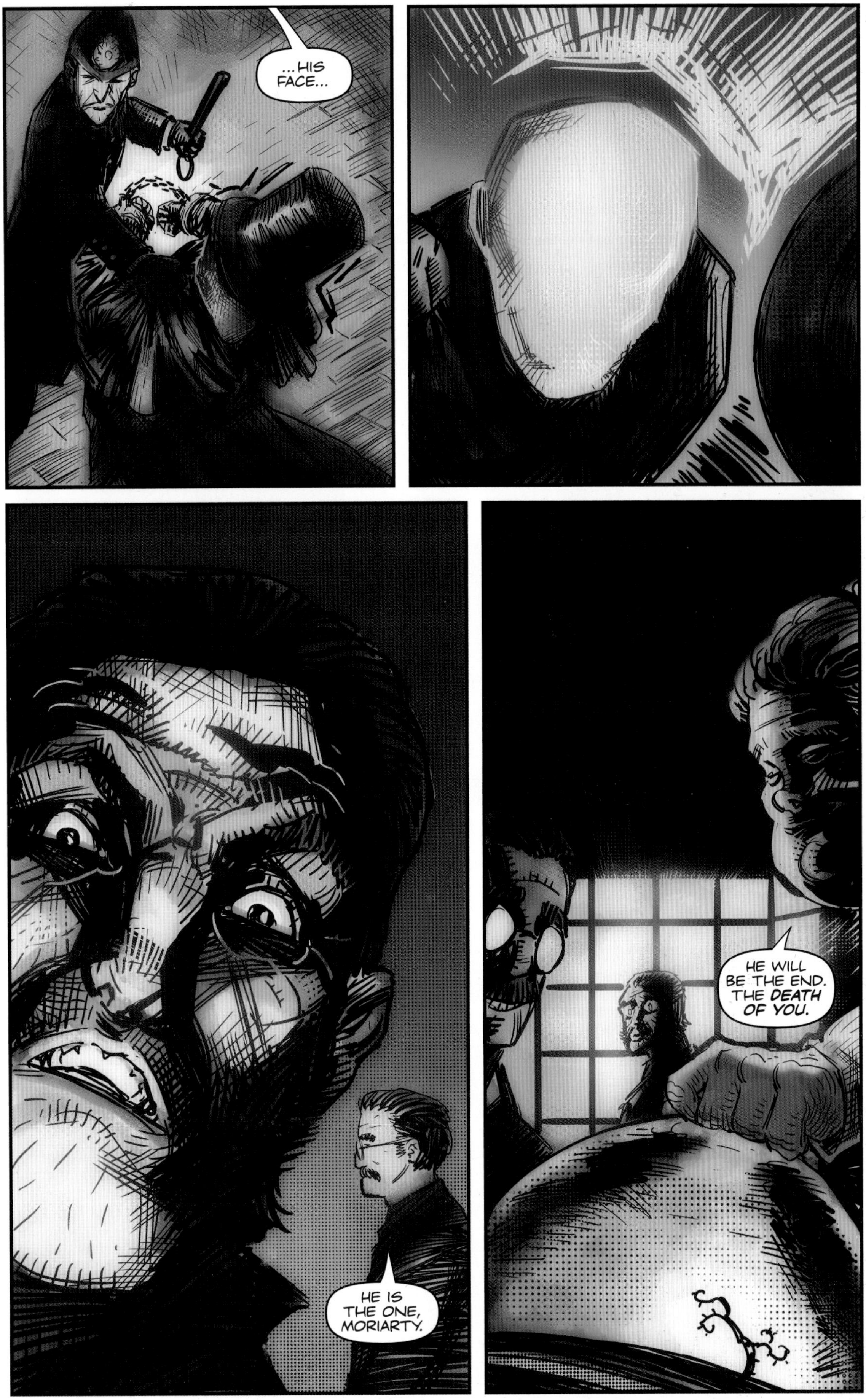
...HIS FACE...
HE IS THE ONE, MORIARTY.
HE WILL BE THE END. THE DEATH OF YOU.

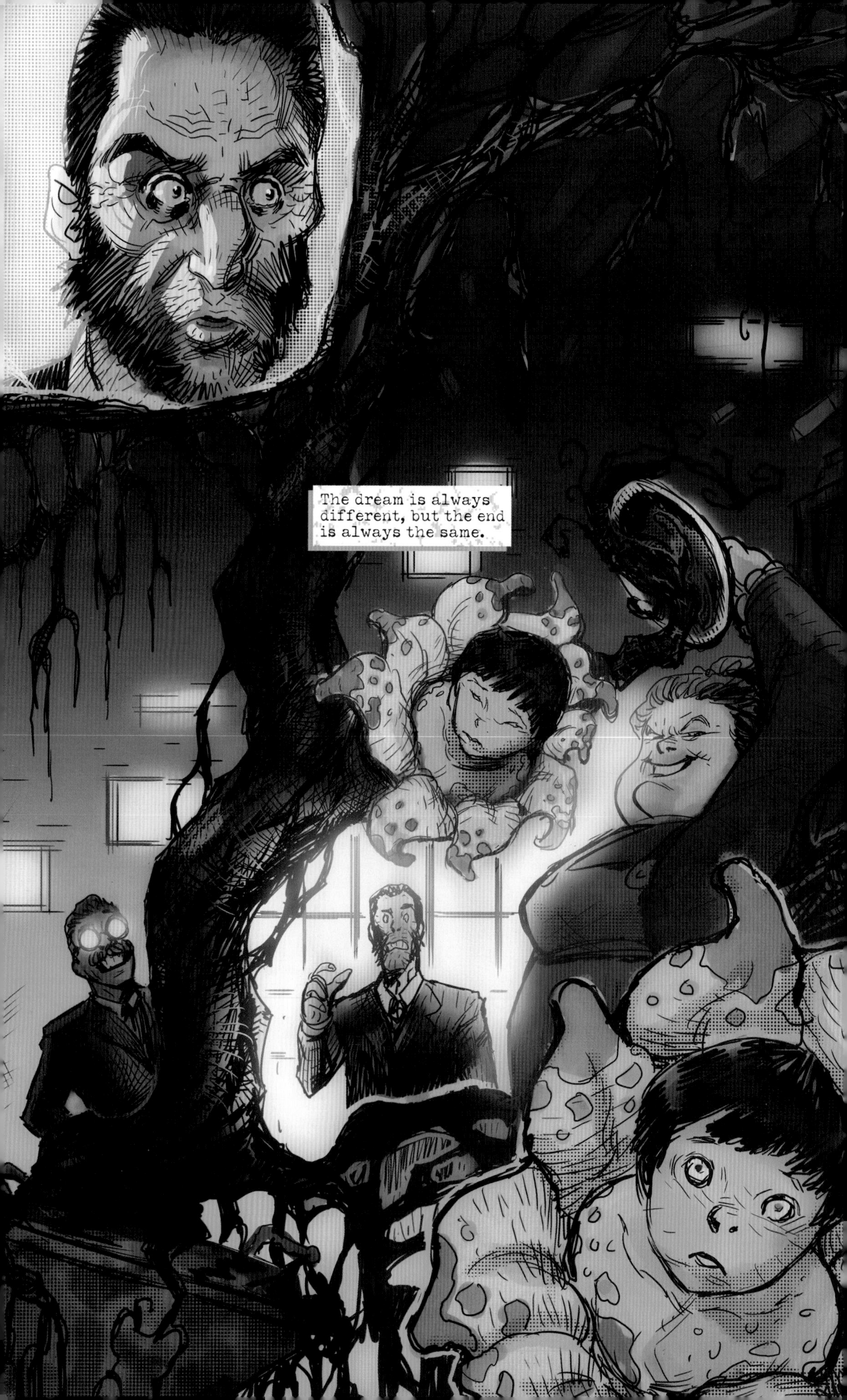
The dream is always different, but the end is always the same.

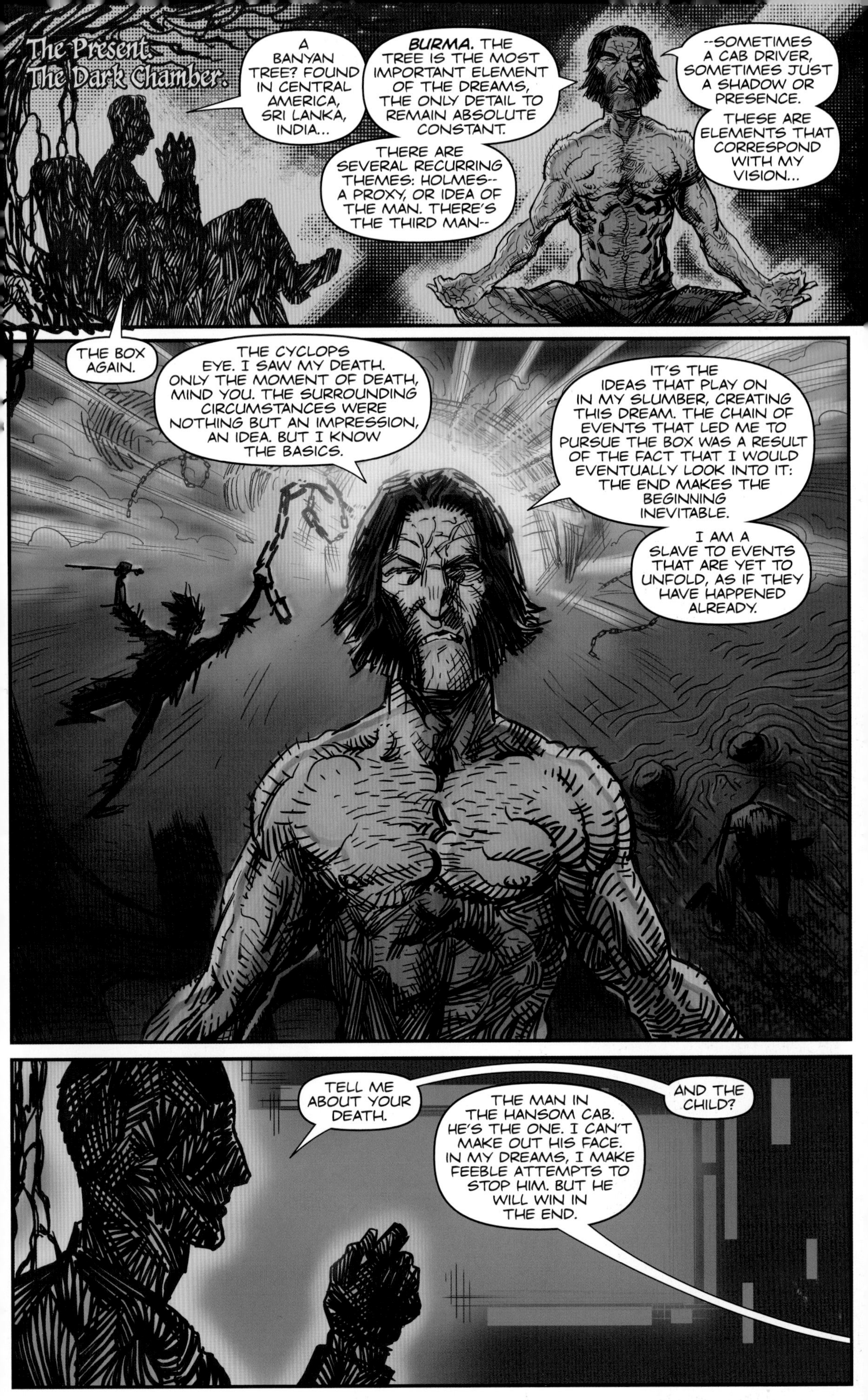
The Present.
The Dark Chamber.
A BANYAN TREE? FOUND IN CENTRAL AMERICA, SRI LANKA, INDIA...
BURMA. THE TREE IS THE MOST IMPORTANT ELEMENT OF THE DREAMS, THE ONLY DETAIL TO REMAIN ABSOLUTE CONSTANT.
THERE ARE SEVERAL RECURRING THEMES: HOLMES--A PROXY, OR IDEA OF THE MAN. THERE'S THE THIRD MAN--
--SOMETIMES A CAB DRIVER, SOMETIMES JUST A SHADOW OR PRESENCE.
THESE ARE ELEMENTS THAT CORRESPOND WITH MY VISION...
THE BOX AGAIN.
THE CYCLOPS EYE. I SAW MY DEATH. ONLY THE MOMENT OF DEATH, MIND YOU. THE SURROUNDING CIRCUMSTANCES WERE NOTHING BUT AN IMPRESSION, AN IDEA. BUT I KNOW THE BASICS.
IT'S THE IDEAS THAT PLAY ON IN MY SLUMBER, CREATING THIS DREAM. THE CHAIN OF EVENTS THAT LED ME TO PURSUE THE BOX WAS A RESULT OF THE FACT THAT I WOULD EVENTUALLY LOOK INTO IT: THE END MAKES THE BEGINNING INEVITABLE.
I AM A SLAVE TO EVENTS THAT ARE YET TO UNFOLD, AS IF THEY HAVE HAPPENED ALREADY.
TELL ME ABOUT YOUR DEATH.
AND THE CHILD?
THE MAN IN THE HANSOM CAB. HE'S THE ONE. I CAN'T MAKE OUT HIS FACE. IN MY DREAMS, I MAKE FEEBLE ATTEMPTS TO STOP HIM. BUT HE WILL WIN IN THE END.

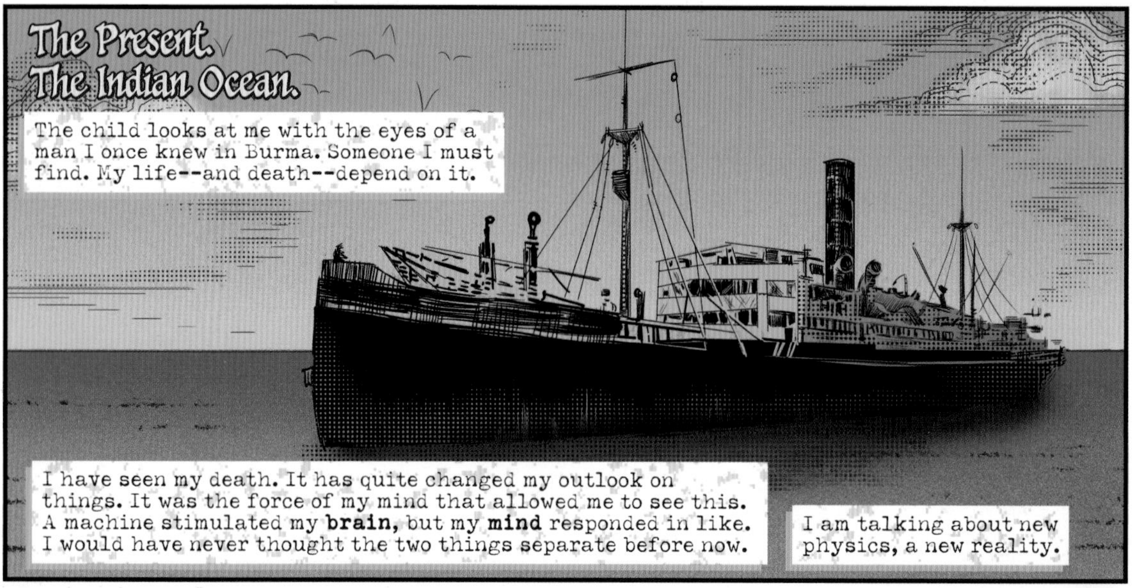
The Present.
The Indian Ocean.
The child looks at me with the eyes of a man I once knew in Burma. Someone I must find. My life--and death--depend on it.
I have seen my death. It has quite changed my outlook on things. It was the force of my mind that allowed me to see this. A machine stimulated my **brain**, but my **mind** responded in like. I would have never thought the two things separate before now.
I am talking about new physics, a new reality.

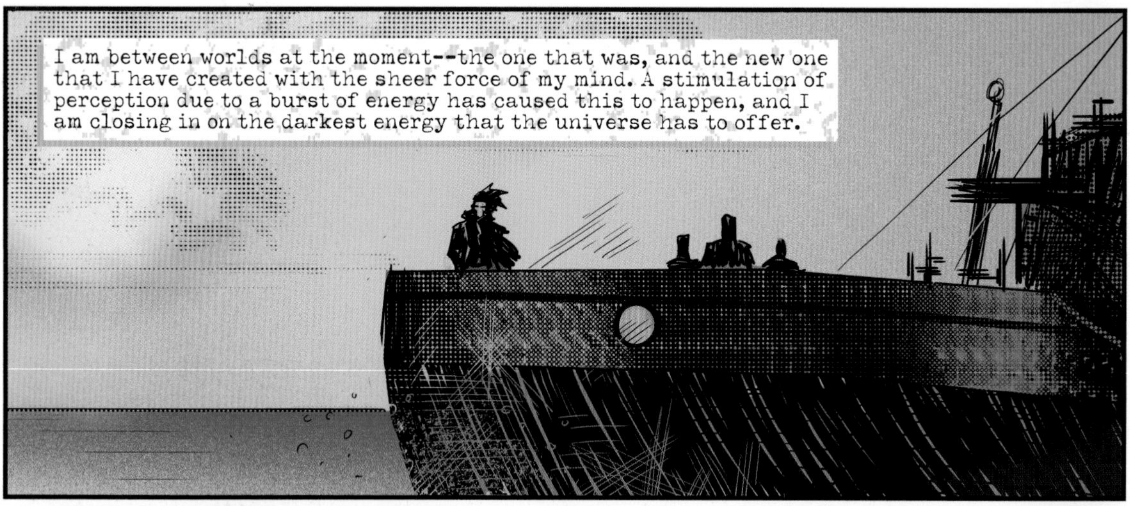
I am between worlds at the moment--the one that was, and the new one that I have created with the sheer force of my mind. A stimulation of perception due to a burst of energy has caused this to happen, and I am closing in on the darkest energy that the universe has to offer.

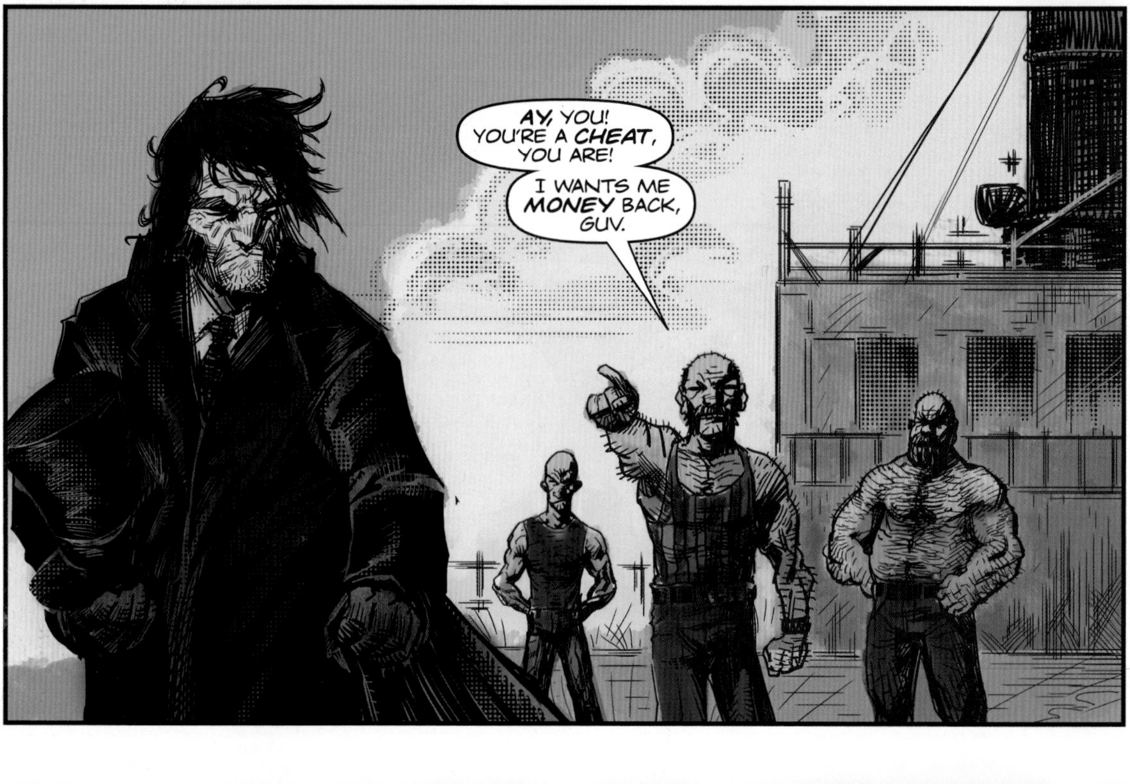
AY, YOU! YOU'RE A CHEAT, YOU ARE!
I WANTS ME MONEY BACK, GUV.

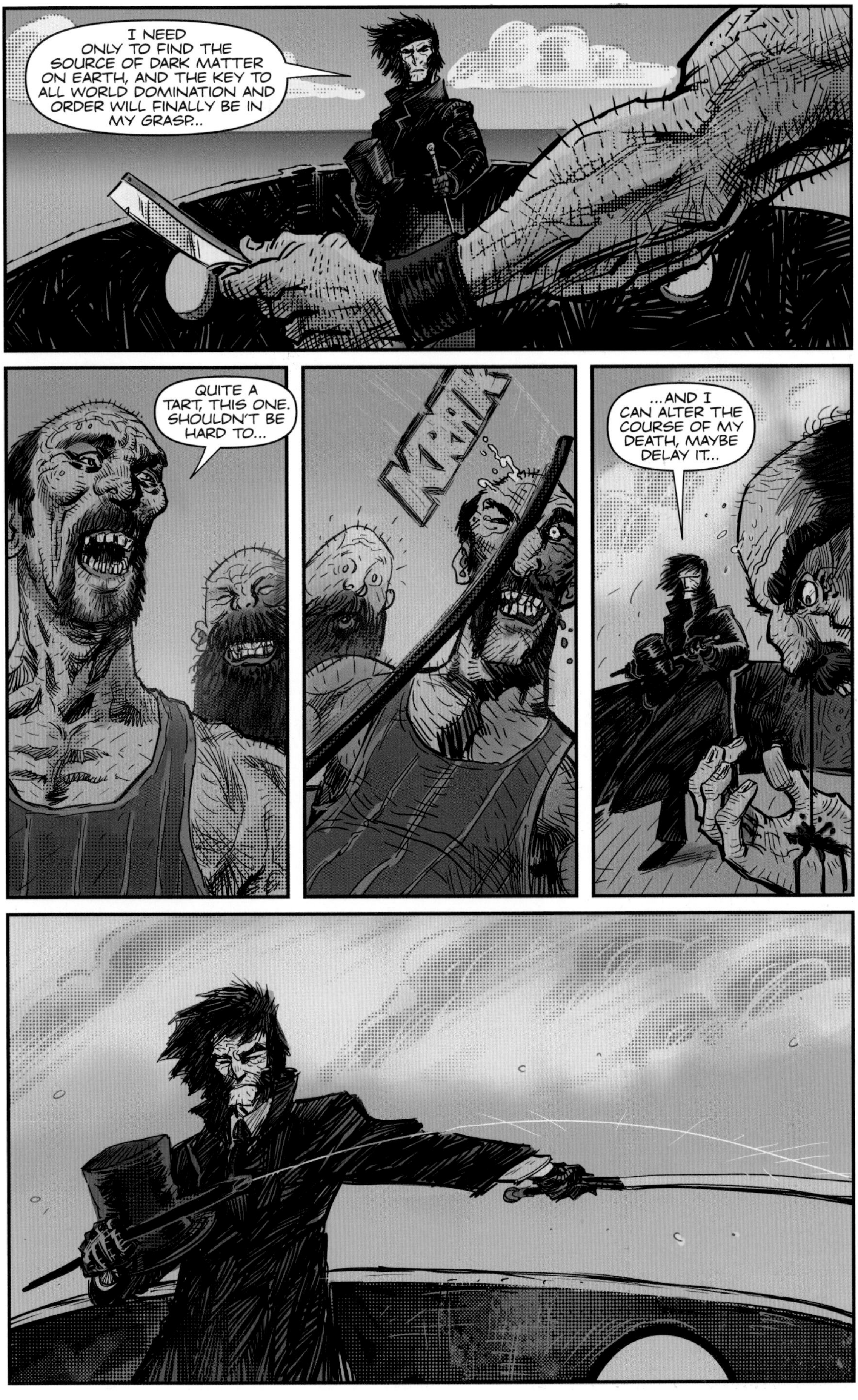
I NEED ONLY TO FIND THE SOURCE OF DARK MATTER ON EARTH, AND THE KEY TO ALL WORLD DOMINATION AND ORDER WILL FINALLY BE IN MY GRASP...
QUITE A TART, THIS ONE. SHOULDN'T BE HARD TO...
...AND I CAN ALTER THE COURSE OF MY DEATH, MAYBE DELAY IT...

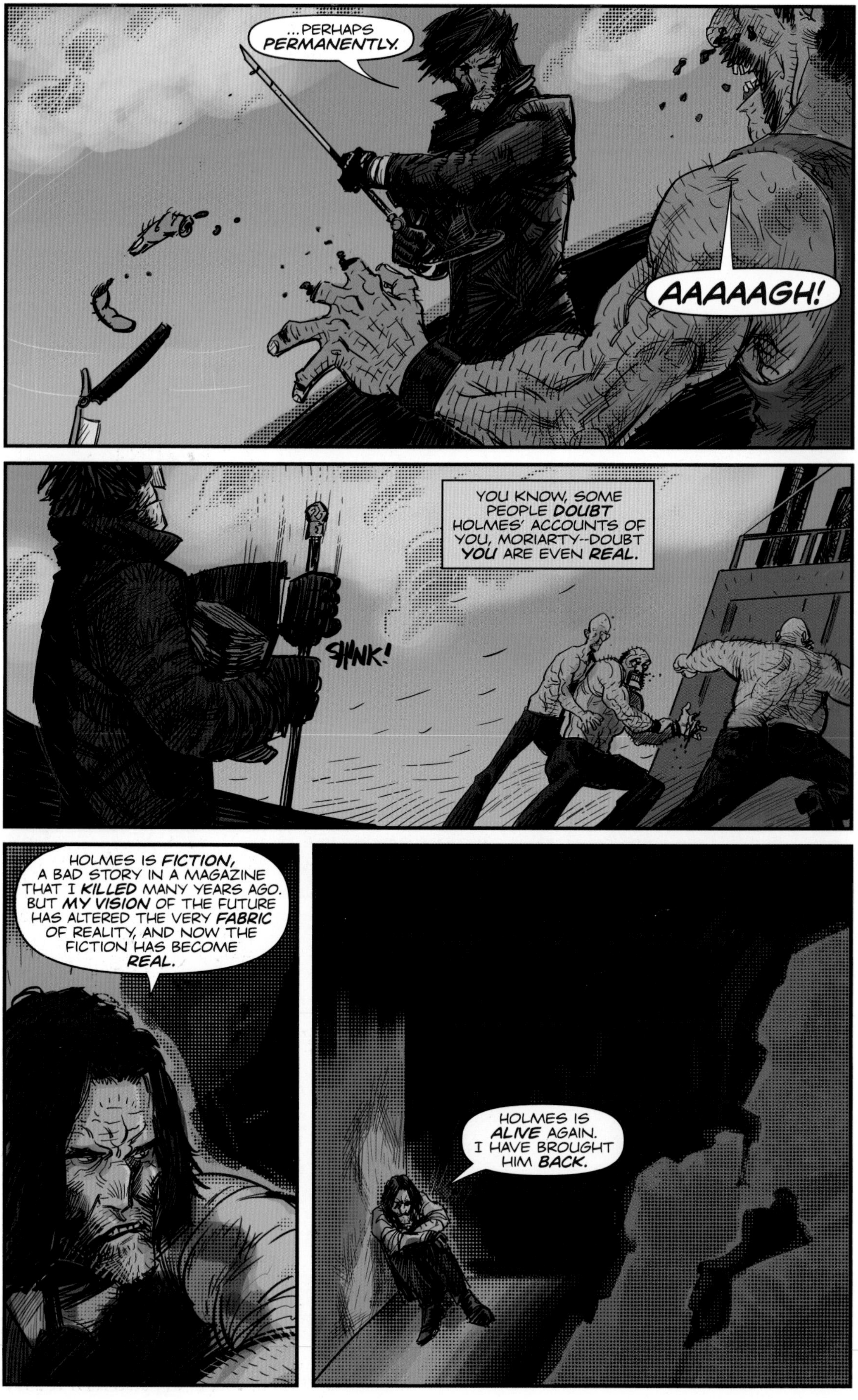
...PERHAPS PERMANENTLY.
AAAAAGH!
YOU KNOW, SOME PEOPLE DOUBT HOLMES' ACCOUNTS OF YOU, MORIARTY--DOUBT YOU ARE EVEN REAL.
SHNK!
HOLMES IS FICTION, A BAD STORY IN A MAGAZINE THAT I KILLED MANY YEARS AGO. BUT MY VISION OF THE FUTURE HAS ALTERED THE VERY FABRIC OF REALITY, AND NOW THE FICTION HAS BECOME REAL.
HOLMES IS ALIVE AGAIN. I HAVE BROUGHT HIM BACK.

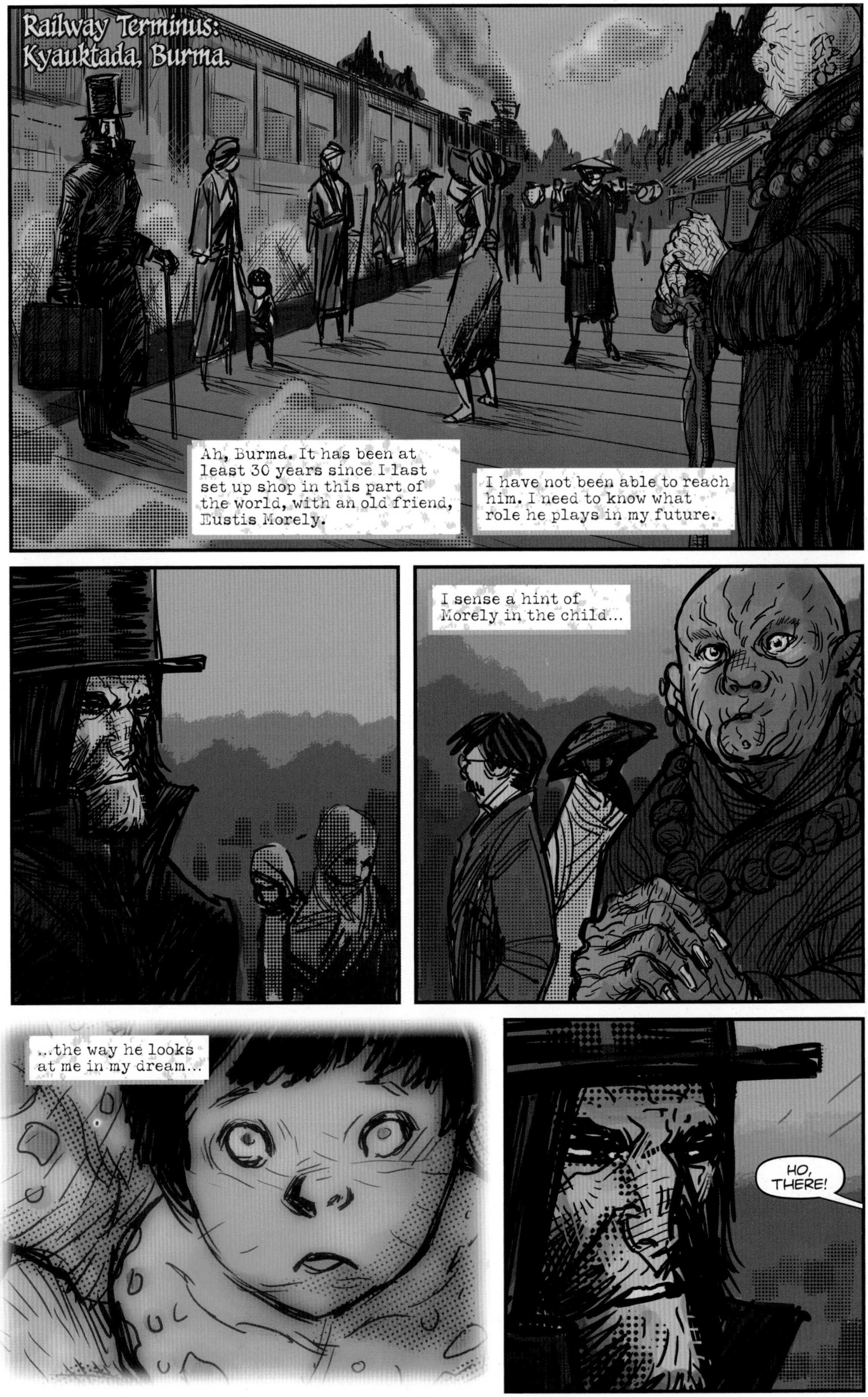
Railway Terminus:
Kyauktada, Burma.
Ah, Burma. It has been at least 30 years since I last set up shop in this part of the world, with an old friend, Eustis Morely.
I have not been able to reach him. I need to know what role he plays in my future.
I sense a hint of Morely in the child...
...the way he looks at me in my dream...
HO, THERE!

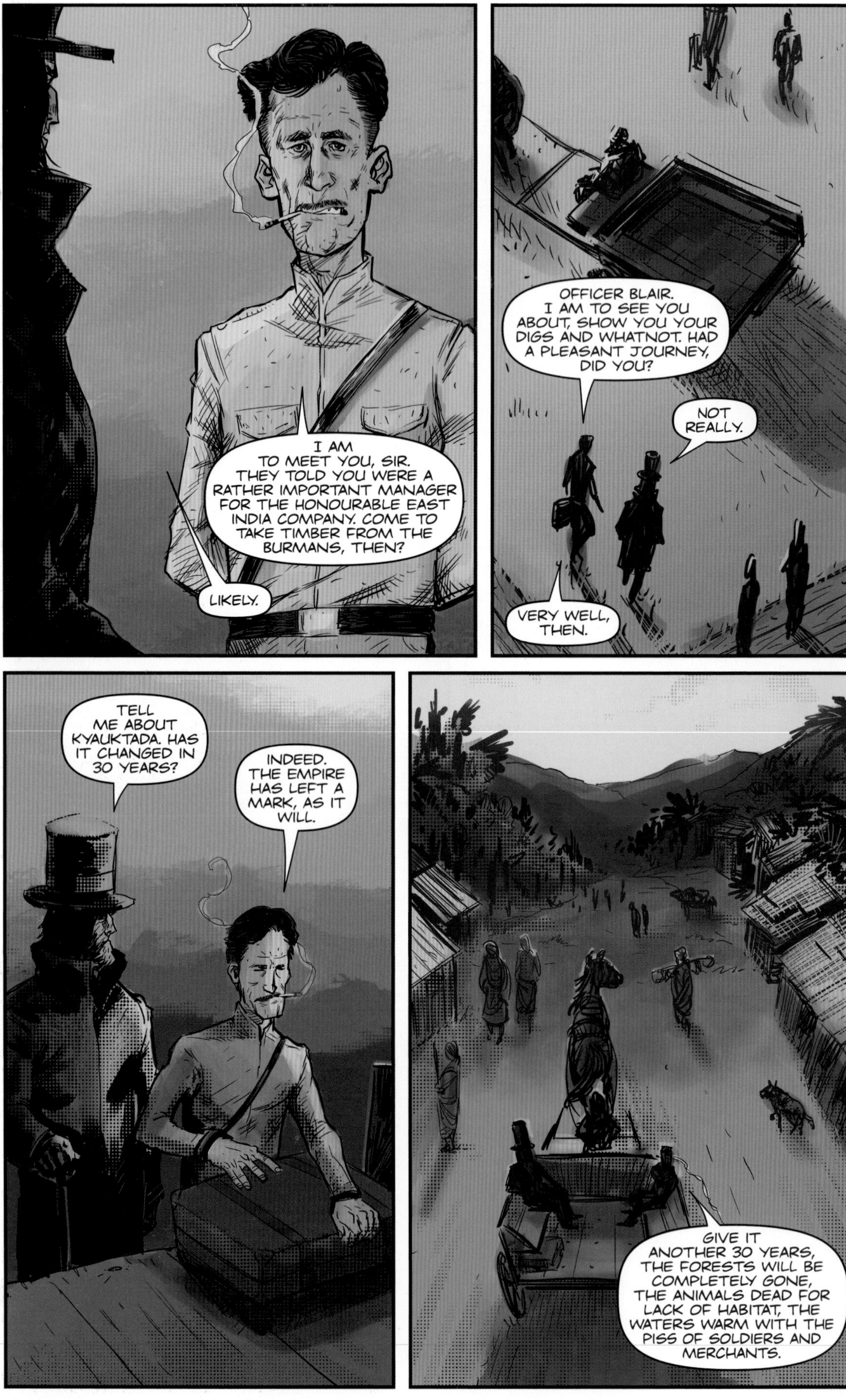
I AM TO MEET YOU, SIR. THEY TOLD YOU WERE A RATHER IMPORTANT MANAGER FOR THE HONOURABLE EAST INDIA COMPANY. COME TO TAKE TIMBER FROM THE BURMANS, THEN?
LIKELY.
OFFICER BLAIR. I AM TO SEE YOU ABOUT, SHOW YOU YOUR DIGS AND WHATNOT. HAD A PLEASANT JOURNEY, DID YOU?
NOT REALLY.
VERY WELL, THEN.
TELL ME ABOUT KYAUKTADA. HAS IT CHANGED IN 30 YEARS?
INDEED. THE EMPIRE HAS LEFT A MARK, AS IT WILL.
GIVE IT ANOTHER 30 YEARS, THE FORESTS WILL BE COMPLETELY GONE, THE ANIMALS DEAD FOR LACK OF HABITAT, THE WATERS WARM WITH THE PISS OF SOLDIERS AND MERCHANTS.

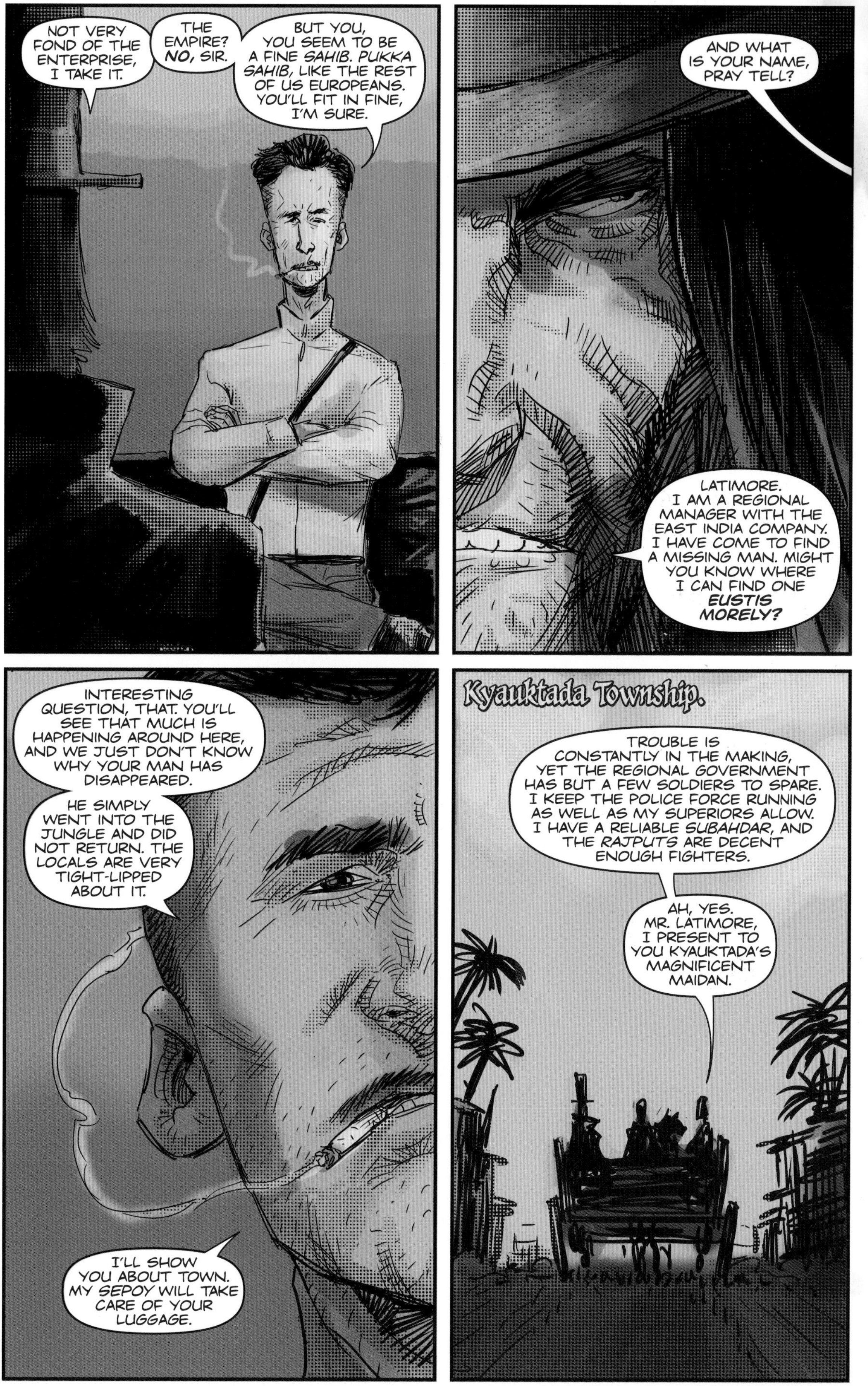
NOT VERY FOND OF THE ENTERPRISE, I TAKE IT.
THE EMPIRE? NO, SIR.
BUT YOU, YOU SEEM TO BE A FINE SAHIB. PUKKA SAHIB, LIKE THE REST OF US EUROPEANS. YOU'LL FIT IN FINE, I'M SURE.
AND WHAT IS YOUR NAME, PRAY TELL?
LATIMORE. I AM A REGIONAL MANAGER WITH THE EAST INDIA COMPANY. I HAVE COME TO FIND A MISSING MAN. MIGHT YOU KNOW WHERE I CAN FIND ONE EUSTIS MORELY?
INTERESTING QUESTION, THAT. YOU'LL SEE THAT MUCH IS HAPPENING AROUND HERE, AND WE JUST DON'T KNOW WHY YOUR MAN HAS DISAPPEARED.
HE SIMPLY WENT INTO THE JUNGLE AND DID NOT RETURN. THE LOCALS ARE VERY TIGHT-LIPPED ABOUT IT.
I'LL SHOW YOU ABOUT TOWN. MY SEPOY WILL TAKE CARE OF YOUR LUGGAGE.
Kyauktada Township.
TROUBLE IS CONSTANTLY IN THE MAKING, YET THE REGIONAL GOVERNMENT HAS BUT A FEW SOLDIERS TO SPARE. I KEEP THE POLICE FORCE RUNNING AS WELL AS MY SUPERIORS ALLOW. I HAVE A RELIABLE SUBAHDAR, AND THE RAJPUTS ARE DECENT ENOUGH FIGHTERS.
AH, YES. MR. LATIMORE, I PRESENT TO YOU KYAUKTADA'S MAGNIFICENT MAIDAN.

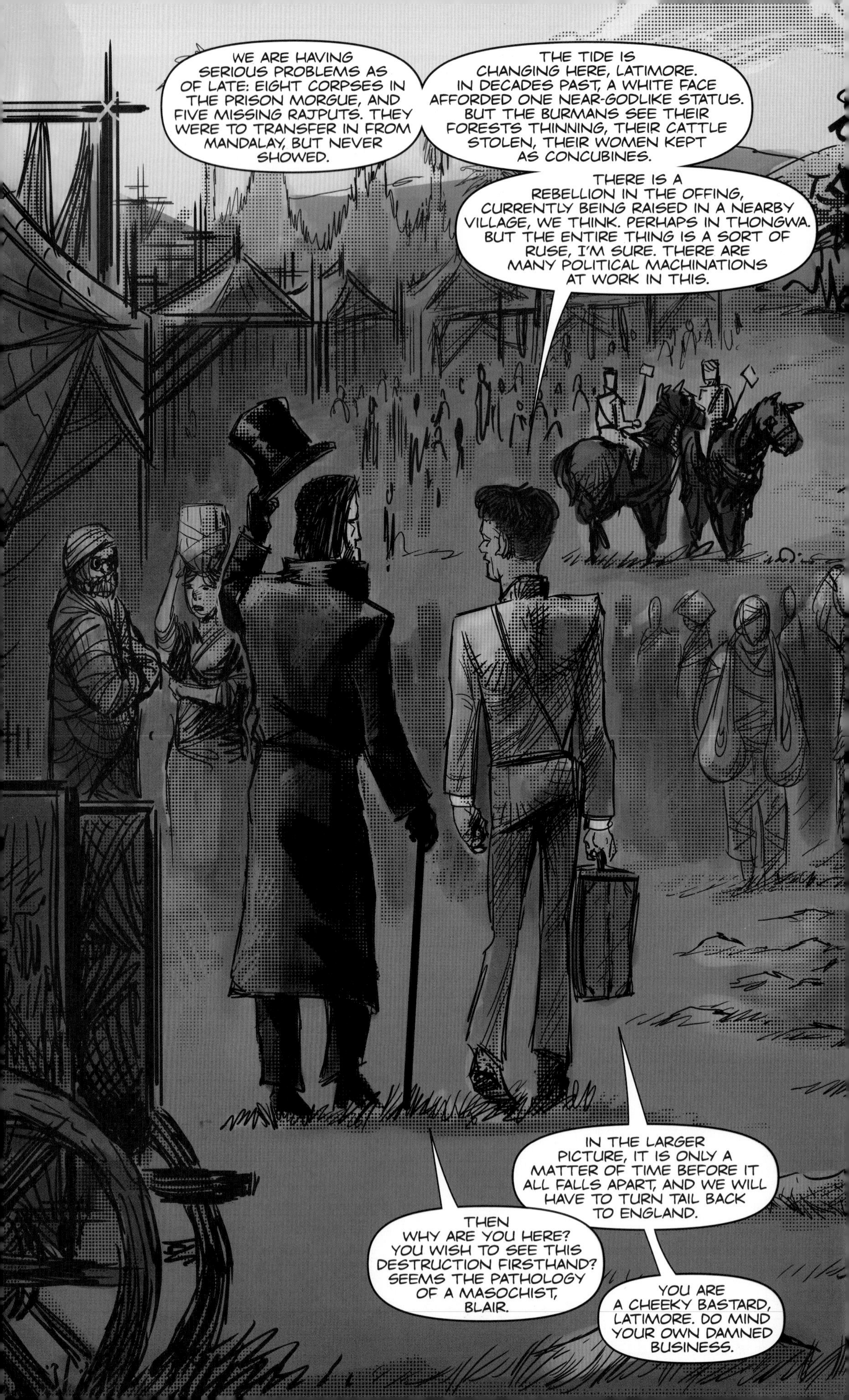
WE ARE HAVING SERIOUS PROBLEMS AS OF LATE: EIGHT CORPSES IN THE PRISON MORGUE, AND FIVE MISSING RAJPUTS. THEY WERE TO TRANSFER IN FROM MANDALAY, BUT NEVER SHOWED.
THE TIDE IS CHANGING HERE, LATIMORE. IN DECADES PAST, A WHITE FACE AFFORDED ONE NEAR-GODLIKE STATUS. BUT THE BURMANS SEE THEIR FORESTS THINNING, THEIR CATTLE STOLEN, THEIR WOMEN KEPT AS CONCUBINES.
THERE IS A REBELLION IN THE OFFING, CURRENTLY BEING RAISED IN A NEARBY VILLAGE, WE THINK. PERHAPS IN THONGWA. BUT THE ENTIRE THING IS A SORT OF RUSE, I'M SURE. THERE ARE MANY POLITICAL MACHINATIONS AT WORK IN THIS.
IN THE LARGER PICTURE, IT IS ONLY A MATTER OF TIME BEFORE IT ALL FALLS APART, AND WE WILL HAVE TO TURN TAIL BACK TO ENGLAND.
THEN WHY ARE YOU HERE? YOU WISH TO SEE THIS DESTRUCTION FIRSTHAND? SEEMS THE PATHOLOGY OF A MASOCHIST, BLAIR.
YOU ARE A CHEEKY BASTARD, LATIMORE. DO MIND YOUR OWN DAMNED BUSINESS.

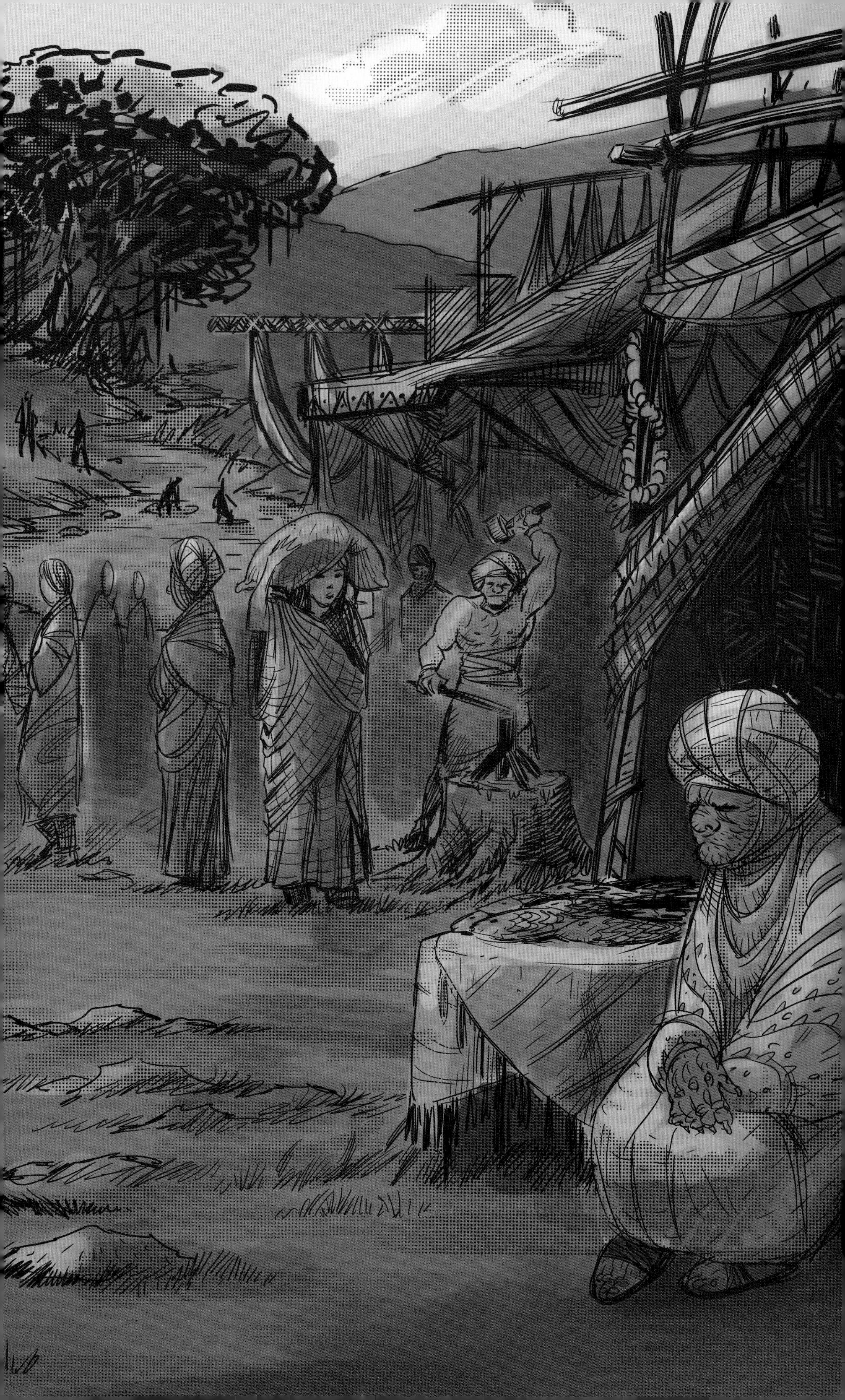

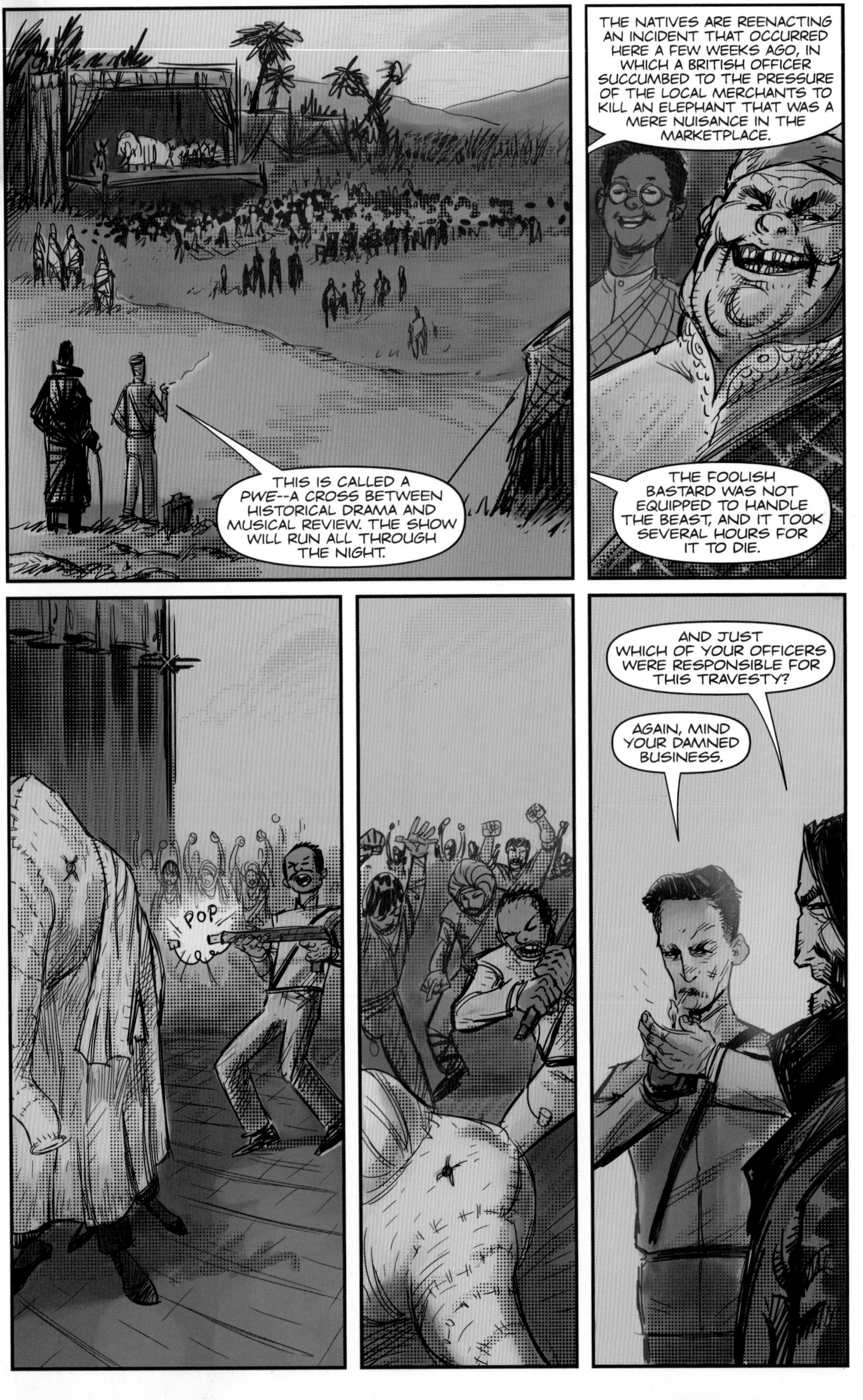
THIS IS CALLED A PWE--A CROSS BETWEEN HISTORICAL DRAMA AND MUSICAL REVIEW. THE SHOW WILL RUN ALL THROUGH THE NIGHT.
THE NATIVES ARE REENACTING AN INCIDENT THAT OCCURRED HERE A FEW WEEKS AGO, IN WHICH A BRITISH OFFICER SUCCUMBED TO THE PRESSURE OF THE LOCAL MERCHANTS TO KILL AN ELEPHANT THAT WAS A MERE NUISANCE IN THE MARKETPLACE.
THE FOOLISH BASTARD WAS NOT EQUIPPED TO HANDLE THE BEAST, AND IT TOOK SEVERAL HOURS FOR IT TO DIE.
POP
AND JUST WHICH OF YOUR OFFICERS WERE RESPONSIBLE FOR THIS TRAVESTY?
AGAIN, MIND YOUR DAMNED BUSINESS.

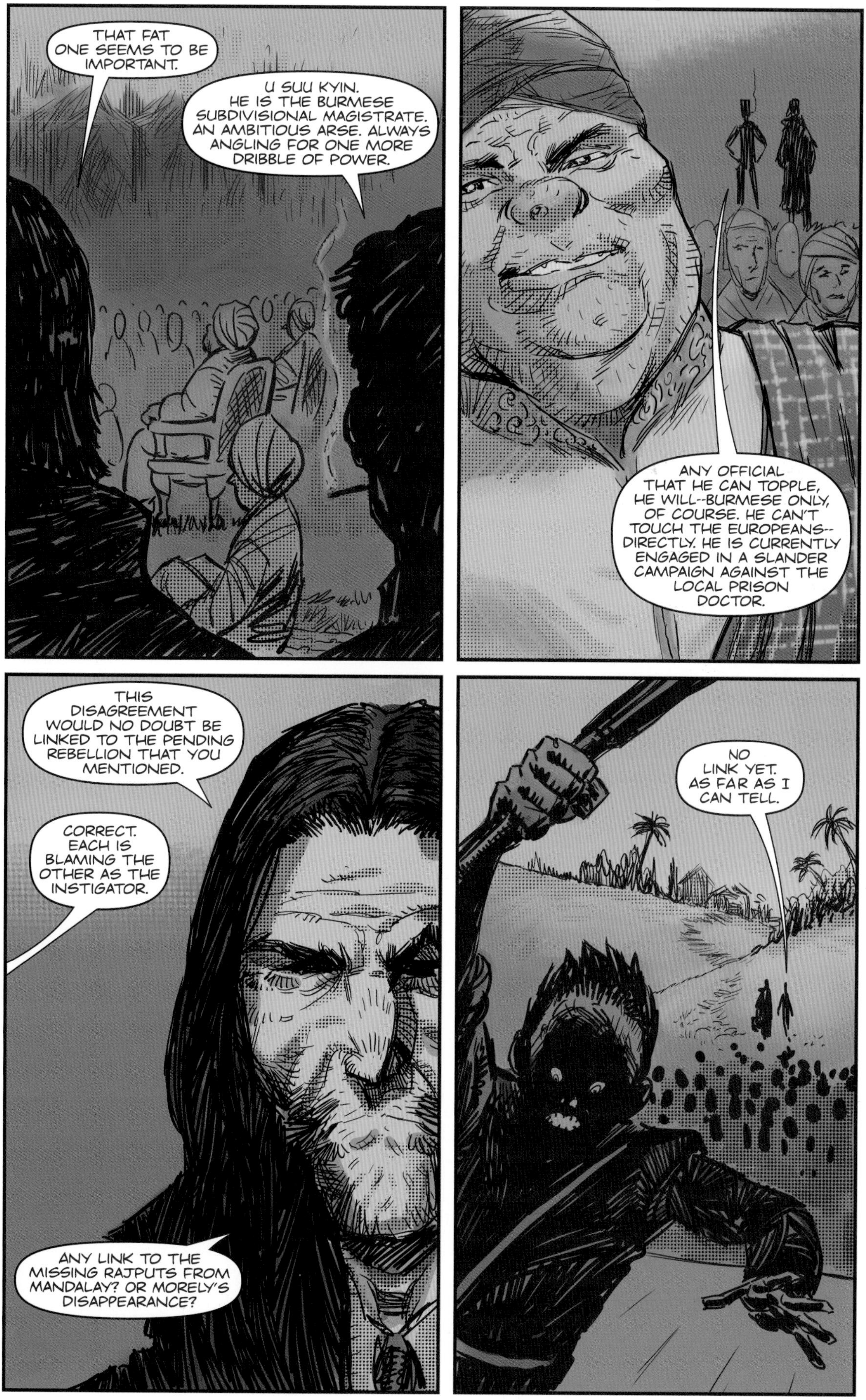
THAT FAT ONE SEEMS TO BE IMPORTANT.
U SUU KYIN. HE IS THE BURMESE SUBDIVISIONAL MAGISTRATE. AN AMBITIOUS ARSE. ALWAYS ANGLING FOR ONE MORE DRIBBLE OF POWER.
ANY OFFICIAL THAT HE CAN TOPPLE, HE WILL--BURMESE ONLY, OF COURSE. HE CAN'T TOUCH THE EUROPEANS--DIRECTLY. HE IS CURRENTLY ENGAGED IN A SLANDER CAMPAIGN AGAINST THE LOCAL PRISON DOCTOR.
THIS DISAGREEMENT WOULD NO DOUBT BE LINKED TO THE PENDING REBELLION THAT YOU MENTIONED.
CORRECT. EACH IS BLAMING THE OTHER AS THE INSTIGATOR.
ANY LINK TO THE MISSING RAJPUTS FROM MANDALAY? OR MORELY'S DISAPPEARANCE?
NO LINK YET. AS FAR AS I CAN TELL.

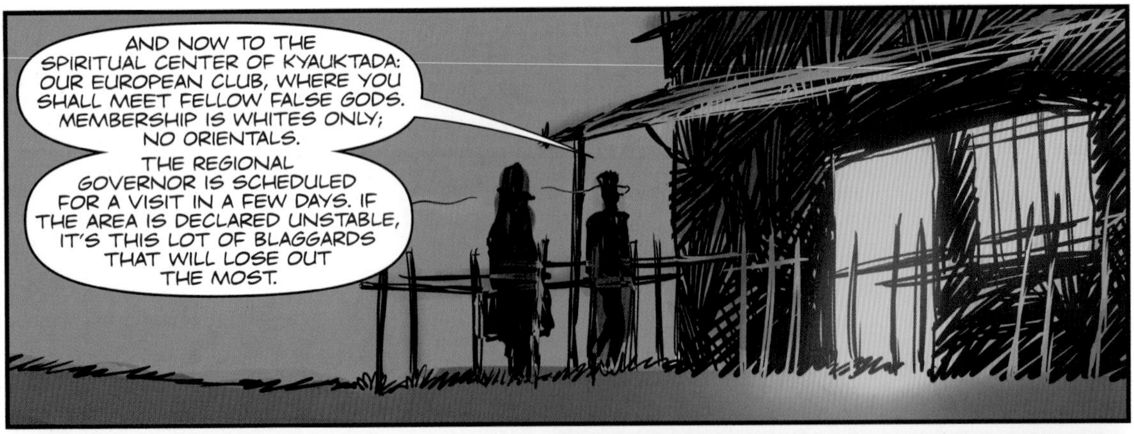
AND NOW TO THE SPIRITUAL CENTER OF KYAUKTADA: OUR EUROPEAN CLUB, WHERE YOU SHALL MEET FELLOW FALSE GODS. MEMBERSHIP IS WHITES ONLY; NO ORIENTALS.
THE REGIONAL GOVERNOR IS SCHEDULED FOR A VISIT IN A FEW DAYS. IF THE AREA IS DECLARED UNSTABLE, IT'S THIS LOT OF BLAGGARDS THAT WILL LOSE OUT THE MOST.

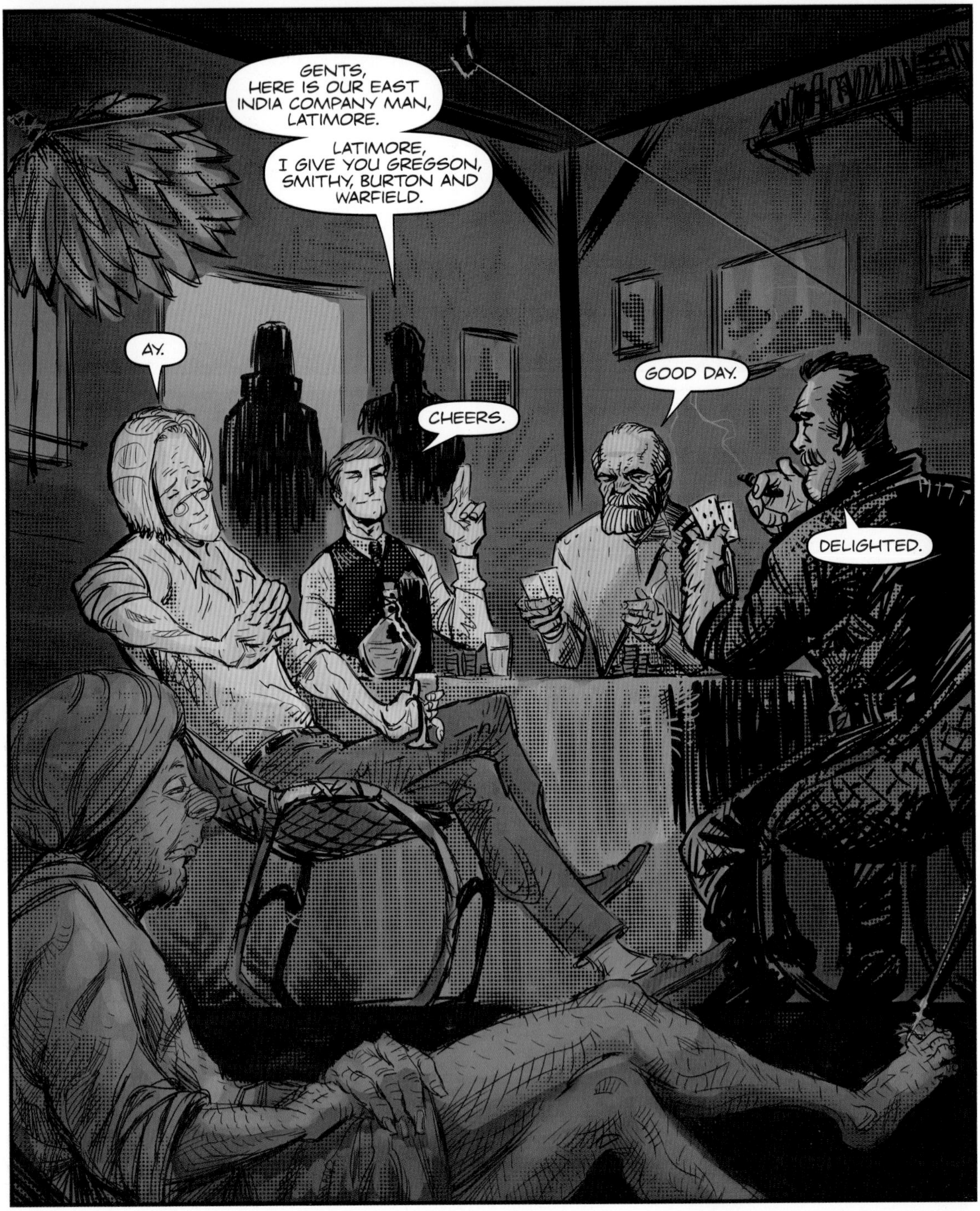
GENTS, HERE IS OUR EAST INDIA COMPANY MAN, LATIMORE.
LATIMORE, I GIVE YOU GREGSON, SMITHY, BURTON AND WARFIELD.
AY.
CHEERS.
GOOD DAY.
DELIGHTED.

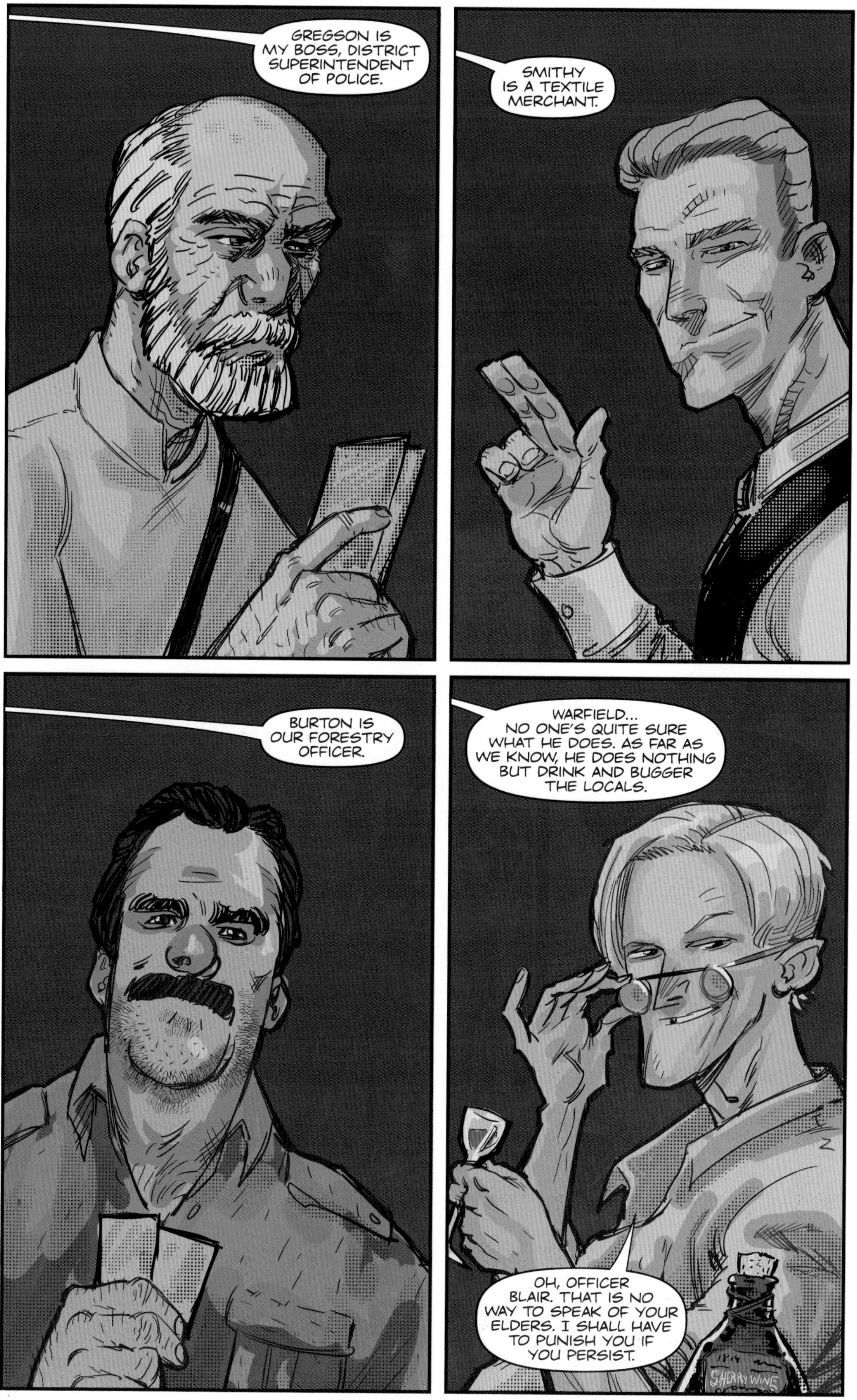
GREGSON IS MY BOSS, DISTRICT SUPERINTENDENT OF POLICE.
SMITHY IS A TEXTILE MERCHANT.
BURTON IS OUR FORESTRY OFFICER.
WARFIELD... NO ONE'S QUITE SURE WHAT HE DOES. AS FAR AS WE KNOW, HE DOES NOTHING BUT DRINK AND BUGGER THE LOCALS.
OH, OFFICER BLAIR. THAT IS NO WAY TO SPEAK OF YOUR ELDERS. I SHALL HAVE TO PUNISH YOU IF YOU PERSIST.
SHERRY WINE

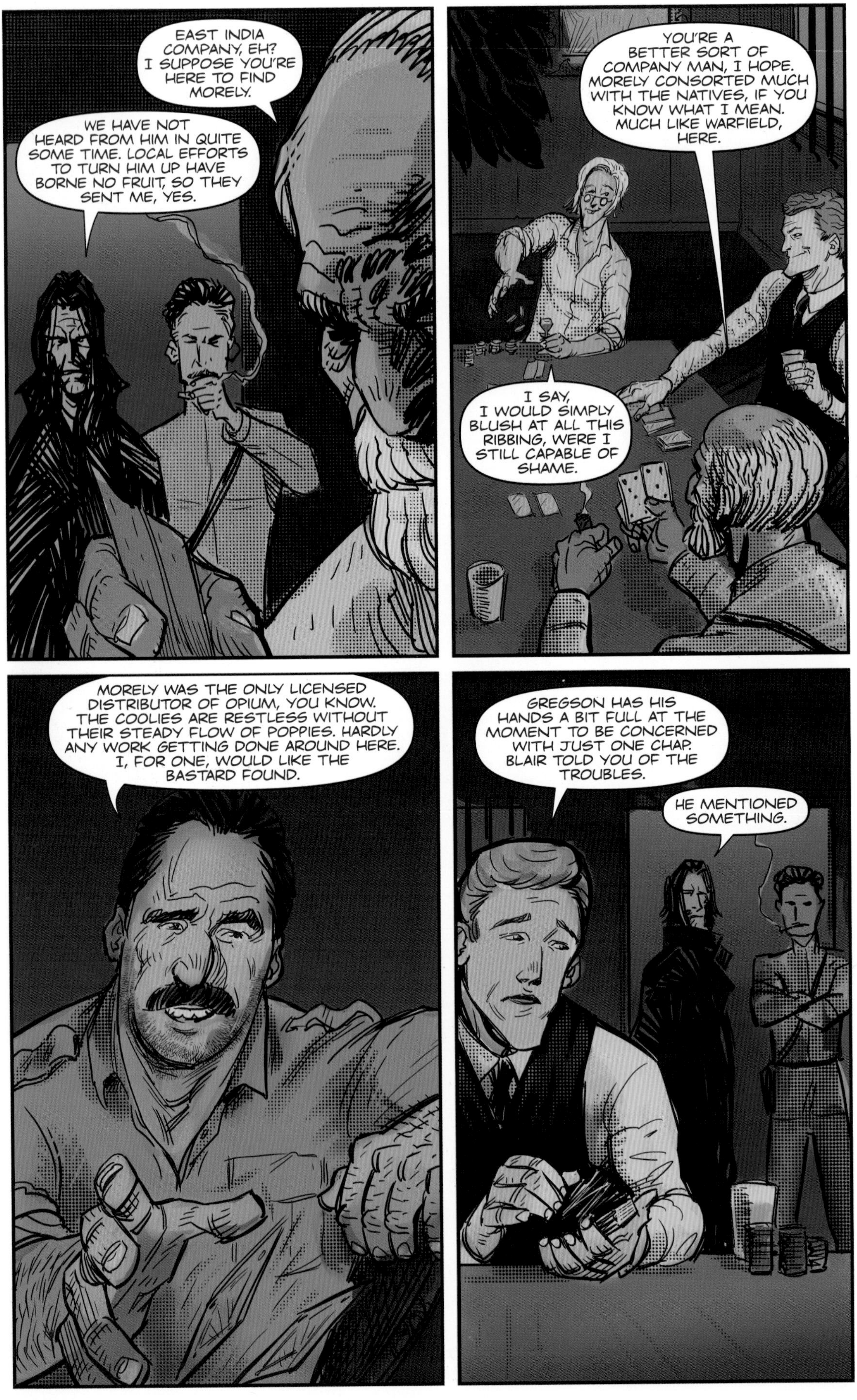
EAST INDIA COMPANY, EH? I SUPPOSE YOU'RE HERE TO FIND MORELY.
WE HAVE NOT HEARD FROM HIM IN QUITE SOME TIME. LOCAL EFFORTS TO TURN HIM UP HAVE BORNE NO FRUIT, SO THEY SENT ME, YES.
YOU'RE A BETTER SORT OF COMPANY MAN, I HOPE. MORELY CONSORTED MUCH WITH THE NATIVES, IF YOU KNOW WHAT I MEAN. MUCH LIKE WARFIELD, HERE.
I SAY, I WOULD SIMPLY BLUSH AT ALL THIS RIBBING, WERE I STILL CAPABLE OF SHAME.
MORELY WAS THE ONLY LICENSED DISTRIBUTOR OF OPIUM, YOU KNOW. THE COOLIES ARE RESTLESS WITHOUT THEIR STEADY FLOW OF POPPIES. HARDLY ANY WORK GETTING DONE AROUND HERE. I, FOR ONE, WOULD LIKE THE BASTARD FOUND.
GREGSON HAS HIS HANDS A BIT FULL AT THE MOMENT TO BE CONCERNED WITH JUST ONE CHAP. BLAIR TOLD YOU OF THE TROUBLES.
HE MENTIONED SOMETHING.

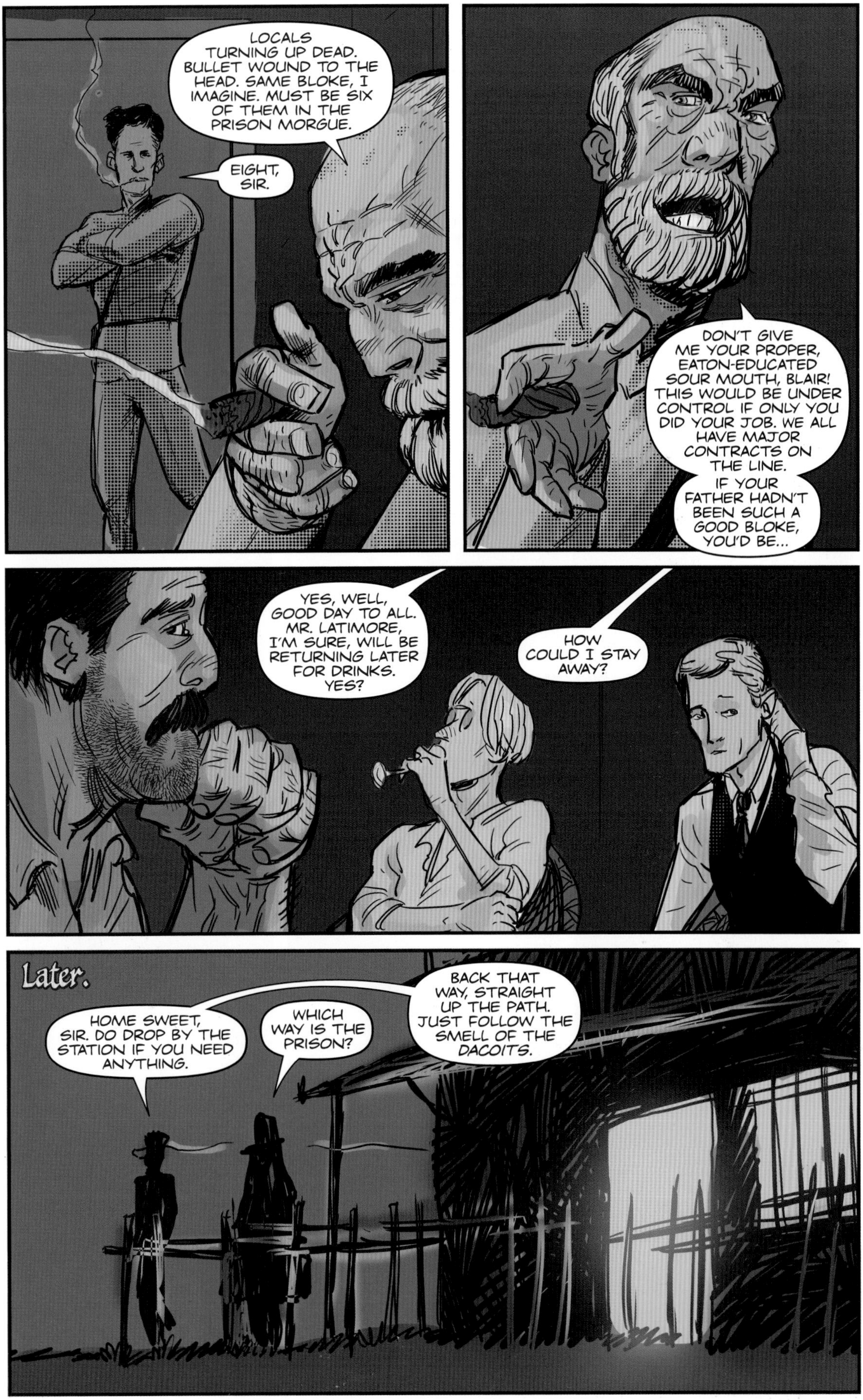
LOCALS TURNING UP DEAD. BULLET WOUND TO THE HEAD. SAME BLOKE, I IMAGINE. MUST BE SIX OF THEM IN THE PRISON MORGUE.
EIGHT, SIR.
DON'T GIVE ME YOUR PROPER, EATON-EDUCATED SOUR MOUTH, BLAIR! THIS WOULD BE UNDER CONTROL IF ONLY YOU DID YOUR JOB. WE ALL HAVE MAJOR CONTRACTS ON THE LINE.
IF YOUR FATHER HADN'T BEEN SUCH A GOOD BLOKE, YOU'D BE...
YES, WELL, GOOD DAY TO ALL. MR. LATIMORE, I'M SURE, WILL BE RETURNING LATER FOR DRINKS. YES?
HOW COULD I STAY AWAY?
Later.
HOME SWEET, SIR. DO DROP BY THE STATION IF YOU NEED ANYTHING.
WHICH WAY IS THE PRISON?
BACK THAT WAY, STRAIGHT UP THE PATH. JUST FOLLOW THE SMELL OF THE DACOITS.

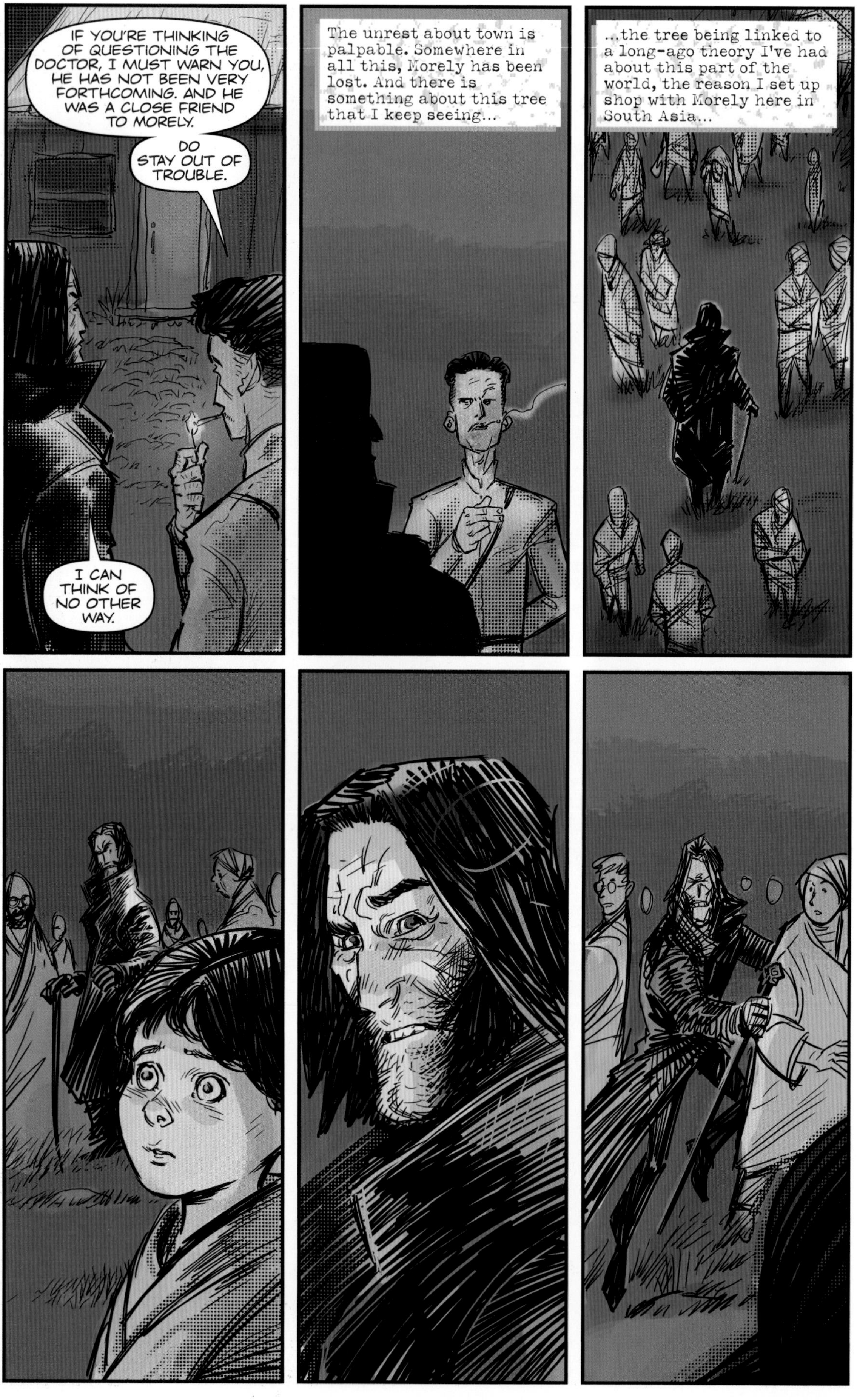
IF YOU'RE THINKING OF QUESTIONING THE DOCTOR, I MUST WARN YOU, HE HAS NOT BEEN VERY FORTHCOMING. AND HE WAS A CLOSE FRIEND TO MORELY.
DO STAY OUT OF TROUBLE.
I CAN THINK OF NO OTHER WAY.
The unrest about town is palpable. Somewhere in all this, Morely has been lost. And there is something about this tree that I keep seeing...
...the tree being linked to a long-ago theory I've had about this part of the world, the reason I set up shop with Morely here in South Asia...

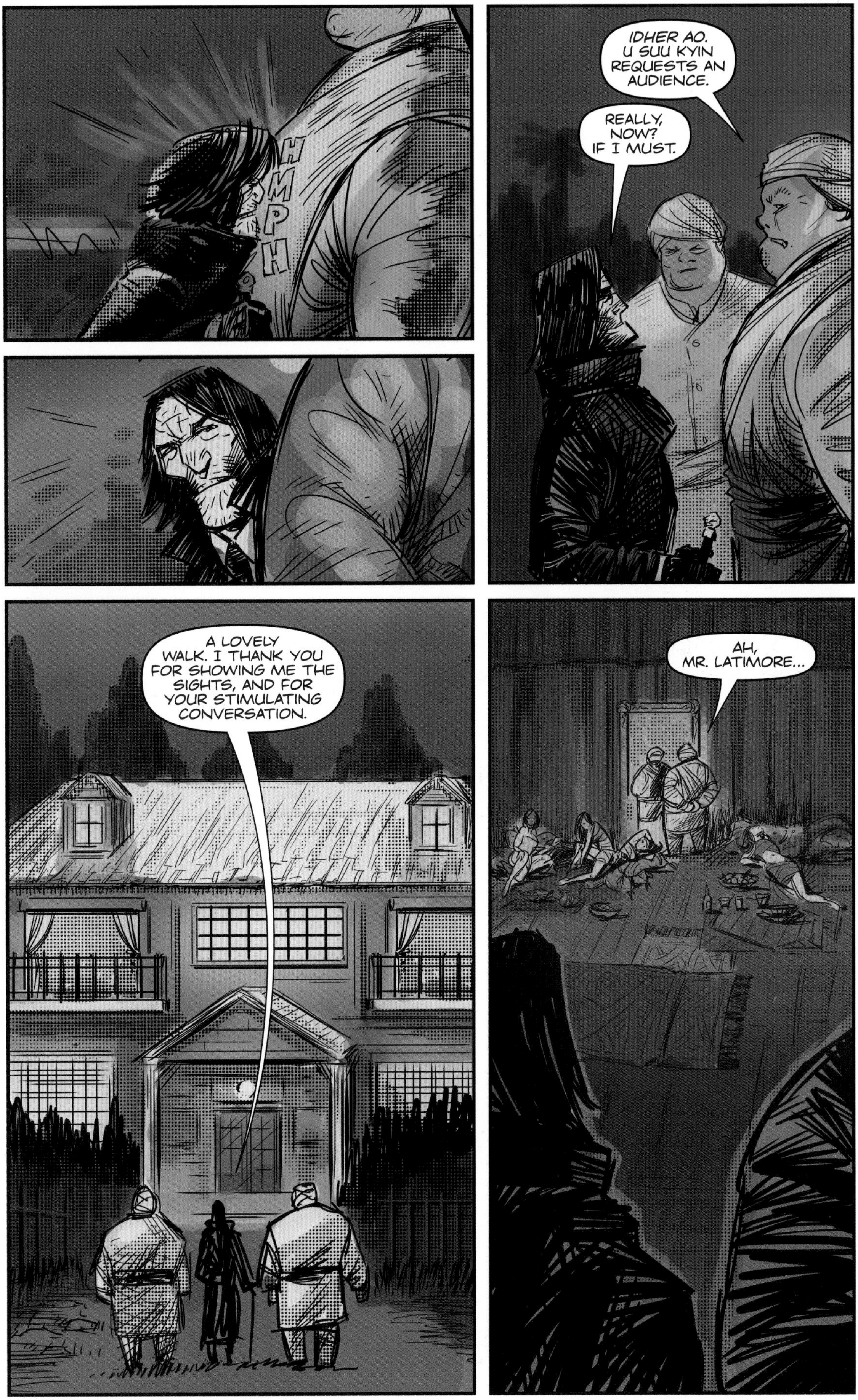
HMMPH
IDHER AO. U SUU KYIN REQUESTS AN AUDIENCE.
REALLY, NOW? IF I MUST.
A LOVELY WALK. I THANK YOU FOR SHOWING ME THE SIGHTS, AND FOR YOUR STIMULATING CONVERSATION.
AH, MR. LATIMORE...

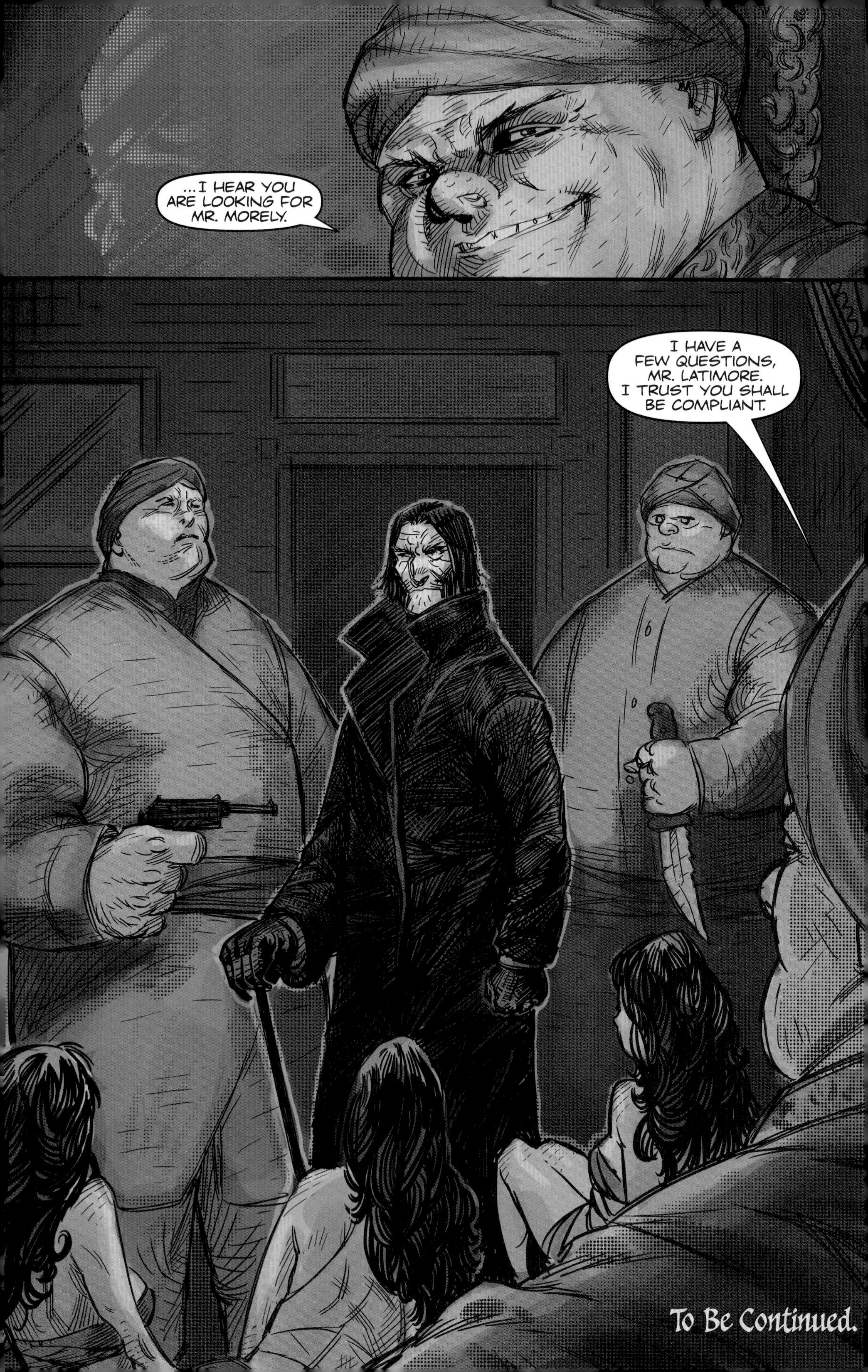
...I HEAR YOU ARE LOOKING FOR MR. MORELY.
I HAVE A FEW QUESTIONS, MR. LATIMORE. I TRUST YOU SHALL BE COMPLIANT.
To Be Continued.

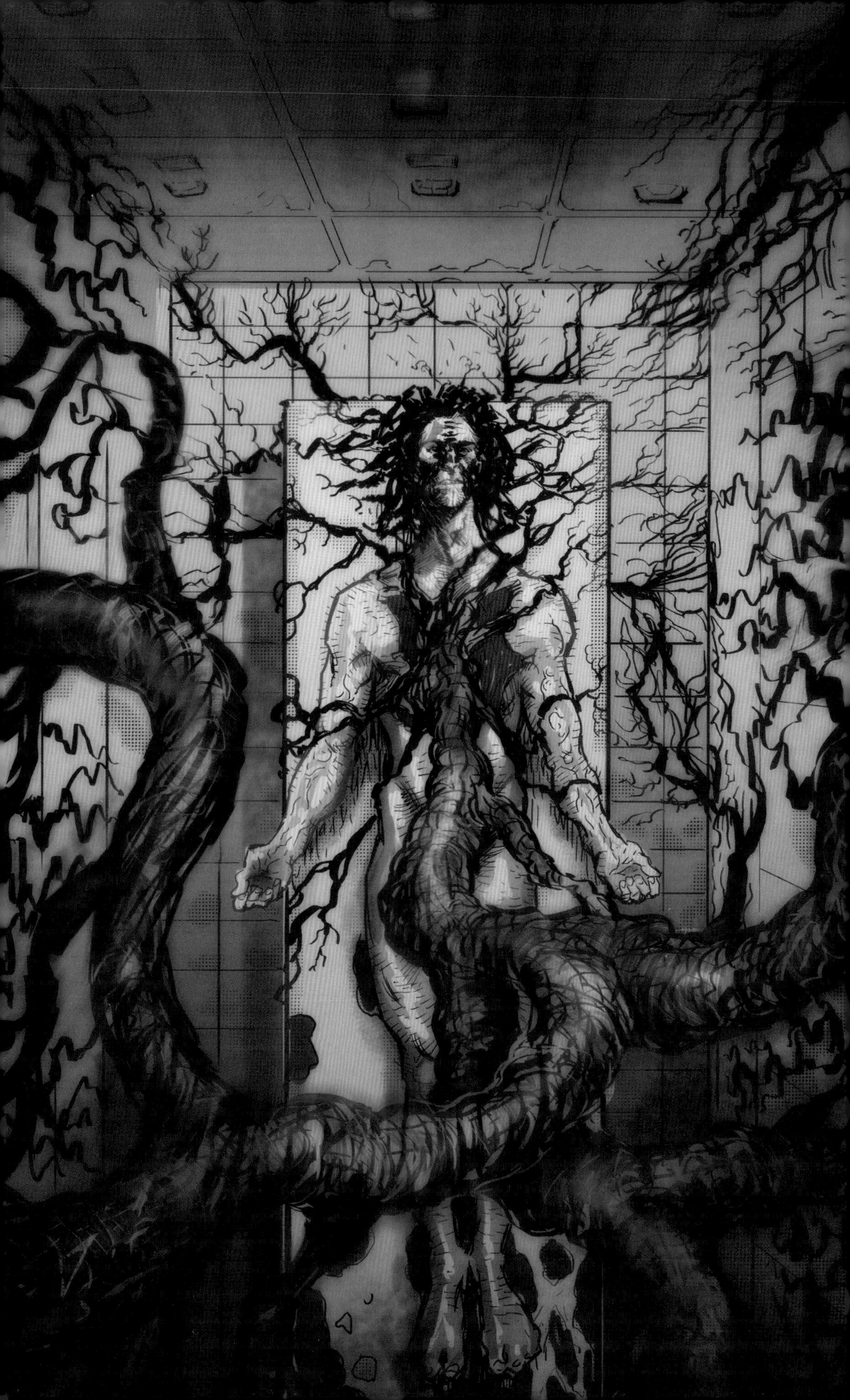

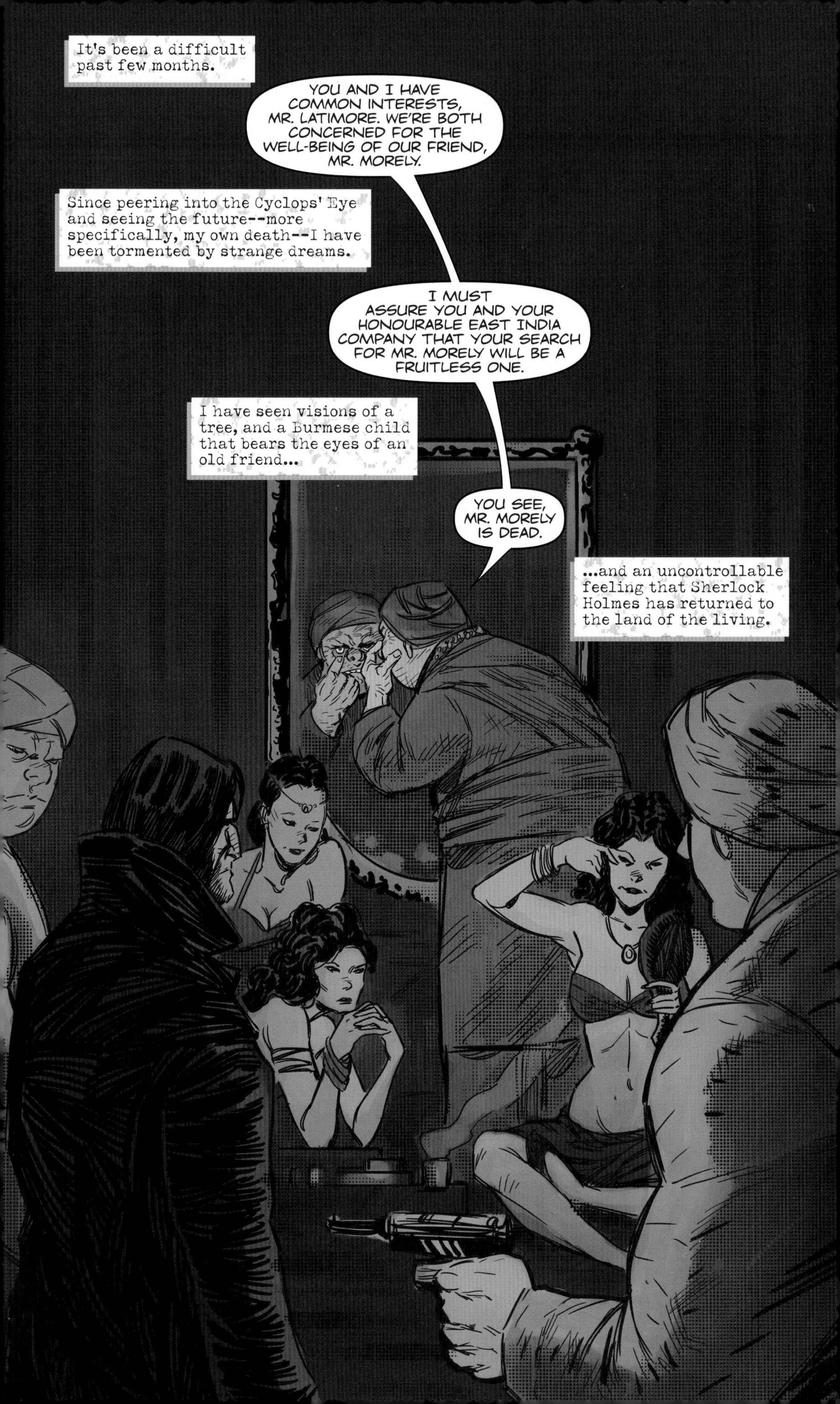

It's been a difficult past few months.
YOU AND I HAVE COMMON INTERESTS, MR. LATIMORE. WE'RE BOTH CONCERNED FOR THE WELL-BEING OF OUR FRIEND, MR. MORELY.
Since peering into the Cyclops' Eye and seeing the future--more specifically, my own death--I have been tormented by strange dreams.
I MUST ASSURE YOU AND YOUR HONOURABLE EAST INDIA COMPANY THAT YOUR SEARCH FOR MR. MORELY WILL BE A FRUITLESS ONE.
I have seen visions of a tree, and a Burmese child that bears the eyes of an old friend...
YOU SEE, MR. MORELY IS DEAD.
...and an uncontrollable feeling that Sherlock Holmes has returned to the land of the living.

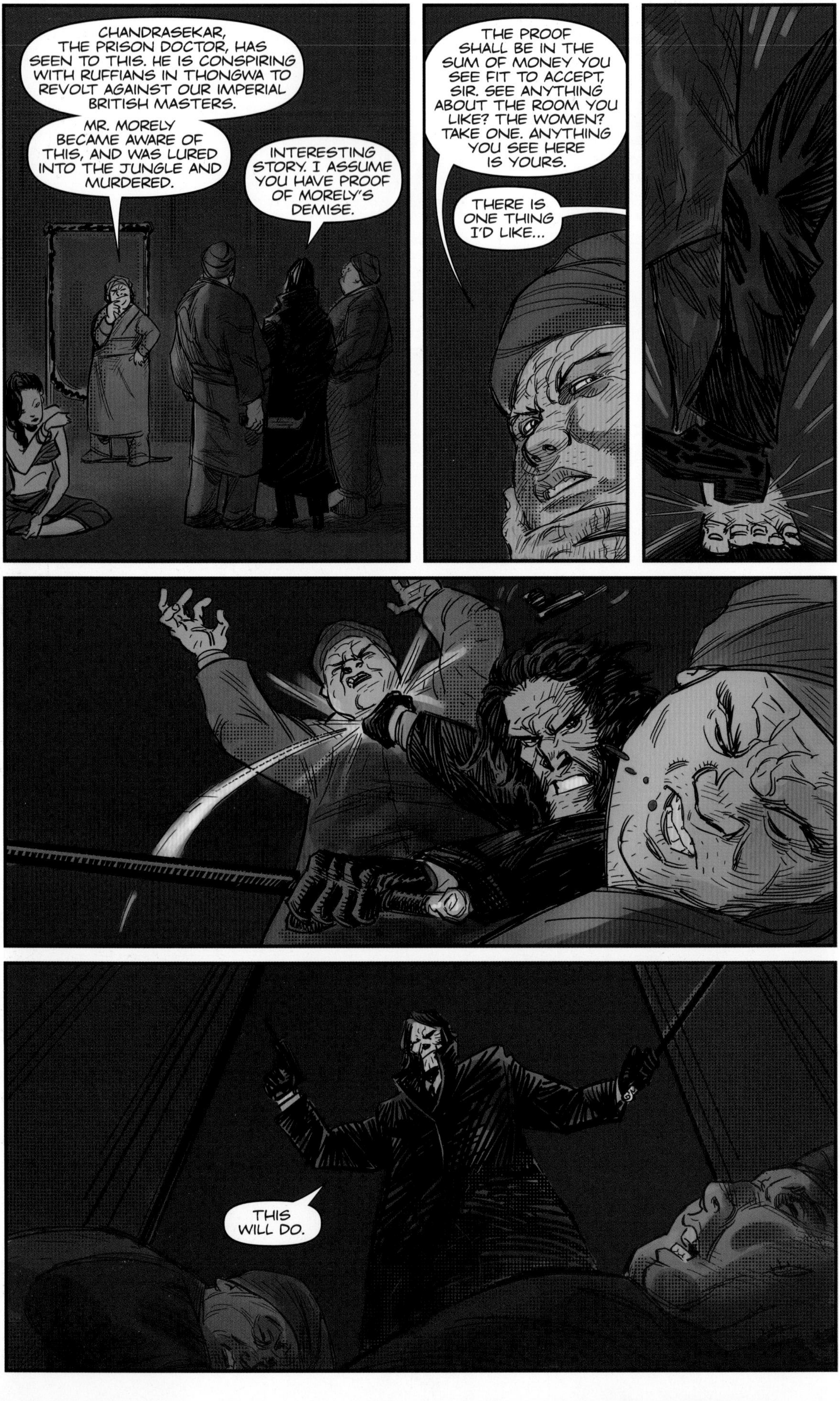
CHANDRASEKAR, THE PRISON DOCTOR, HAS SEEN TO THIS. HE IS CONSPIRING WITH RUFFIANS IN THONGWA TO REVOLT AGAINST OUR IMPERIAL BRITISH MASTERS.
MR. MORELY BECAME AWARE OF THIS, AND WAS LURED INTO THE JUNGLE AND MURDERED.
INTERESTING STORY. I ASSUME YOU HAVE PROOF OF MORELY'S DEMISE.
THE PROOF SHALL BE IN THE SUM OF MONEY YOU SEE FIT TO ACCEPT, SIR. SEE ANYTHING ABOUT THE ROOM YOU LIKE? THE WOMEN? TAKE ONE. ANYTHING YOU SEE HERE IS YOURS.
THERE IS ONE THING I'D LIKE...
THIS WILL DO.

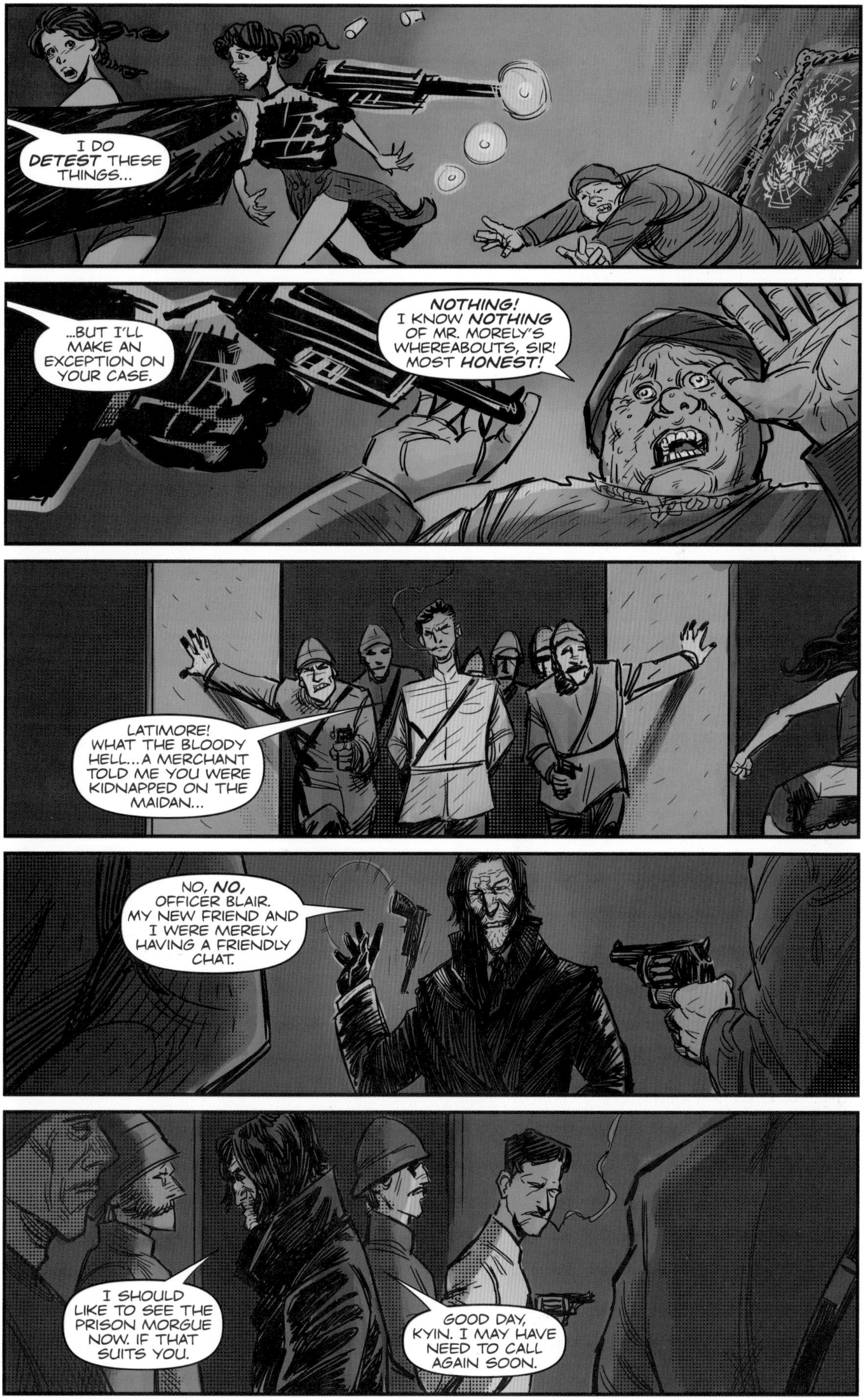
I DO DETEST THESE THINGS...
...BUT I'LL MAKE AN EXCEPTION ON YOUR CASE.
NOTHING! I KNOW NOTHING OF MR. MORELY'S WHEREABOUTS, SIR! MOST HONEST!
LATIMORE! WHAT THE BLOODY HELL...A MERCHANT TOLD ME YOU WERE KIDNAPPED ON THE MAIDAN...
NO, NO, OFFICER BLAIR. MY NEW FRIEND AND I WERE MERELY HAVING A FRIENDLY CHAT.
I SHOULD LIKE TO SEE THE PRISON MORGUE NOW. IF THAT SUITS YOU.
GOOD DAY, KYIN. I MAY HAVE NEED TO CALL AGAIN SOON.

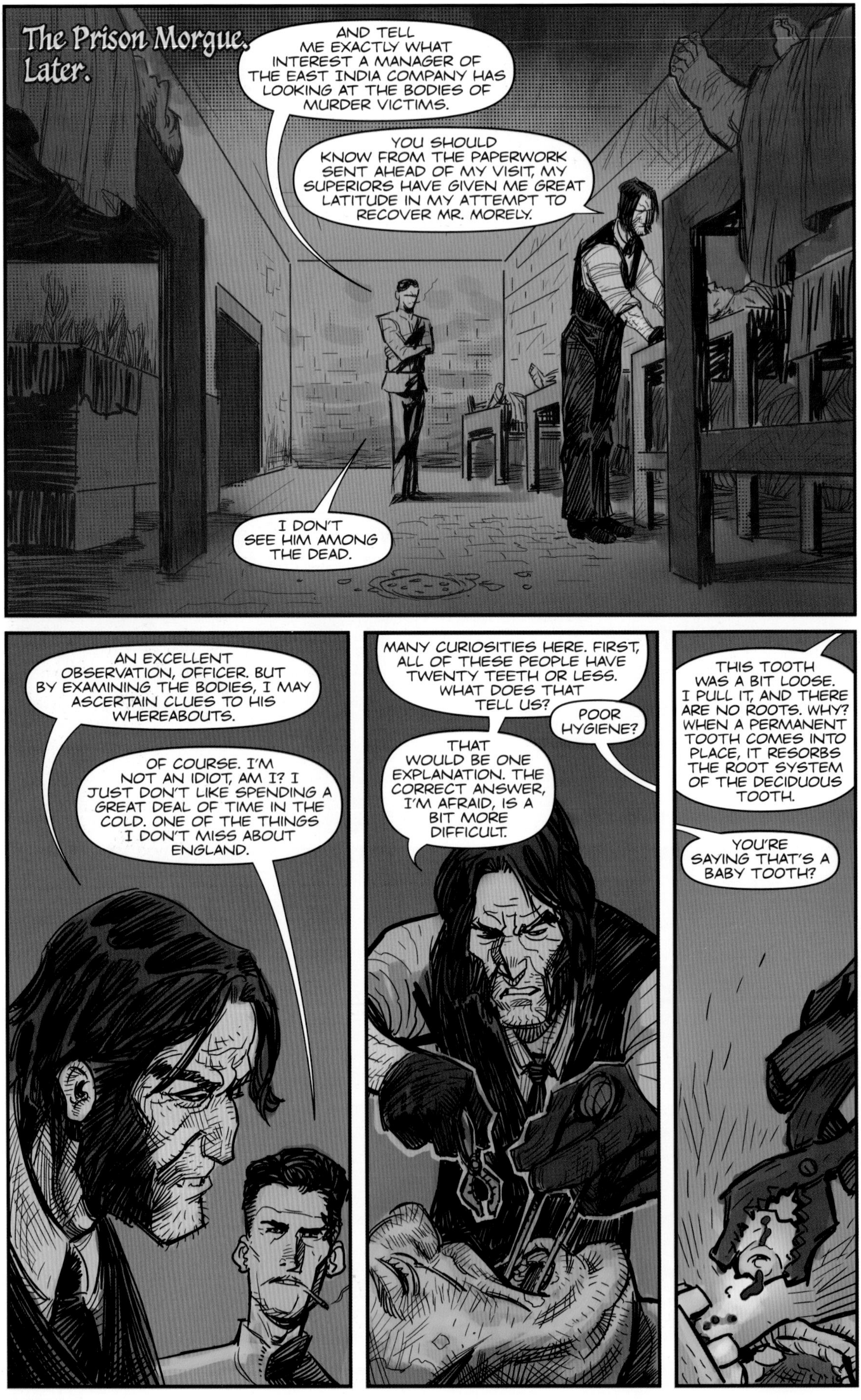
The Prison Morgue. Later.
AND TELL ME EXACTLY WHAT INTEREST A MANAGER OF THE EAST INDIA COMPANY HAS LOOKING AT THE BODIES OF MURDER VICTIMS.
YOU SHOULD KNOW FROM THE PAPERWORK SENT AHEAD OF MY VISIT, MY SUPERIORS HAVE GIVEN ME GREAT LATITUDE IN MY ATTEMPT TO RECOVER MR. MORELY.
I DON'T SEE HIM AMONG THE DEAD.
AN EXCELLENT OBSERVATION, OFFICER. BUT BY EXAMINING THE BODIES, I MAY ASCERTAIN CLUES TO HIS WHEREABOUTS.
OF COURSE. I'M NOT AN IDIOT, AM I? I JUST DON'T LIKE SPENDING A GREAT DEAL OF TIME IN THE COLD. ONE OF THE THINGS I DON'T MISS ABOUT ENGLAND.
MANY CURIOSITIES HERE. FIRST, ALL OF THESE PEOPLE HAVE TWENTY TEETH OR LESS. WHAT DOES THAT TELL US?
POOR HYGIENE?
THAT WOULD BE ONE EXPLANATION. THE CORRECT ANSWER, I'M AFRAID, IS A BIT MORE DIFFICULT.
THIS TOOTH WAS A BIT LOOSE. I PULL IT, AND THERE ARE NO ROOTS. WHY? WHEN A PERMANENT TOOTH COMES INTO PLACE, IT RESORBS THE ROOT SYSTEM OF THE DECIDUOUS TOOTH.
YOU'RE SAYING THAT'S A BABY TOOTH?

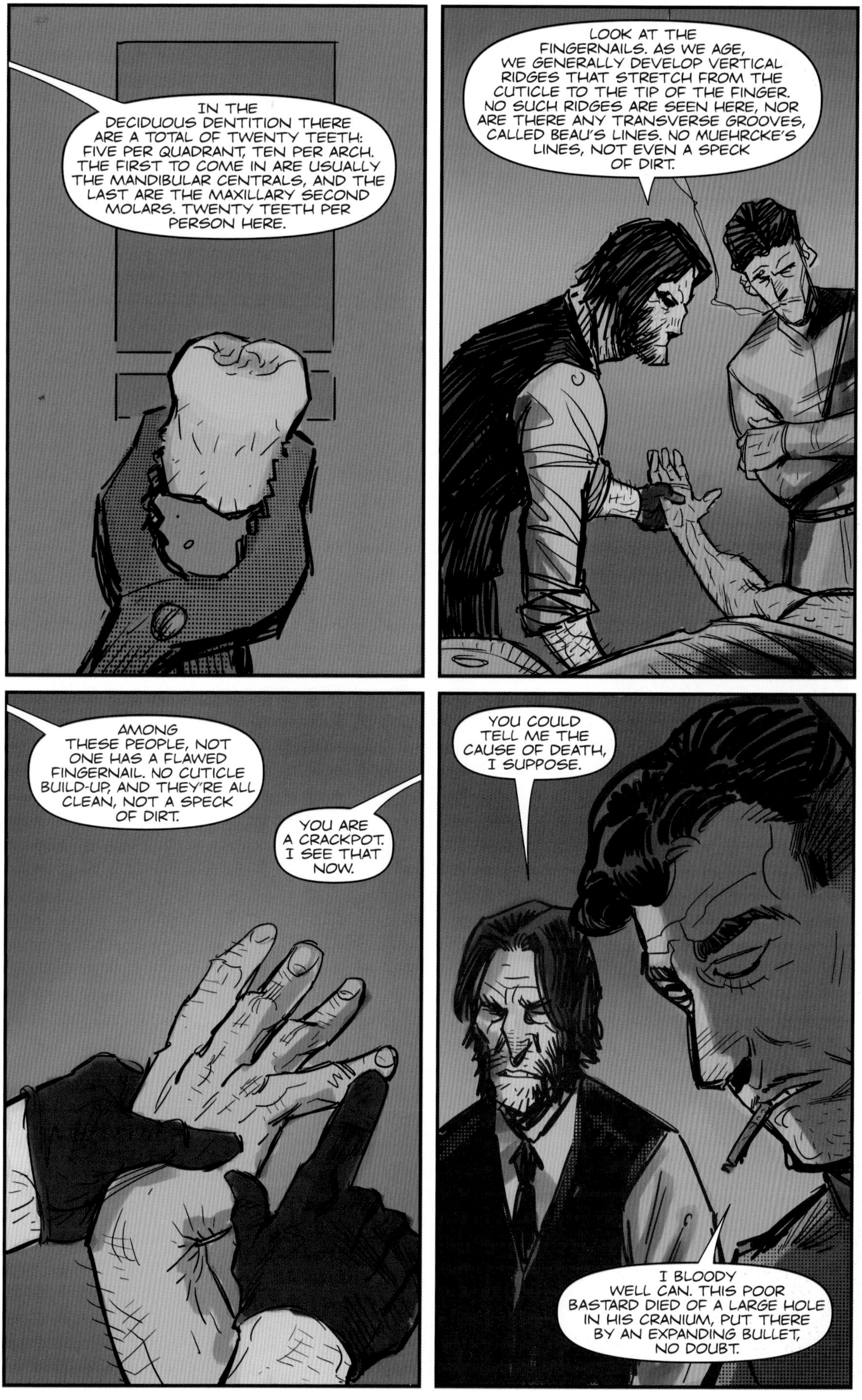
IN THE DECIDUOUS DENTITION THERE ARE A TOTAL OF TWENTY TEETH: FIVE PER QUADRANT, TEN PER ARCH. THE FIRST TO COME IN ARE USUALLY THE MANDIBULAR CENTRALS, AND THE LAST ARE THE MAXILLARY SECOND MOLARS. TWENTY TEETH PER PERSON HERE.
LOOK AT THE FINGERNAILS. AS WE AGE, WE GENERALLY DEVELOP VERTICAL RIDGES THAT STRETCH FROM THE CUTICLE TO THE TIP OF THE FINGER. NO SUCH RIDGES ARE SEEN HERE, NOR ARE THERE ANY TRANSVERSE GROOVES, CALLED BEAU'S LINES. NO MUEHRCKE'S LINES, NOT EVEN A SPECK OF DIRT.
AMONG THESE PEOPLE, NOT ONE HAS A FLAWED FINGERNAIL. NO CUTICLE BUILD-UP, AND THEY'RE ALL CLEAN, NOT A SPECK OF DIRT.
YOU ARE A CRACKPOT. I SEE THAT NOW.
YOU COULD TELL ME THE CAUSE OF DEATH, I SUPPOSE.
I BLOODY WELL CAN. THIS POOR BASTARD DIED OF A LARGE HOLE IN HIS CRANIUM, PUT THERE BY AN EXPANDING BULLET, NO DOUBT.

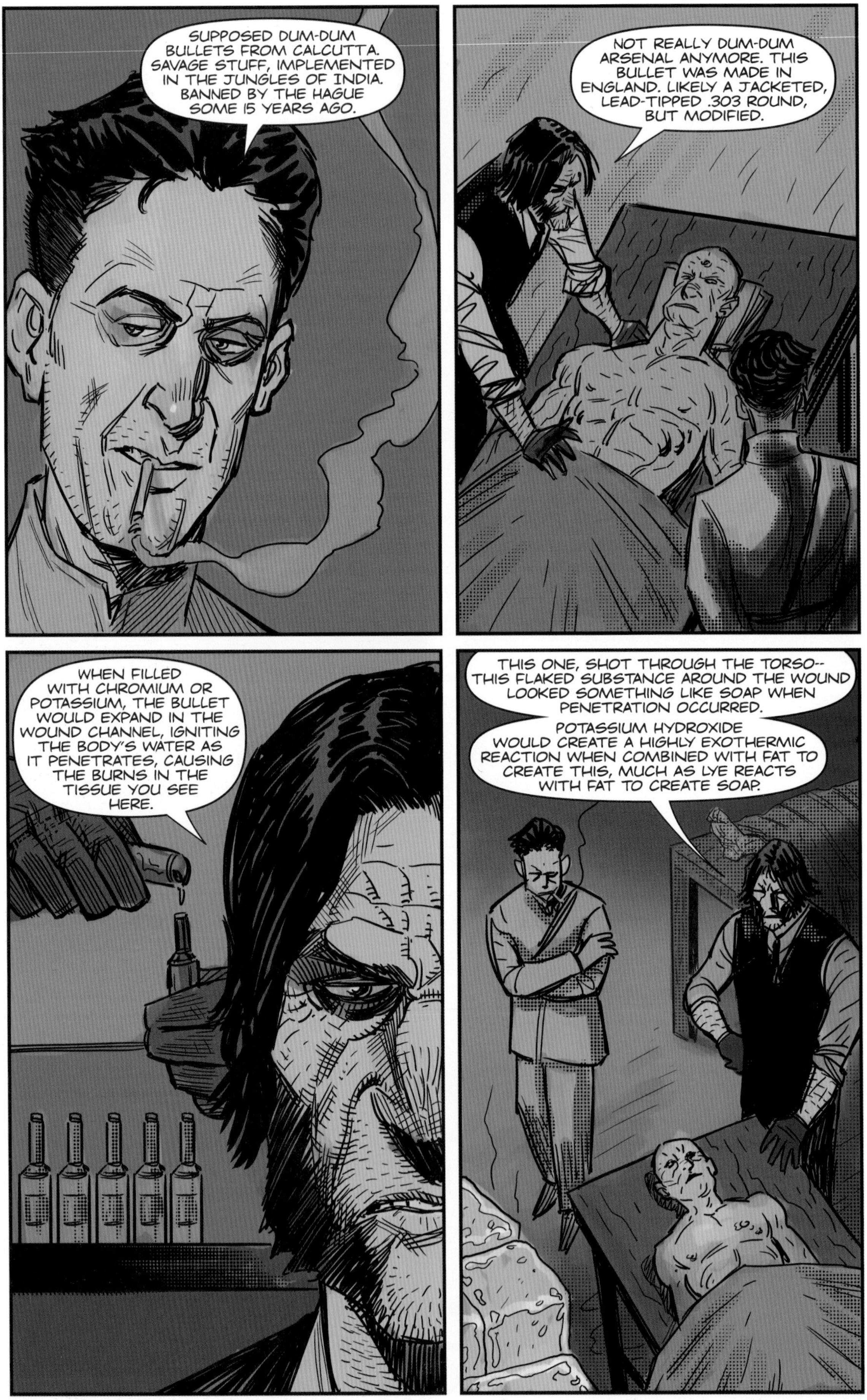
SUPPOSED DUM-DUM BULLETS FROM CALCUTTA. SAVAGE STUFF, IMPLEMENTED IN THE JUNGLES OF INDIA. BANNED BY THE HAGUE SOME 15 YEARS AGO.
NOT REALLY DUM-DUM ARSENAL ANYMORE. THIS BULLET WAS MADE IN ENGLAND. LIKELY A JACKETED, LEAD-TIPPED .303 ROUND, BUT MODIFIED.
WHEN FILLED WITH CHROMIUM OR POTASSIUM, THE BULLET WOULD EXPAND IN THE WOUND CHANNEL, IGNITING THE BODY'S WATER AS IT PENETRATES, CAUSING THE BURNS IN THE TISSUE YOU SEE HERE.
THIS ONE, SHOT THROUGH THE TORSO-- THIS FLAKED SUBSTANCE AROUND THE WOUND LOOKED SOMETHING LIKE SOAP WHEN PENETRATION OCCURRED.
POTASSIUM HYDROXIDE WOULD CREATE A HIGHLY EXOTHERMIC REACTION WHEN COMBINED WITH FAT TO CREATE THIS, MUCH AS LYE REACTS WITH FAT TO CREATE SOAP.

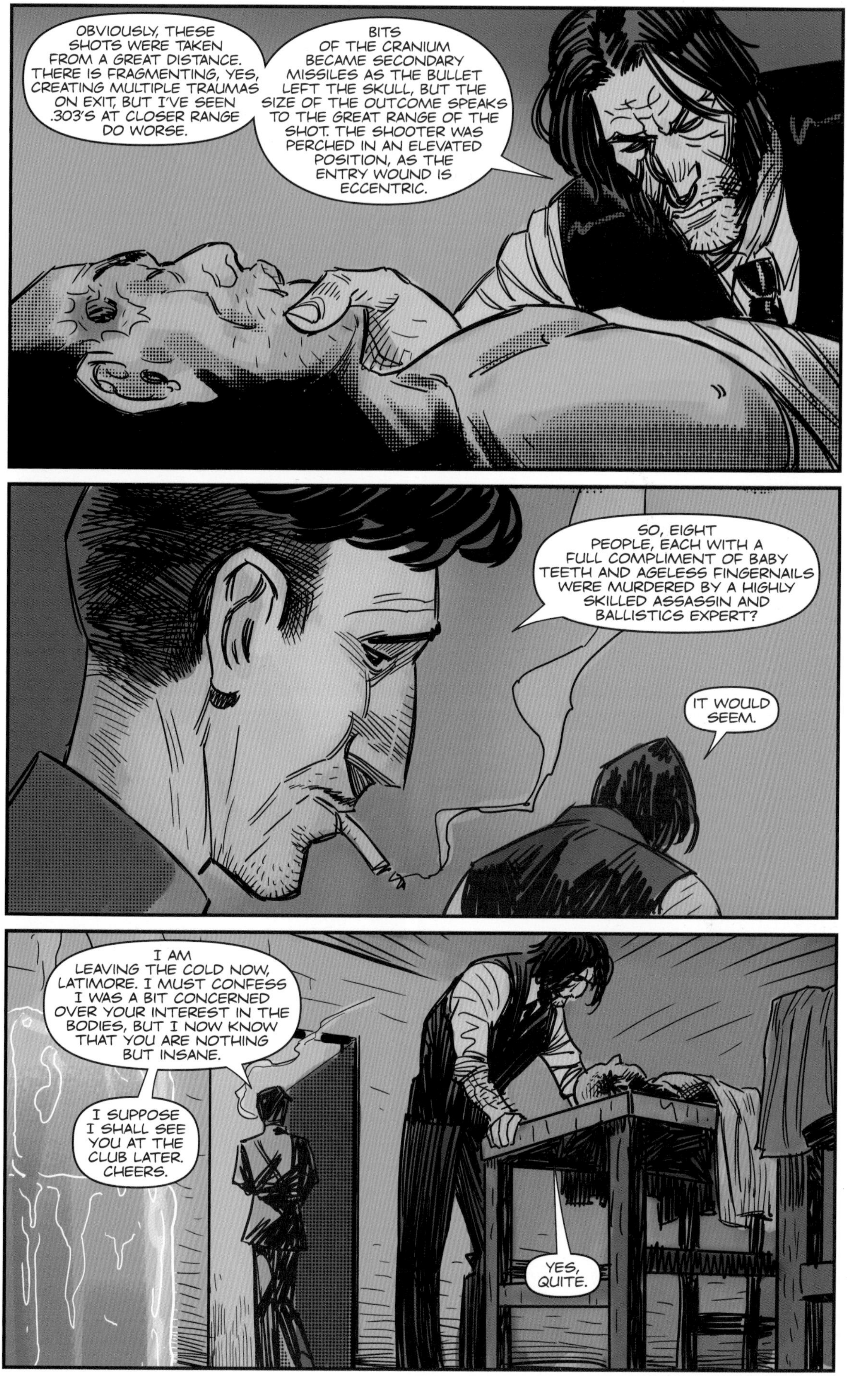
OBVIOUSLY, THESE SHOTS WERE TAKEN FROM A GREAT DISTANCE. THERE IS FRAGMENTING, YES, CREATING MULTIPLE TRAUMAS ON EXIT, BUT I'VE SEEN .303'S AT CLOSER RANGE DO WORSE.
BITS OF THE CRANIUM BECAME SECONDARY MISSILES AS THE BULLET LEFT THE SKULL, BUT THE SIZE OF THE OUTCOME SPEAKS TO THE GREAT RANGE OF THE SHOT. THE SHOOTER WAS PERCHED IN AN ELEVATED POSITION, AS THE ENTRY WOUND IS ECCENTRIC.
SO, EIGHT PEOPLE, EACH WITH A FULL COMPLIMENT OF BABY TEETH AND AGELESS FINGERNAILS WERE MURDERED BY A HIGHLY SKILLED ASSASSIN AND BALLISTICS EXPERT?
IT WOULD SEEM.
I AM LEAVING THE COLD NOW, LATIMORE. I MUST CONFESS I WAS A BIT CONCERNED OVER YOUR INTEREST IN THE BODIES, BUT I NOW KNOW THAT YOU ARE NOTHING BUT INSANE.
I SUPPOSE I SHALL SEE YOU AT THE CLUB LATER. CHEERS.
YES, QUITE.

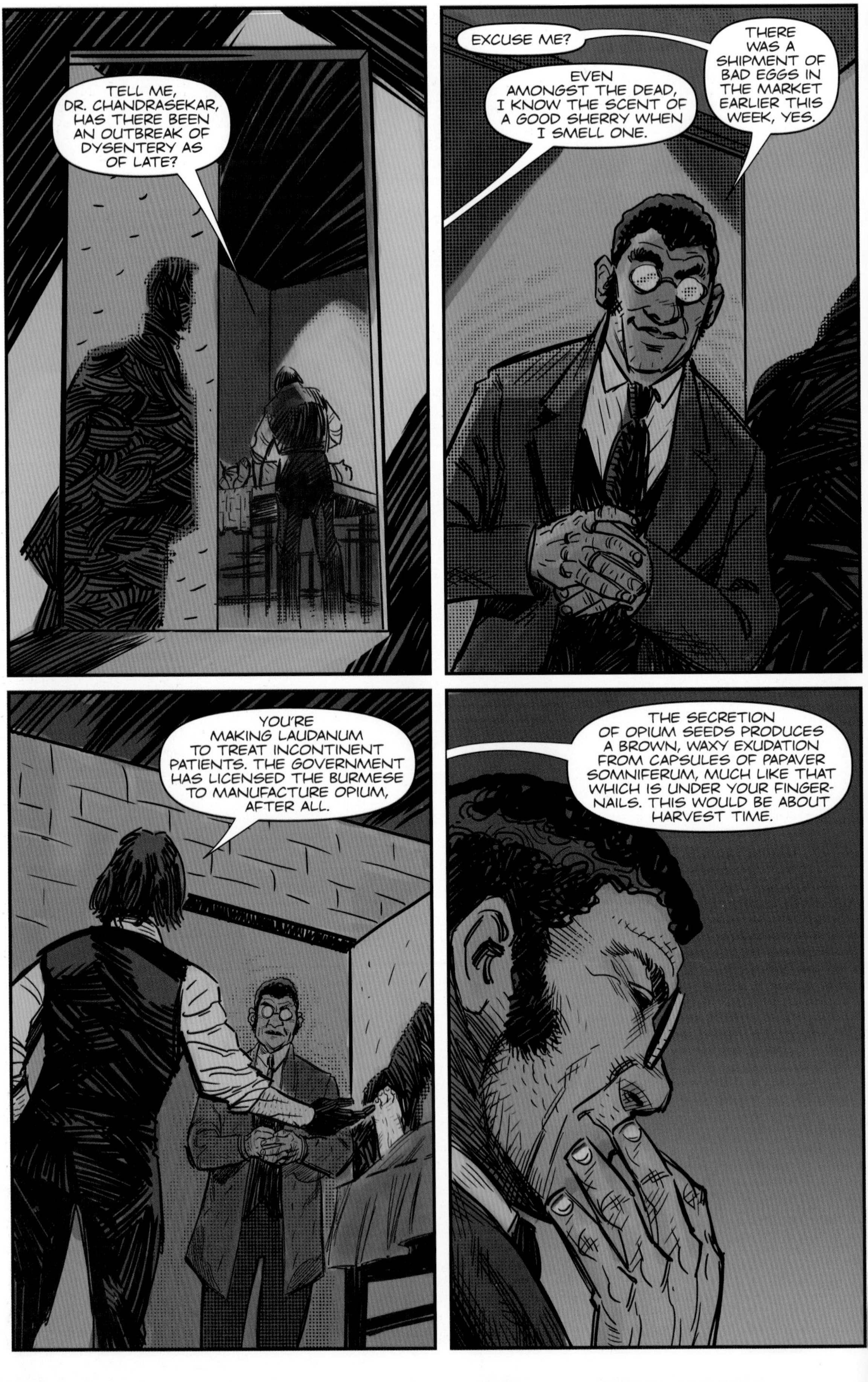
TELL ME, DR. CHANDRASEKAR, HAS THERE BEEN AN OUTBREAK OF DYSENTERY AS OF LATE?
EXCUSE ME?
THERE WAS A SHIPMENT OF BAD EGGS IN THE MARKET EARLIER THIS WEEK, YES.
EVEN AMONGST THE DEAD, I KNOW THE SCENT OF A GOOD SHERRY WHEN I SMELL ONE.
YOU'RE MAKING LAUDANUM TO TREAT INCONTINENT PATIENTS. THE GOVERNMENT HAS LICENSED THE BURMESE TO MANUFACTURE OPIUM, AFTER ALL.
THE SECRETION OF OPIUM SEEDS PRODUCES A BROWN, WAXY EXUDATION FROM CAPSULES OF PAPAVER SOMNIFERUM, MUCH LIKE THAT WHICH IS UNDER YOUR FINGER-NAILS. THIS WOULD BE ABOUT HARVEST TIME.

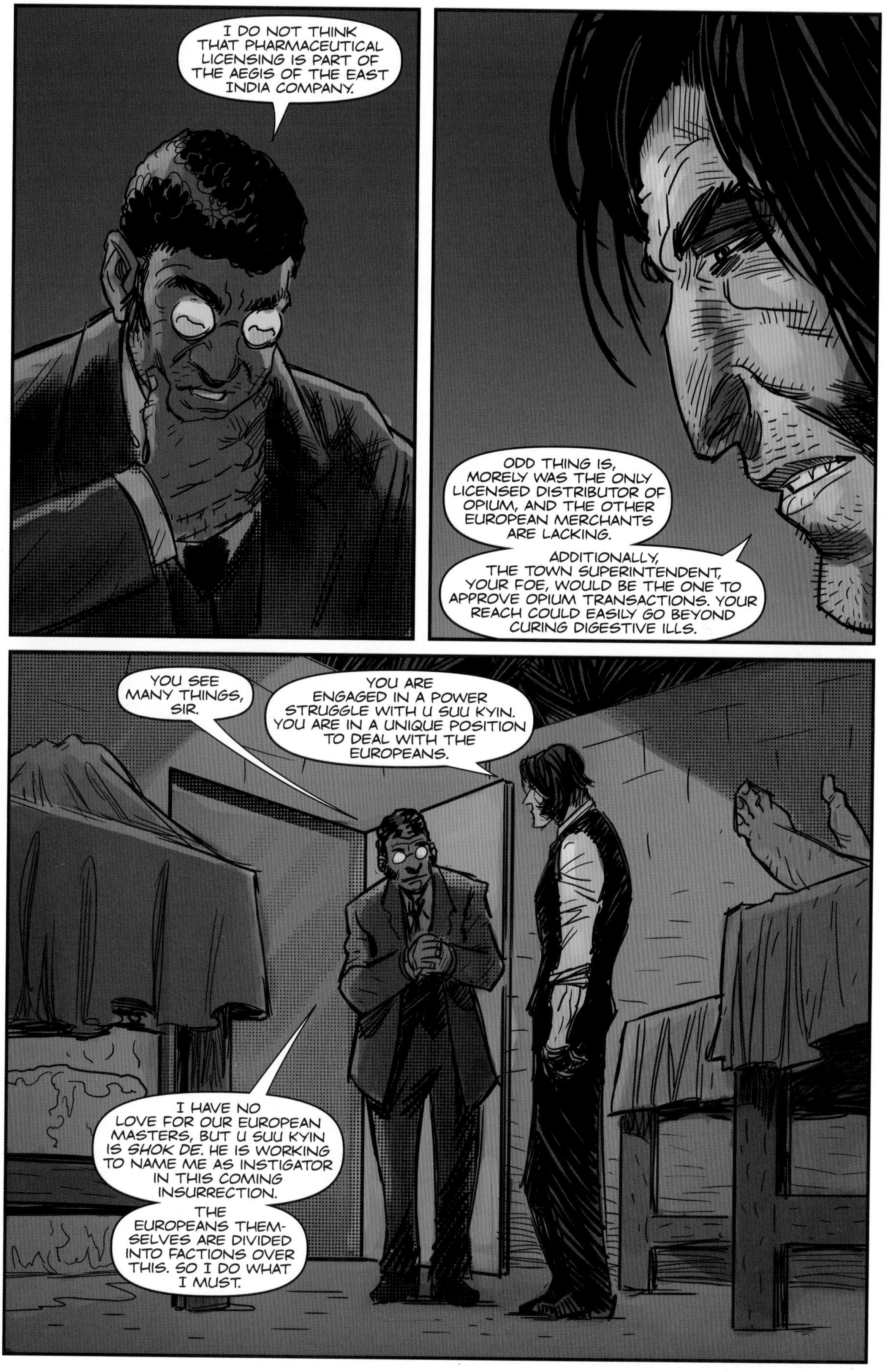
I DO NOT THINK THAT PHARMACEUTICAL LICENSING IS PART OF THE AEGIS OF THE EAST INDIA COMPANY.
ODD THING IS, MORELY WAS THE ONLY LICENSED DISTRIBUTOR OF OPIUM, AND THE OTHER EUROPEAN MERCHANTS ARE LACKING.
ADDITIONALLY, THE TOWN SUPERINTENDENT, YOUR FOE, WOULD BE THE ONE TO APPROVE OPIUM TRANSACTIONS. YOUR REACH COULD EASILY GO BEYOND CURING DIGESTIVE ILLS.
YOU SEE MANY THINGS, SIR.
YOU ARE ENGAGED IN A POWER STRUGGLE WITH U SUU KYIN. YOU ARE IN A UNIQUE POSITION TO DEAL WITH THE EUROPEANS.
I HAVE NO LOVE FOR OUR EUROPEAN MASTERS, BUT U SUU KYIN IS SHOK DE. HE IS WORKING TO NAME ME AS INSTIGATOR IN THIS COMING INSURRECTION.
THE EUROPEANS THEM-SELVES ARE DIVIDED INTO FACTIONS OVER THIS. SO I DO WHAT I MUST.

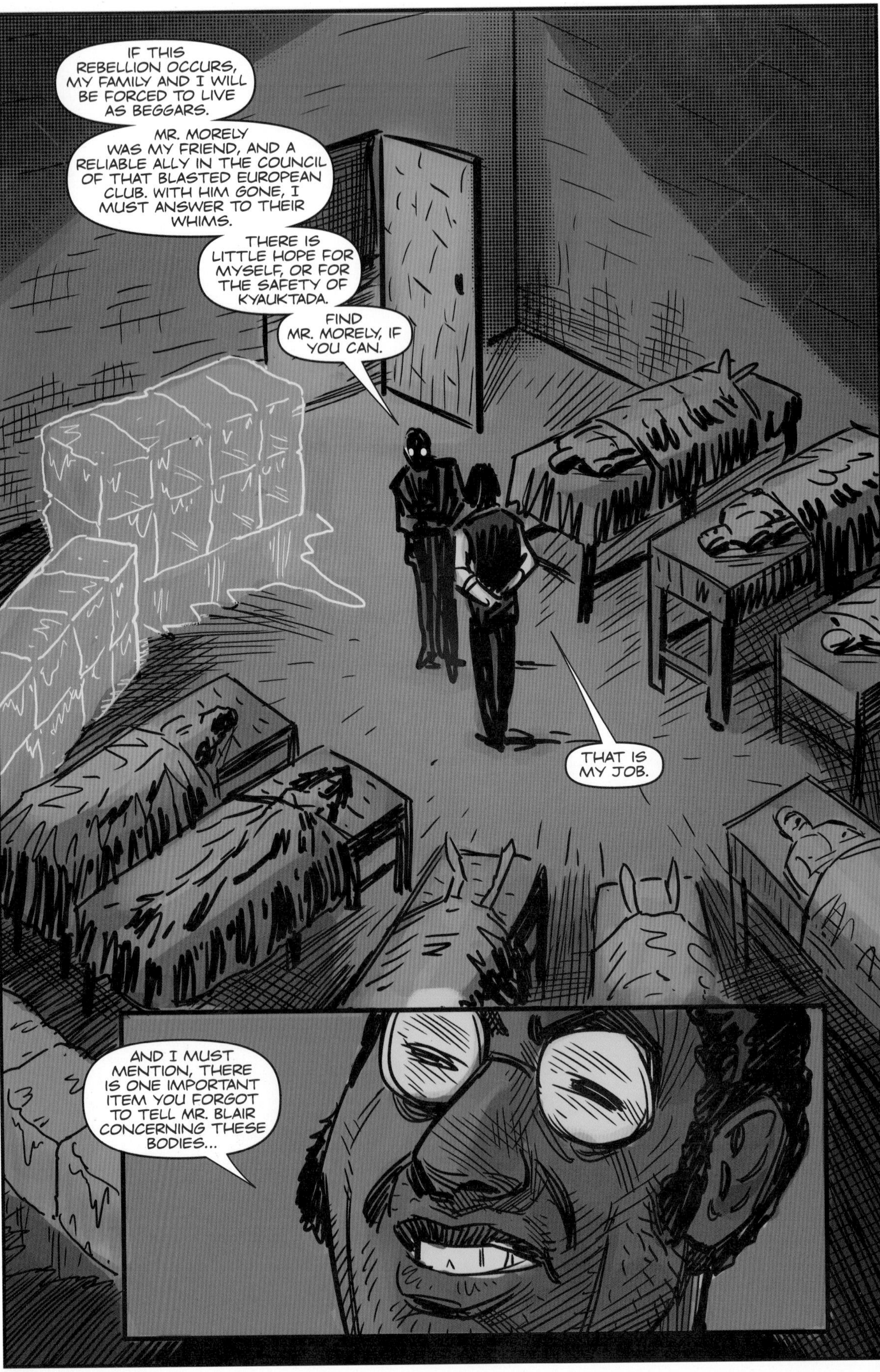
IF THIS REBELLION OCCURS, MY FAMILY AND I WILL BE FORCED TO LIVE AS BEGGARS.
MR. MORELY WAS MY FRIEND, AND A RELIABLE ALLY IN THE COUNCIL OF THAT BLASTED EUROPEAN CLUB. WITH HIM GONE, I MUST ANSWER TO THEIR WHIMS.
THERE IS LITTLE HOPE FOR MYSELF, OR FOR THE SAFETY OF KYAUKTADA.
FIND MR. MORELY, IF YOU CAN.
THAT IS MY JOB.
AND I MUST MENTION, THERE IS ONE IMPORTANT ITEM YOU FORGOT TO TELL MR. BLAIR CONCERNING THESE BODIES...

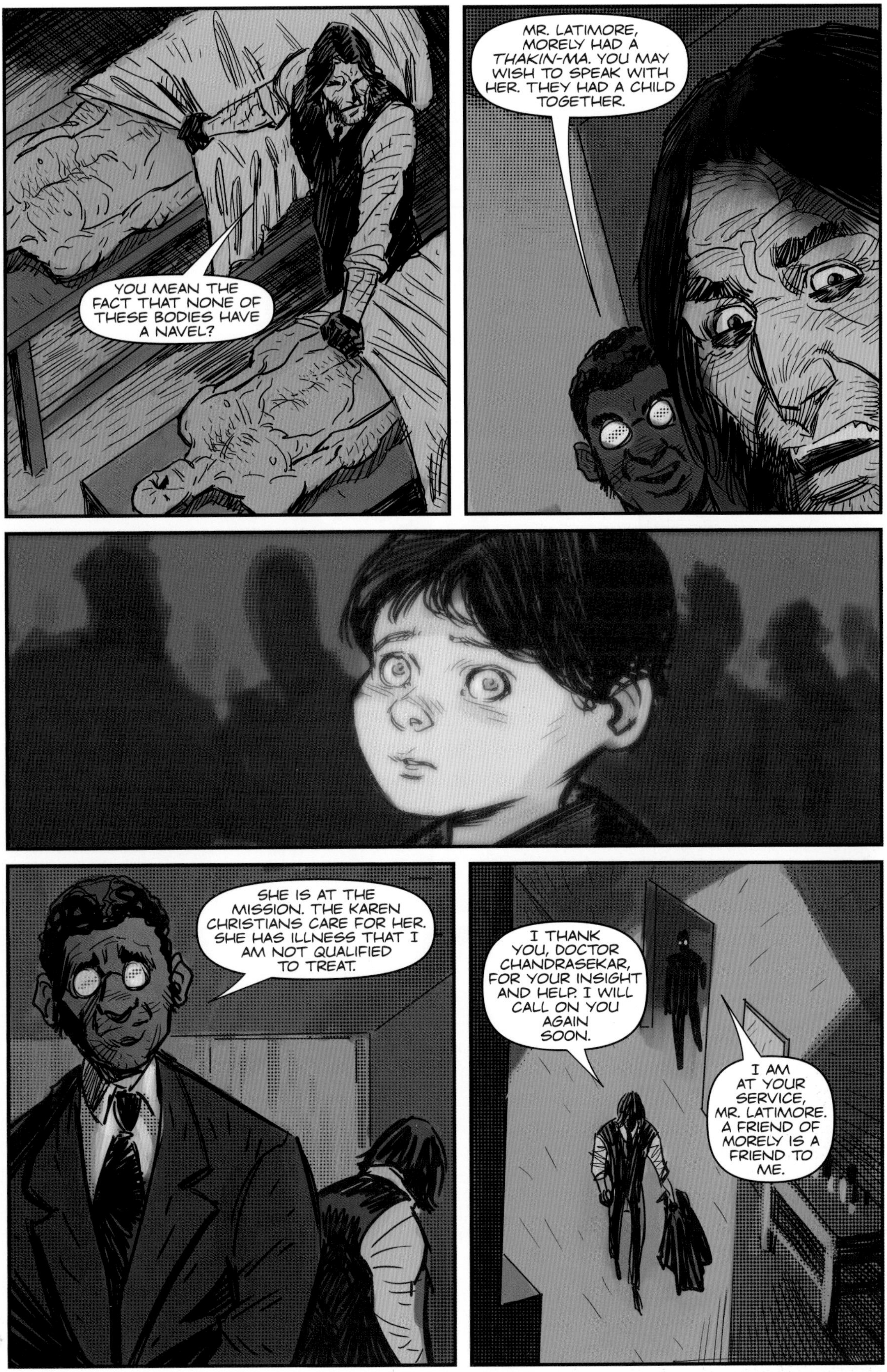
YOU MEAN THE FACT THAT NONE OF THESE BODIES HAVE A NAVEL?
MR. LATIMORE, MORELY HAD A *THAKIN-MA*. YOU MAY WISH TO SPEAK WITH HER. THEY HAD A CHILD TOGETHER.
SHE IS AT THE MISSION. THE KAREN CHRISTIANS CARE FOR HER. SHE HAS ILLNESS THAT I AM NOT QUALIFIED TO TREAT.
I THANK YOU, DOCTOR CHANDRASEKAR, FOR YOUR INSIGHT AND HELP. I WILL CALL ON YOU AGAIN SOON.
I AM AT YOUR SERVICE, MR. LATIMORE. A FRIEND OF MORELY IS A FRIEND TO ME.

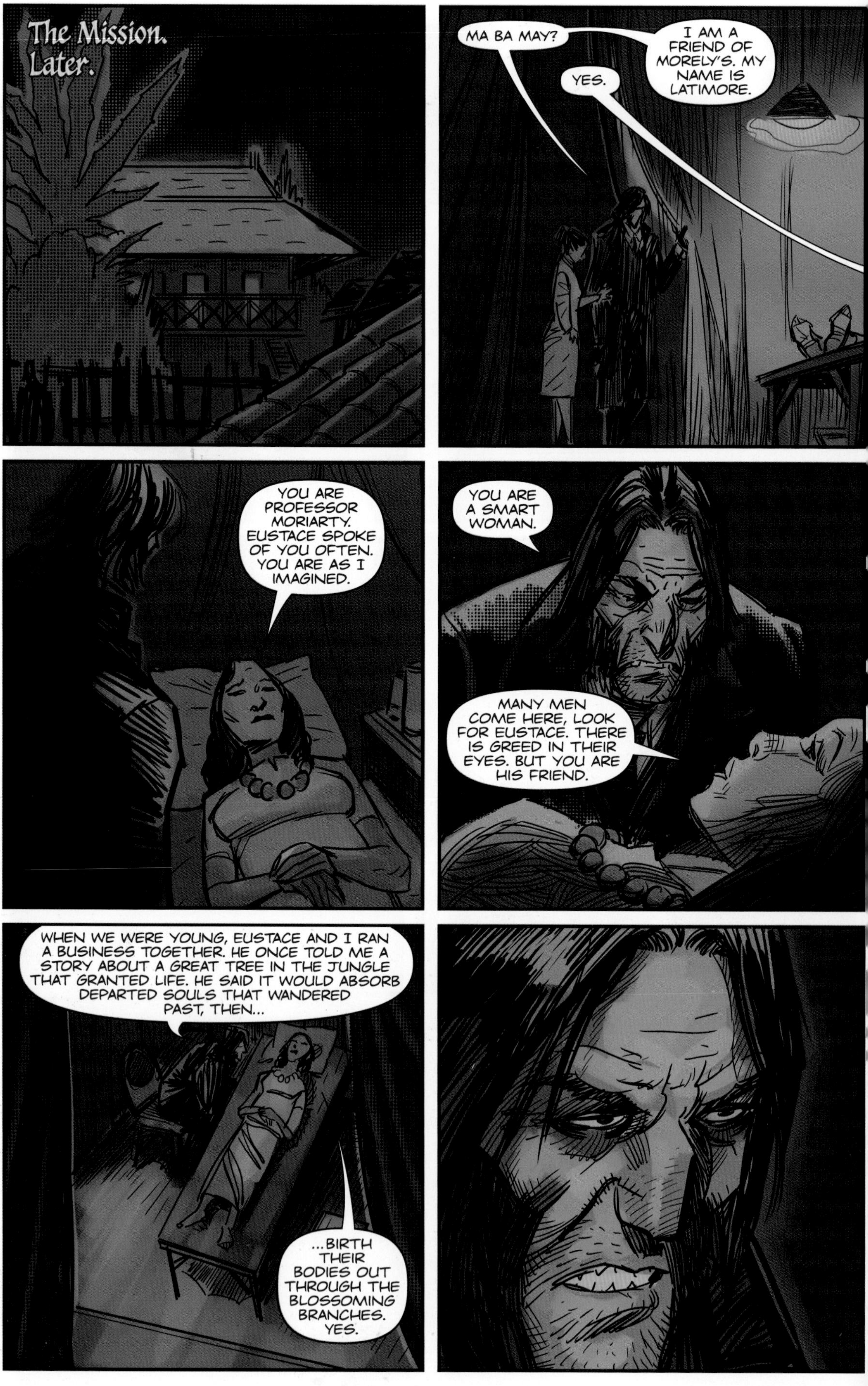
The Mission.
Later.
MA BA MAY?
YES.
I AM A FRIEND OF MORELY'S. MY NAME IS LATIMORE.
YOU ARE PROFESSOR MORIARTY. EUSTACE SPOKE OF YOU OFTEN. YOU ARE AS I IMAGINED.
YOU ARE A SMART WOMAN.
MANY MEN COME HERE, LOOK FOR EUSTACE. THERE IS GREED IN THEIR EYES. BUT YOU ARE HIS FRIEND.
WHEN WE WERE YOUNG, EUSTACE AND I RAN A BUSINESS TOGETHER. HE ONCE TOLD ME A STORY ABOUT A GREAT TREE IN THE JUNGLE THAT GRANTED LIFE. HE SAID IT WOULD ABSORB DEPARTED SOULS THAT WANDERED PAST, THEN...
...BIRTH THEIR BODIES OUT THROUGH THE BLOSSOMING BRANCHES. YES.

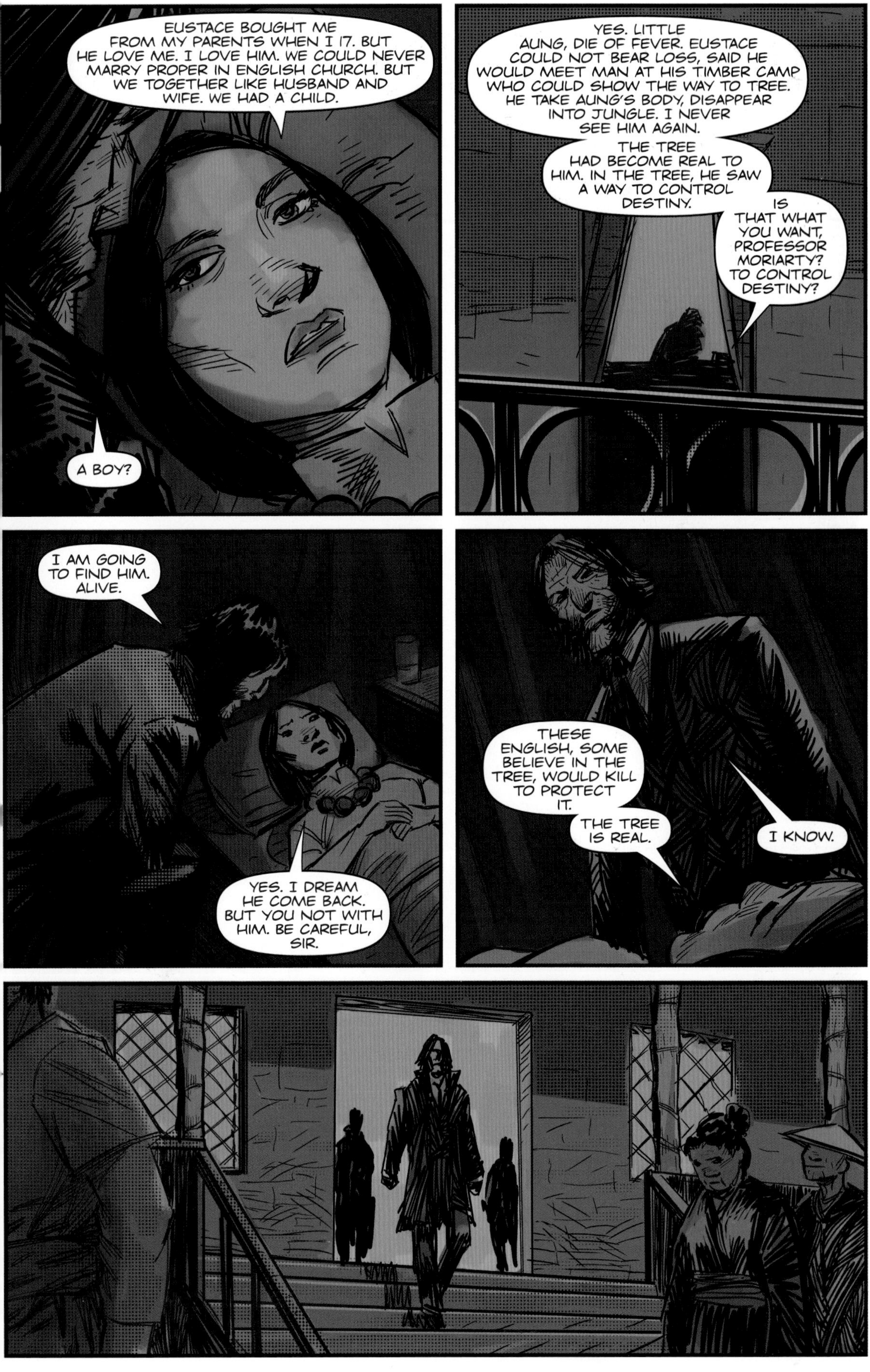
EUSTACE BOUGHT ME FROM MY PARENTS WHEN I 17. BUT HE LOVE ME. I LOVE HIM. WE COULD NEVER MARRY PROPER IN ENGLISH CHURCH. BUT WE TOGETHER LIKE HUSBAND AND WIFE. WE HAD A CHILD.
A BOY?
YES. LITTLE AUNG, DIE OF FEVER. EUSTACE COULD NOT BEAR LOSS, SAID HE WOULD MEET MAN AT HIS TIMBER CAMP WHO COULD SHOW THE WAY TO TREE. HE TAKE AUNG'S BODY, DISAPPEAR INTO JUNGLE. I NEVER SEE HIM AGAIN.
THE TREE HAD BECOME REAL TO HIM. IN THE TREE, HE SAW A WAY TO CONTROL DESTINY.
IS THAT WHAT YOU WANT, PROFESSOR MORIARTY? TO CONTROL DESTINY?
I AM GOING TO FIND HIM. ALIVE.
YES. I DREAM HE COME BACK. BUT YOU NOT WITH HIM. BE CAREFUL, SIR.
THESE ENGLISH, SOME BELIEVE IN THE TREE, WOULD KILL TO PROTECT IT.
THE TREE IS REAL.
I KNOW.

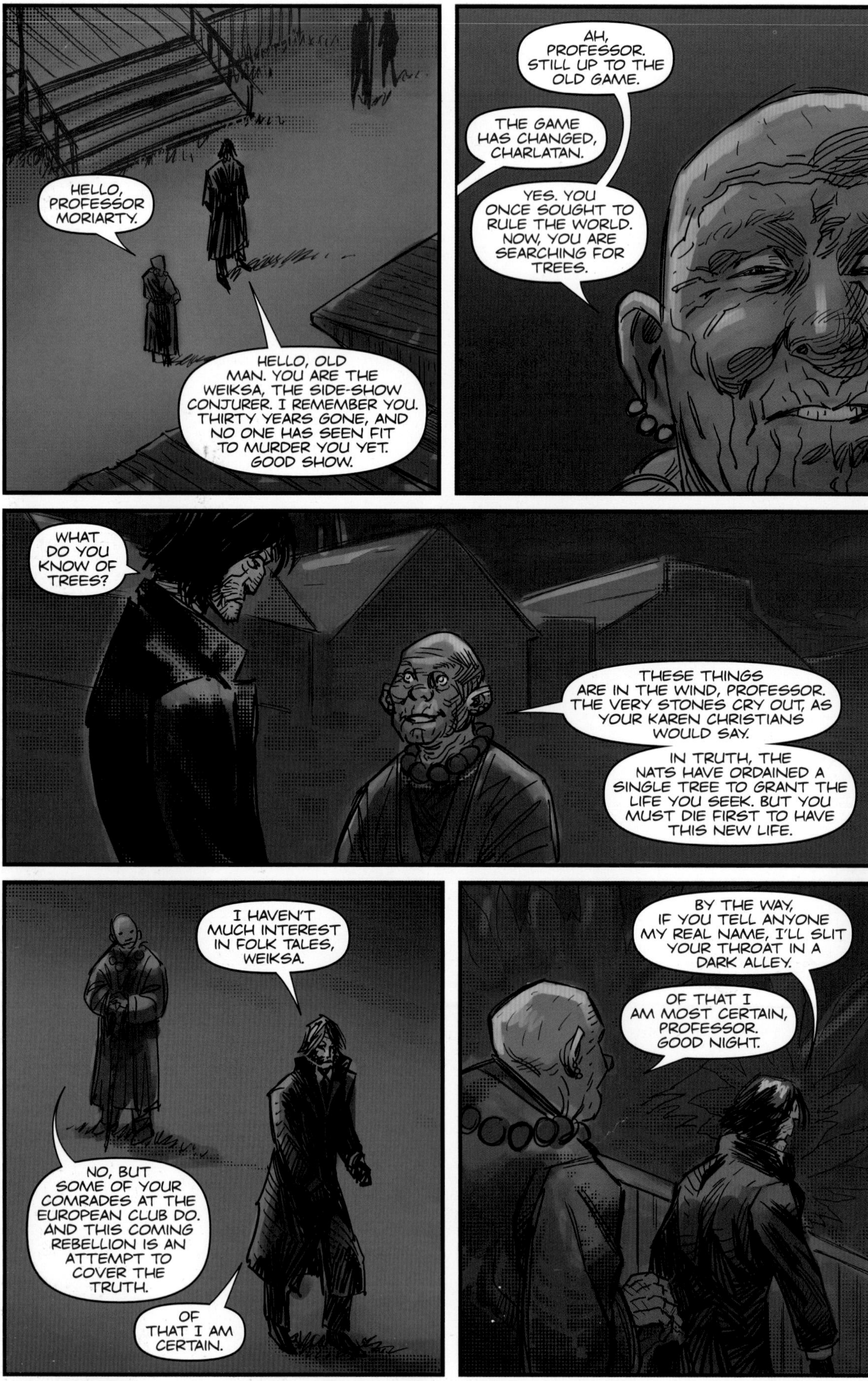
HELLO, PROFESSOR MORIARTY.
HELLO, OLD MAN. YOU ARE THE WEIKSA, THE SIDE-SHOW CONJURER. I REMEMBER YOU. THIRTY YEARS GONE, AND NO ONE HAS SEEN FIT TO MURDER YOU YET. GOOD SHOW.
AH, PROFESSOR. STILL UP TO THE OLD GAME.
THE GAME HAS CHANGED, CHARLATAN.
YES. YOU ONCE SOUGHT TO RULE THE WORLD. NOW, YOU ARE SEARCHING FOR TREES.
WHAT DO YOU KNOW OF TREES?
THESE THINGS ARE IN THE WIND, PROFESSOR. THE VERY STONES CRY OUT, AS YOUR KAREN CHRISTIANS WOULD SAY.
IN TRUTH, THE NATS HAVE ORDAINED A SINGLE TREE TO GRANT THE LIFE YOU SEEK. BUT YOU MUST DIE FIRST TO HAVE THIS NEW LIFE.
I HAVEN'T MUCH INTEREST IN FOLK TALES, WEIKSA.
NO, BUT SOME OF YOUR COMRADES AT THE EUROPEAN CLUB DO. AND THIS COMING REBELLION IS AN ATTEMPT TO COVER THE TRUTH.
OF THAT I AM CERTAIN.
BY THE WAY, IF YOU TELL ANYONE MY REAL NAME, I'LL SLIT YOUR THROAT IN A DARK ALLEY.
OF THAT I AM MOST CERTAIN, PROFESSOR. GOOD NIGHT.

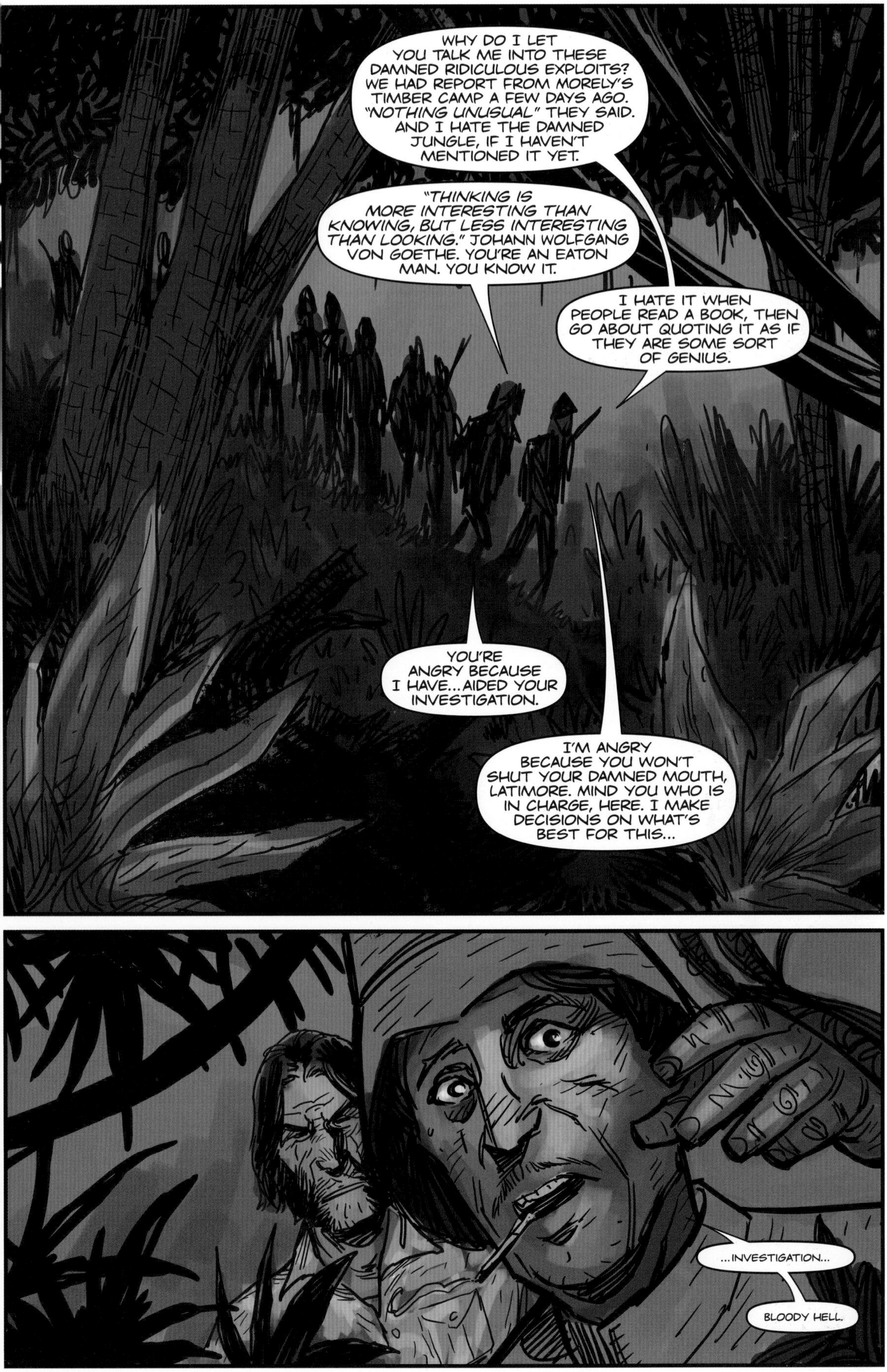
WHY DO I LET YOU TALK ME INTO THESE DAMNED RIDICULOUS EXPLOITS? WE HAD REPORT FROM MORELY'S TIMBER CAMP A FEW DAYS AGO. "NOTHING UNUSUAL" THEY SAID. AND I HATE THE DAMNED JUNGLE, IF I HAVEN'T MENTIONED IT YET.
"THINKING IS MORE INTERESTING THAN KNOWING, BUT LESS INTERESTING THAN LOOKING." JOHANN WOLFGANG VON GOETHE. YOU'RE AN EATON MAN. YOU KNOW IT.
I HATE IT WHEN PEOPLE READ A BOOK, THEN GO ABOUT QUOTING IT AS IF THEY ARE SOME SORT OF GENIUS.
YOU'RE ANGRY BECAUSE I HAVE... AIDED YOUR INVESTIGATION.
I'M ANGRY BECAUSE YOU WON'T SHUT YOUR DAMNED MOUTH, LATIMORE. MIND YOU WHO IS IN CHARGE, HERE. I MAKE DECISIONS ON WHAT'S BEST FOR THIS...
...INVESTIGATION...
BLOODY HELL.

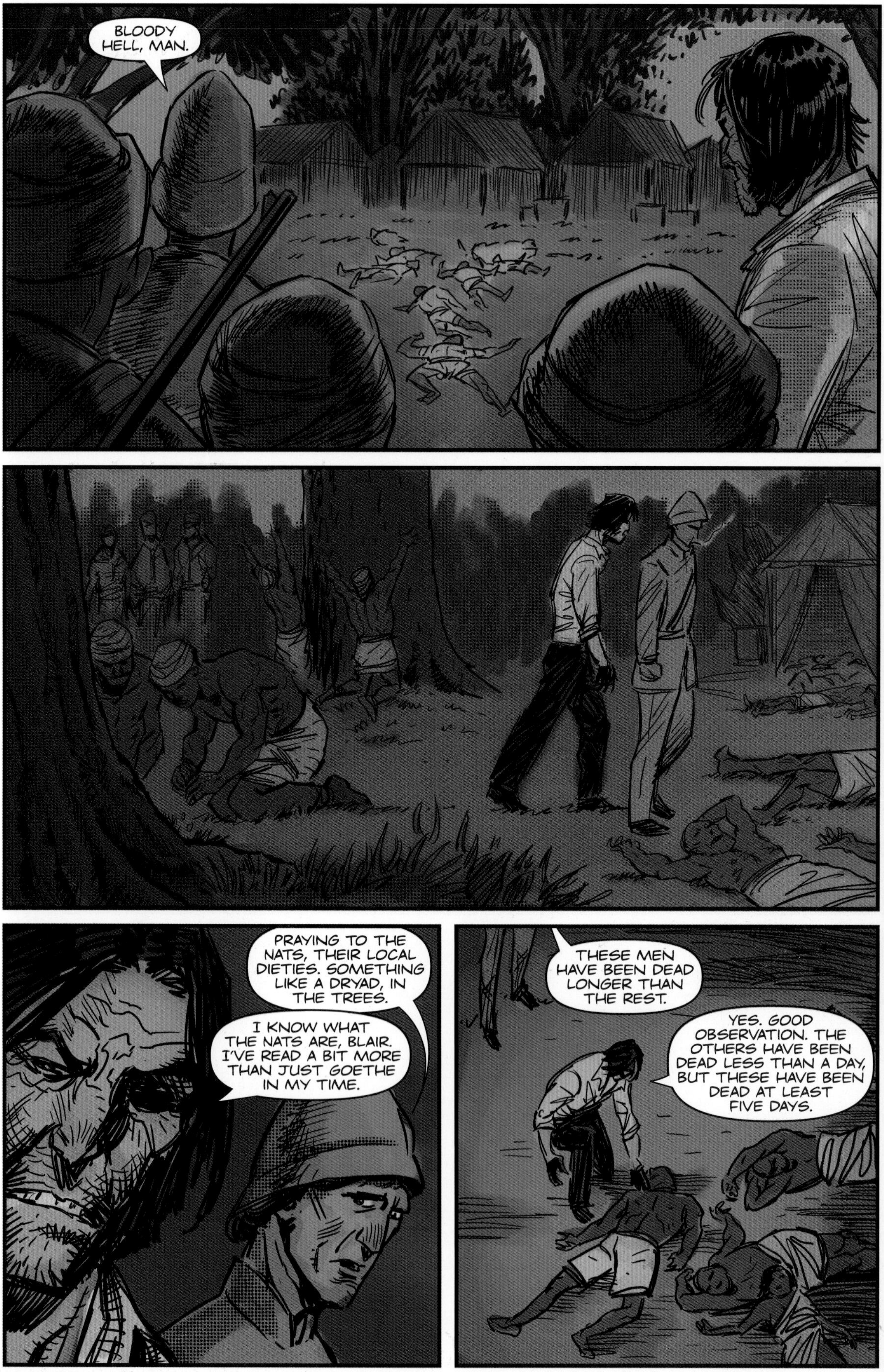
BLOODY HELL, MAN.
PRAYING TO THE NATS, THEIR LOCAL DIETIES. SOMETHING LIKE A DRYAD, IN THE TREES.
I KNOW WHAT THE NATS ARE, BLAIR. I'VE READ A BIT MORE THAN JUST GOETHE IN MY TIME.
THESE MEN HAVE BEEN DEAD LONGER THAN THE REST.
YES. GOOD OBSERVATION. THE OTHERS HAVE BEEN DEAD LESS THAN A DAY, BUT THESE HAVE BEEN DEAD AT LEAST FIVE DAYS.

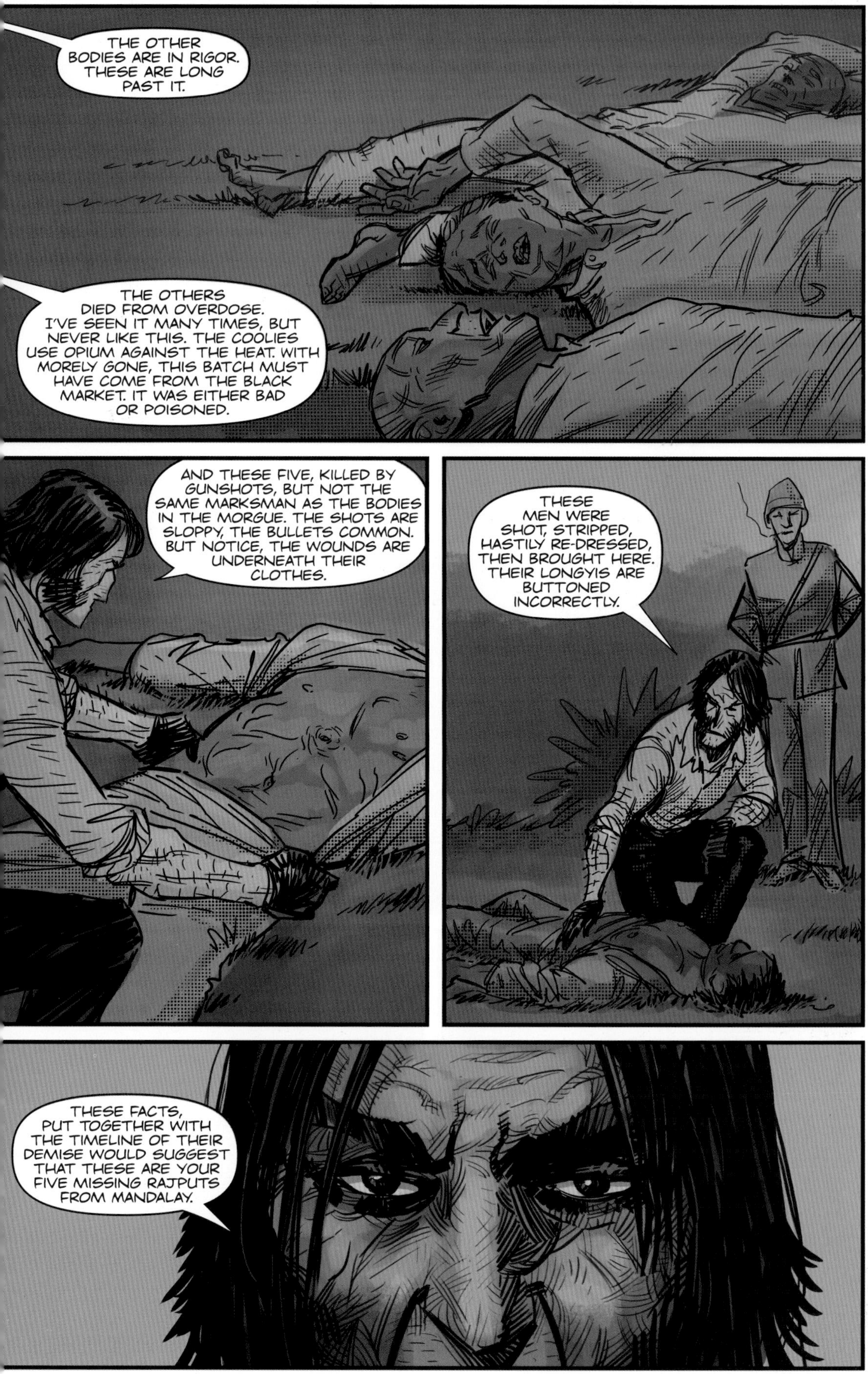
THE OTHER BODIES ARE IN RIGOR. THESE ARE LONG PAST IT.
THE OTHERS DIED FROM OVERDOSE. I'VE SEEN IT MANY TIMES, BUT NEVER LIKE THIS. THE COOLIES USE OPIUM AGAINST THE HEAT. WITH MORELY GONE, THIS BATCH MUST HAVE COME FROM THE BLACK MARKET. IT WAS EITHER BAD OR POISONED.
AND THESE FIVE, KILLED BY GUNSHOTS, BUT NOT THE SAME MARKSMAN AS THE BODIES IN THE MORGUE. THE SHOTS ARE SLOPPY, THE BULLETS COMMON. BUT NOTICE, THE WOUNDS ARE UNDERNEATH THEIR CLOTHES.
THESE MEN WERE SHOT, STRIPPED, HASTILY RE-DRESSED, THEN BROUGHT HERE. THEIR LONGYIS ARE BUTTONED INCORRECTLY.
THESE FACTS, PUT TOGETHER WITH THE TIMELINE OF THEIR DEMISE WOULD SUGGEST THAT THESE ARE YOUR FIVE MISSING RAJPUTS FROM MANDALAY.

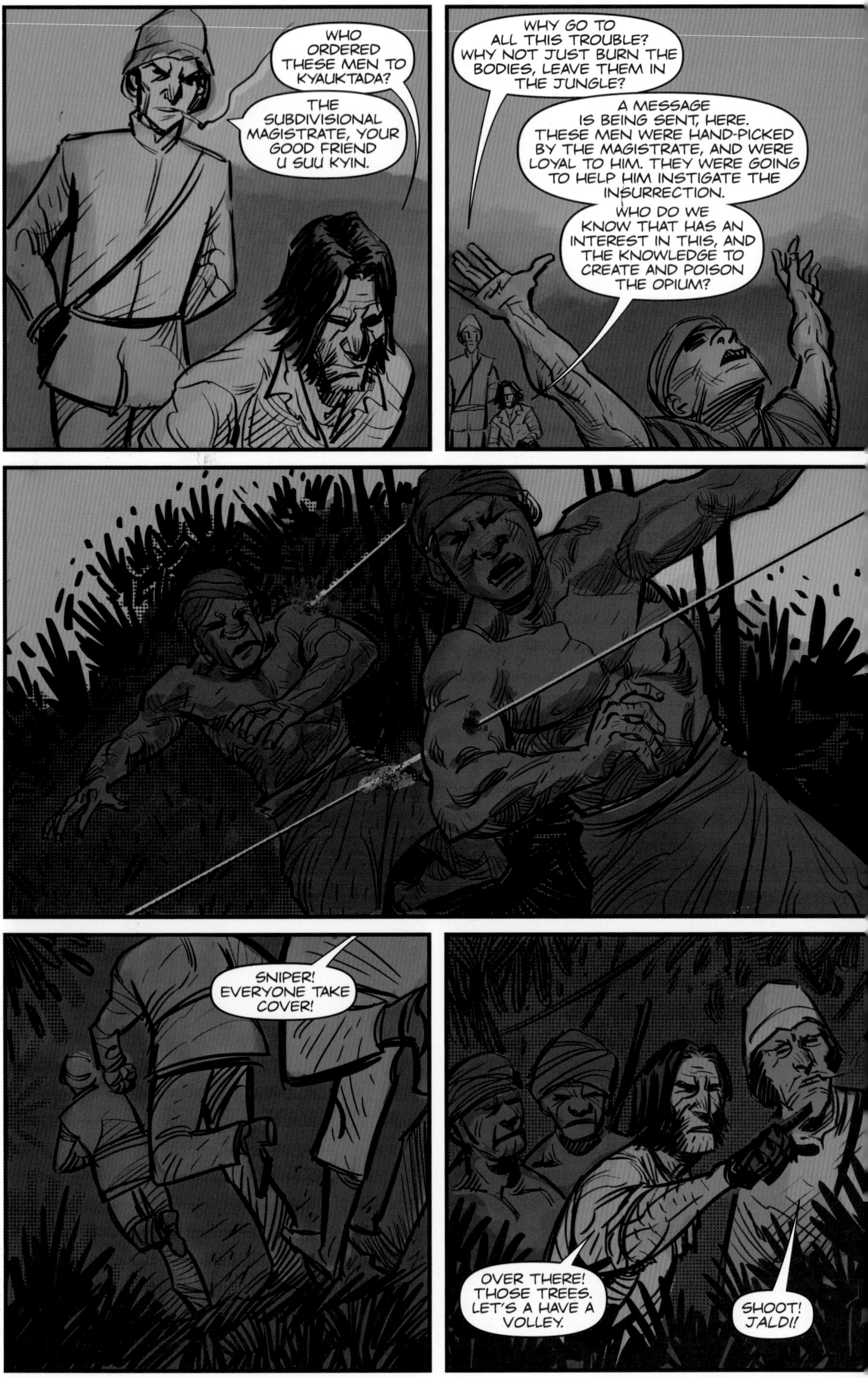
WHO ORDERED THESE MEN TO KYAUKTADA?
THE SUBDIVISIONAL MAGISTRATE, YOUR GOOD FRIEND U SUU KYIN.
WHY GO TO ALL THIS TROUBLE? WHY NOT JUST BURN THE BODIES, LEAVE THEM IN THE JUNGLE?
A MESSAGE IS BEING SENT, HERE. THESE MEN WERE HAND-PICKED BY THE MAGISTRATE, AND WERE LOYAL TO HIM. THEY WERE GOING TO HELP HIM INSTIGATE THE INSURRECTION.
WHO DO WE KNOW THAT HAS AN INTEREST IN THIS, AND THE KNOWLEDGE TO CREATE AND POISON THE OPIUM?
SNIPER! EVERYONE TAKE COVER!
OVER THERE! THOSE TREES. LET'S A HAVE A VOLLEY.
SHOOT! JALDI!

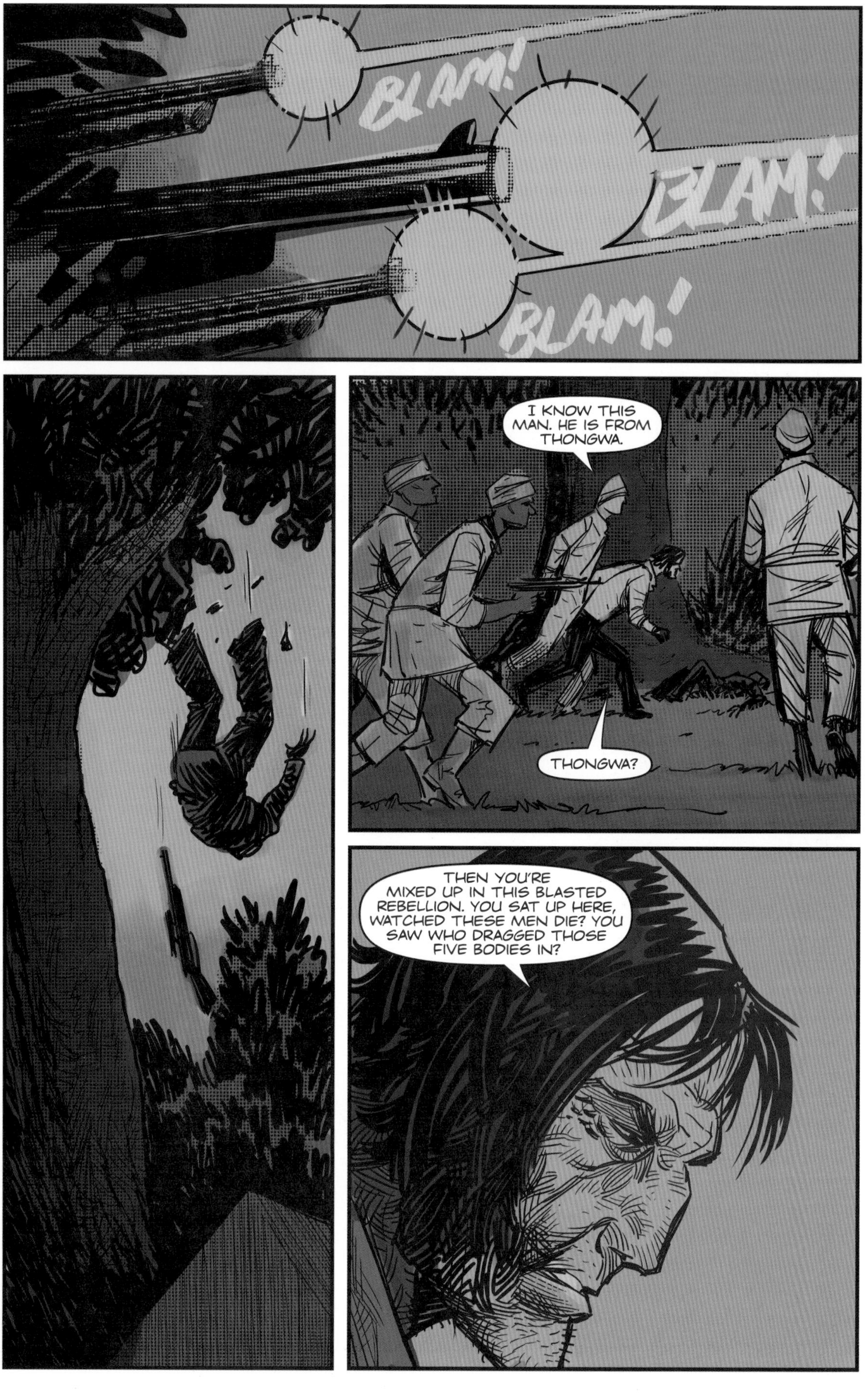
BLAM!
BLAM!
BLAM!
I KNOW THIS MAN. HE IS FROM THONGWA.
THONGWA?
THEN YOU'RE MIXED UP IN THIS BLASTED REBELLION. YOU SAT UP HERE, WATCHED THESE MEN DIE? YOU SAW WHO DRAGGED THOSE FIVE BODIES IN?

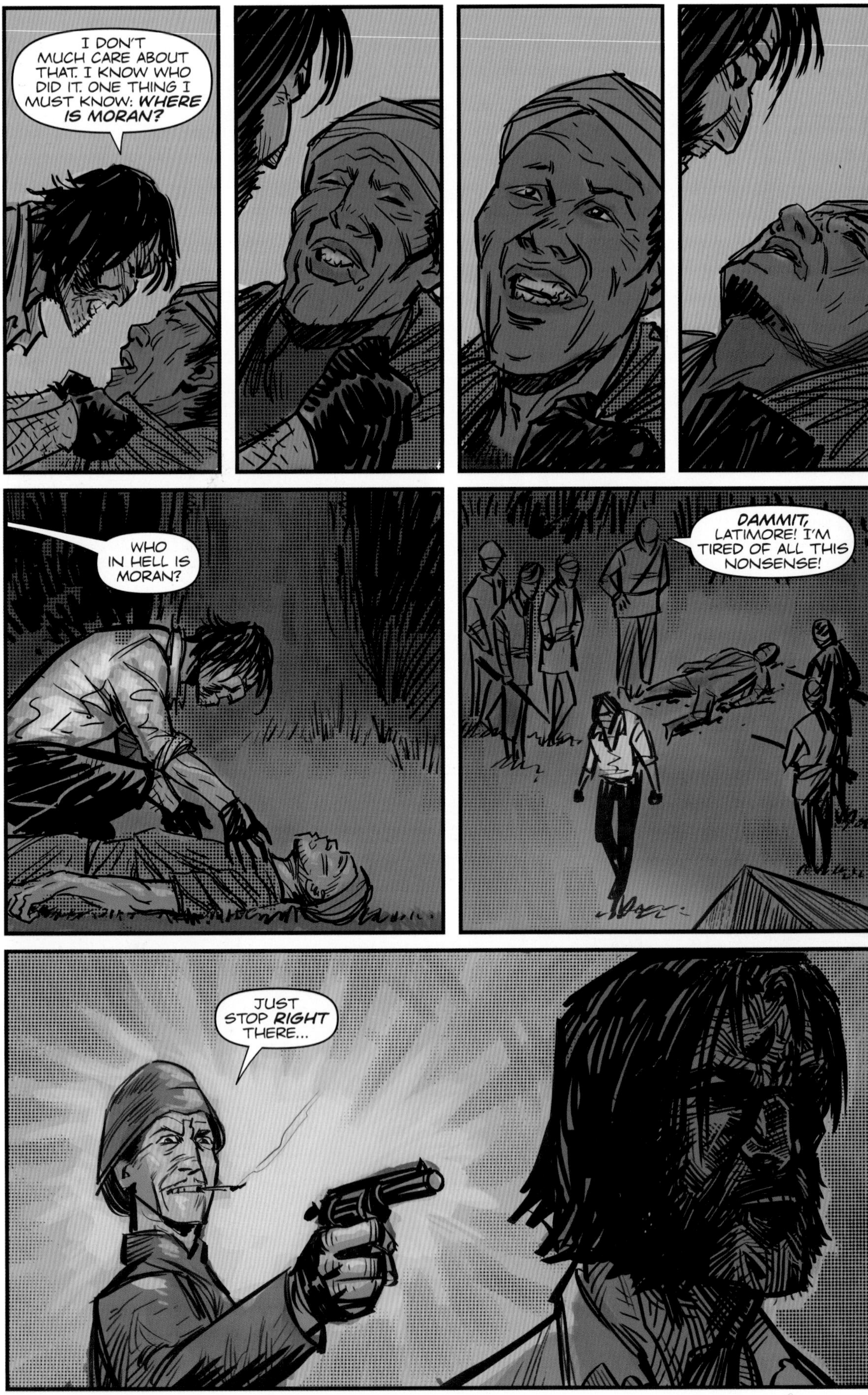
I DON'T MUCH CARE ABOUT THAT. I KNOW WHO DID IT. ONE THING I MUST KNOW: **WHERE IS MORAN?**
WHO IN HELL IS MORAN?
DAMMIT, LATIMORE! I'M TIRED OF ALL THIS NONSENSE!
JUST STOP **RIGHT** THERE...

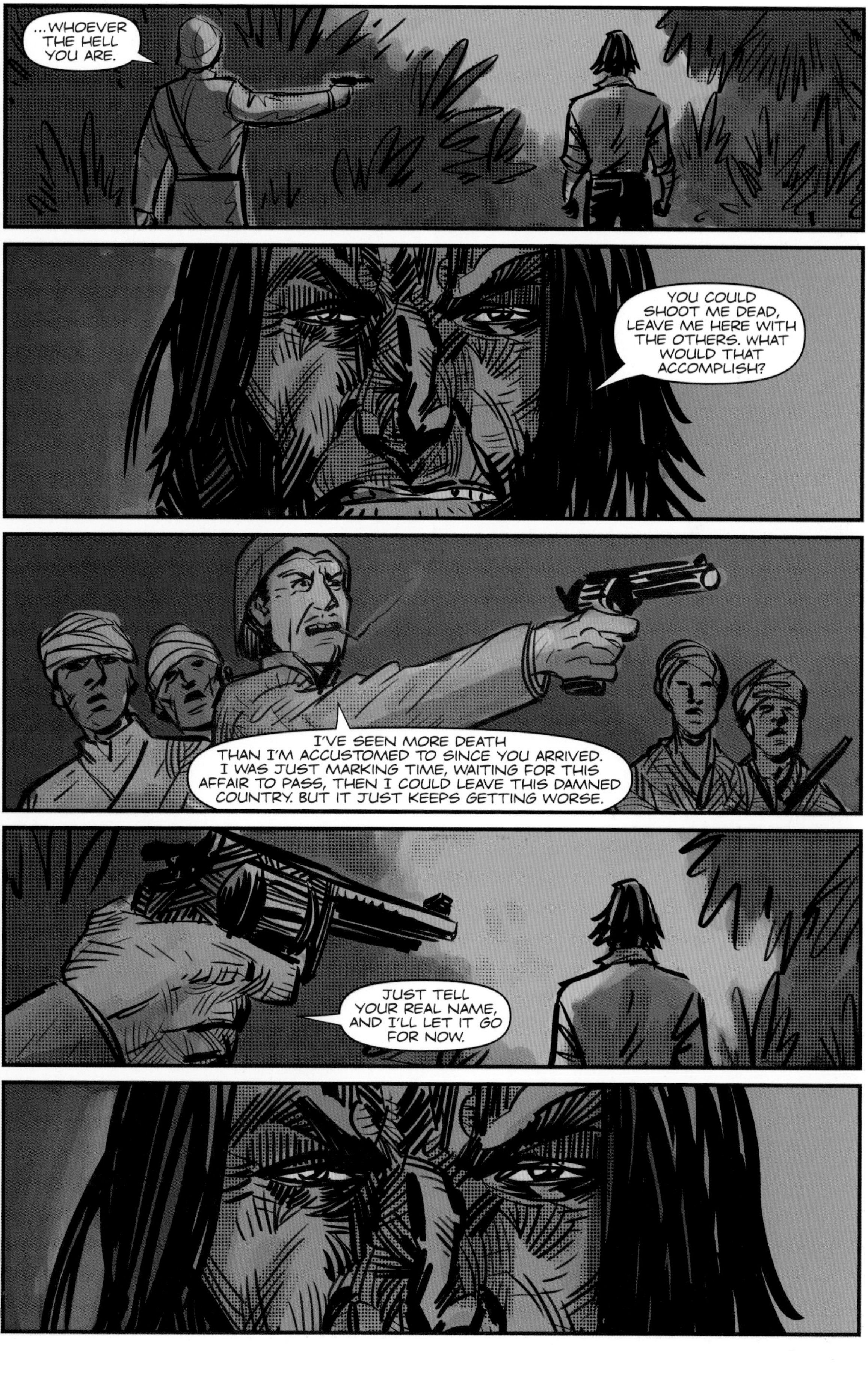
...WHOEVER THE HELL YOU ARE.
YOU COULD SHOOT ME DEAD, LEAVE ME HERE WITH THE OTHERS. WHAT WOULD THAT ACCOMPLISH?
I'VE SEEN MORE DEATH THAN I'M ACCUSTOMED TO SINCE YOU ARRIVED. I WAS JUST MARKING TIME, WAITING FOR THIS AFFAIR TO PASS, THEN I COULD LEAVE THIS DAMNED COUNTRY. BUT IT JUST KEEPS GETTING WORSE.
JUST TELL YOUR REAL NAME, AND I'LL LET IT GO FOR NOW.

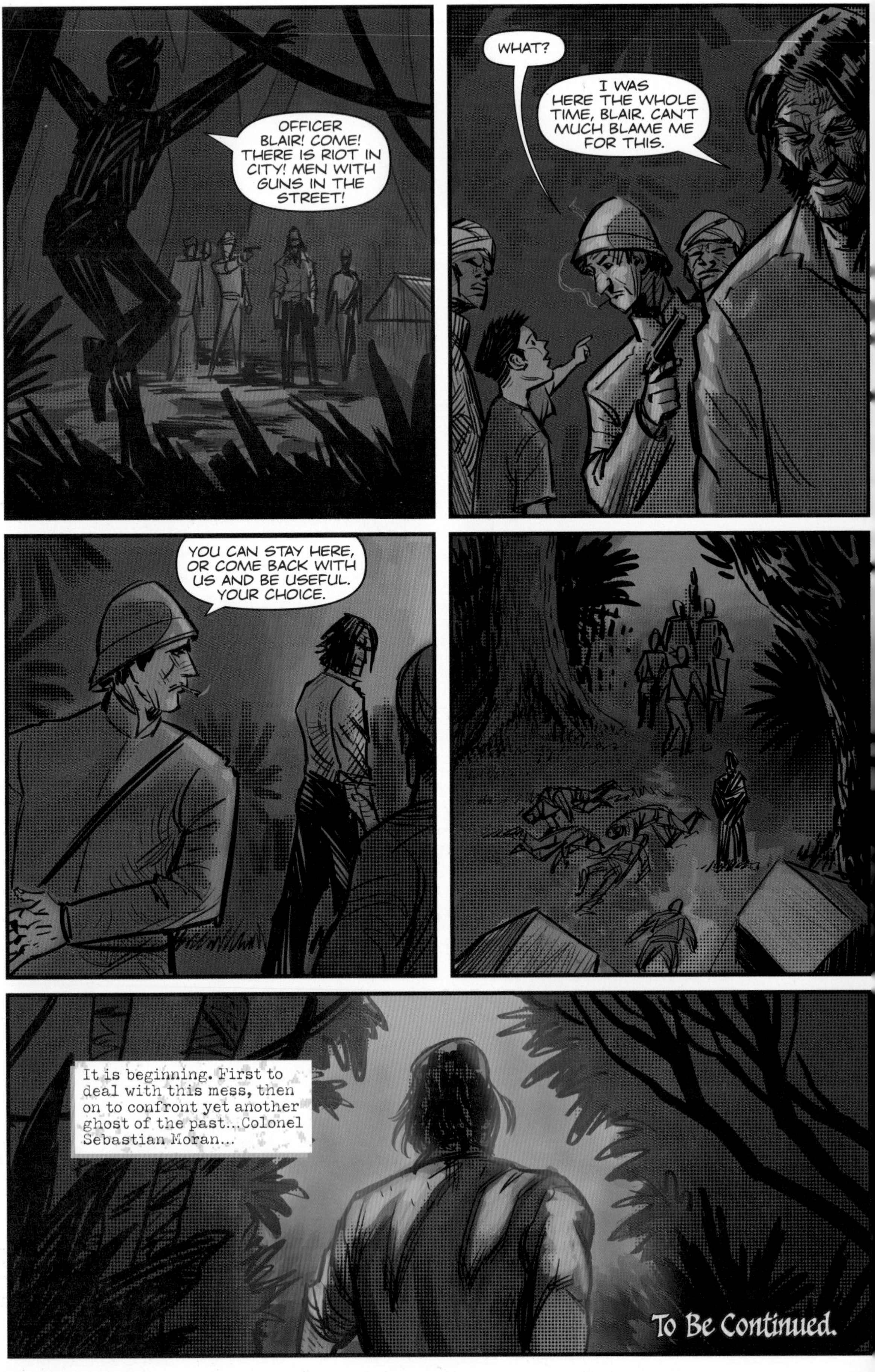
OFFICER BLAIR! COME! THERE IS RIOT IN CITY! MEN WITH GUNS IN THE STREET!
WHAT?
I WAS HERE THE WHOLE TIME, BLAIR. CAN'T MUCH BLAME ME FOR THIS.
YOU CAN STAY HERE, OR COME BACK WITH US AND BE USEFUL. YOUR CHOICE.
It is beginning. First to deal with this mess, then on to confront yet another ghost of the past...Colonel Sebastian Moran...
To Be Continued.

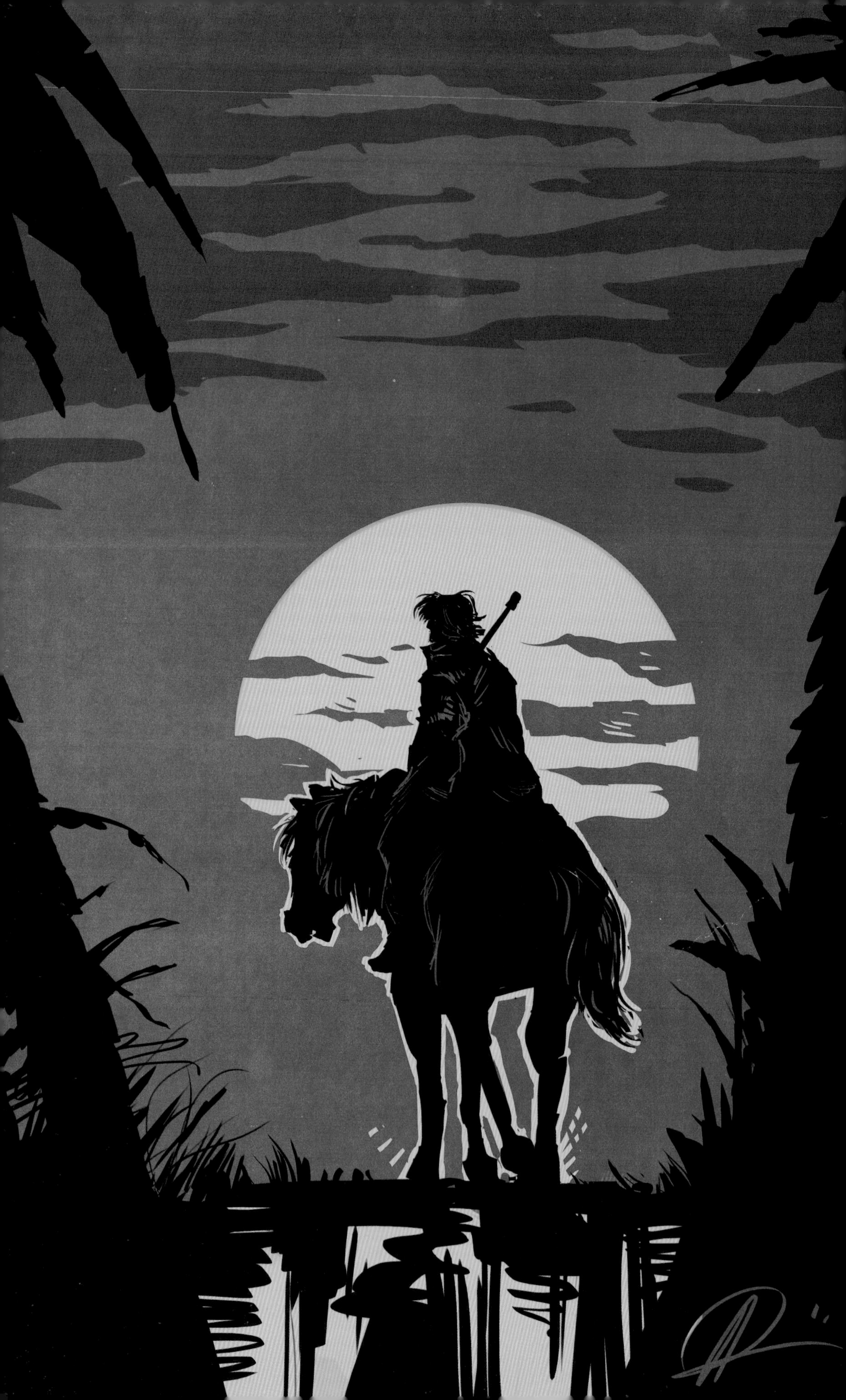

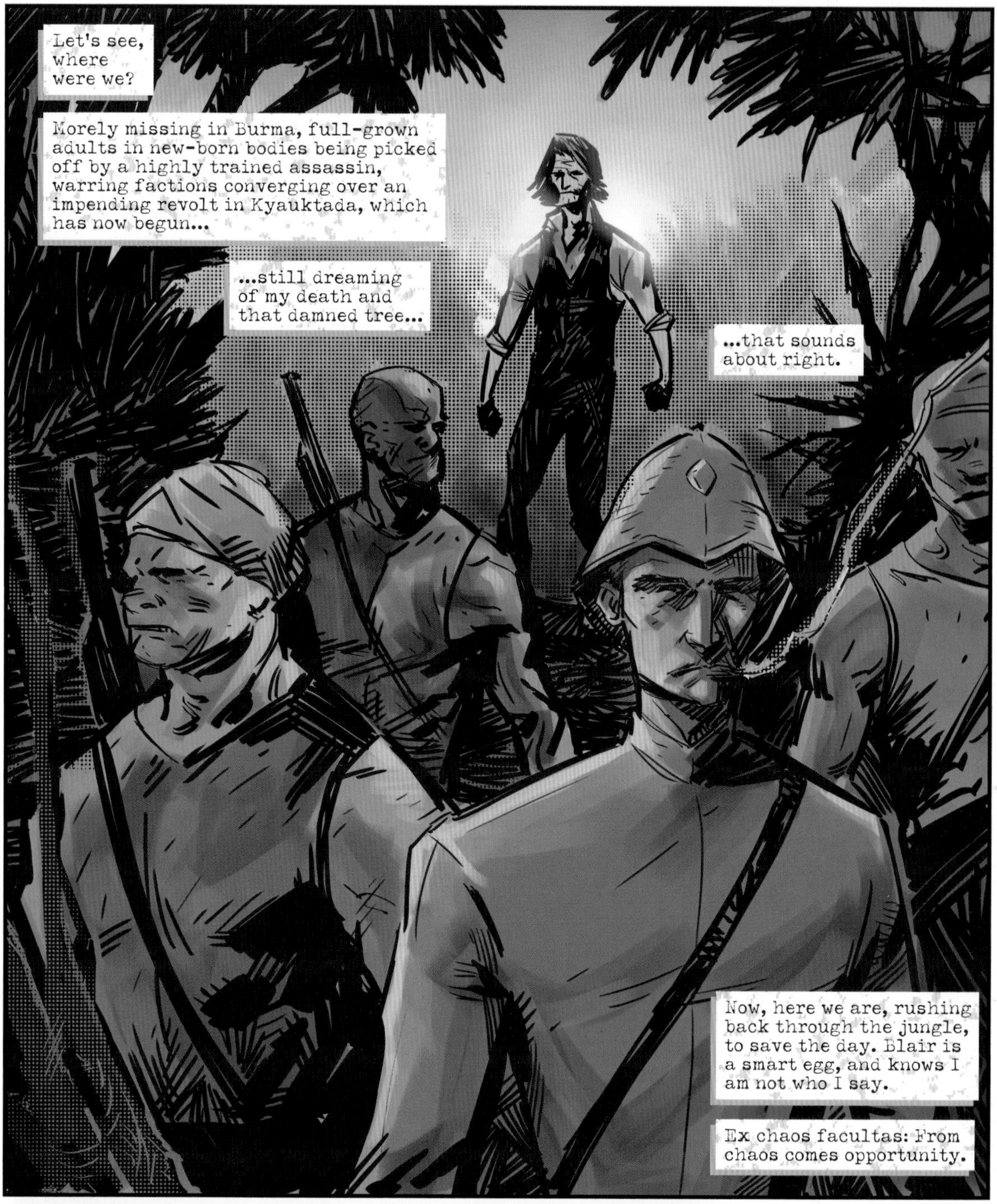
Let's see, where were we?
Morely missing in Burma, full-grown adults in new-born bodies being picked off by a highly trained assassin, warring factions converging over an impending revolt in Kyauktada, which has now begun...
...still dreaming of my death and that damned tree...
...that sounds about right.
Now, here we are, rushing back through the jungle, to save the day. Blair is a smart egg, and knows I am not who I say.
Ex chaos facultas: From chaos comes opportunity.

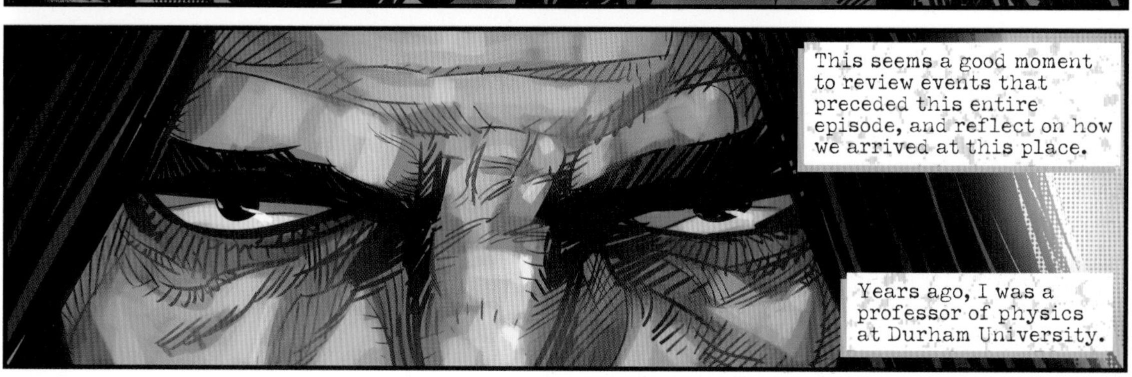
This seems a good moment to review events that preceded this entire episode, and reflect on how we arrived at this place.
Years ago, I was a professor of physics at Durham University.

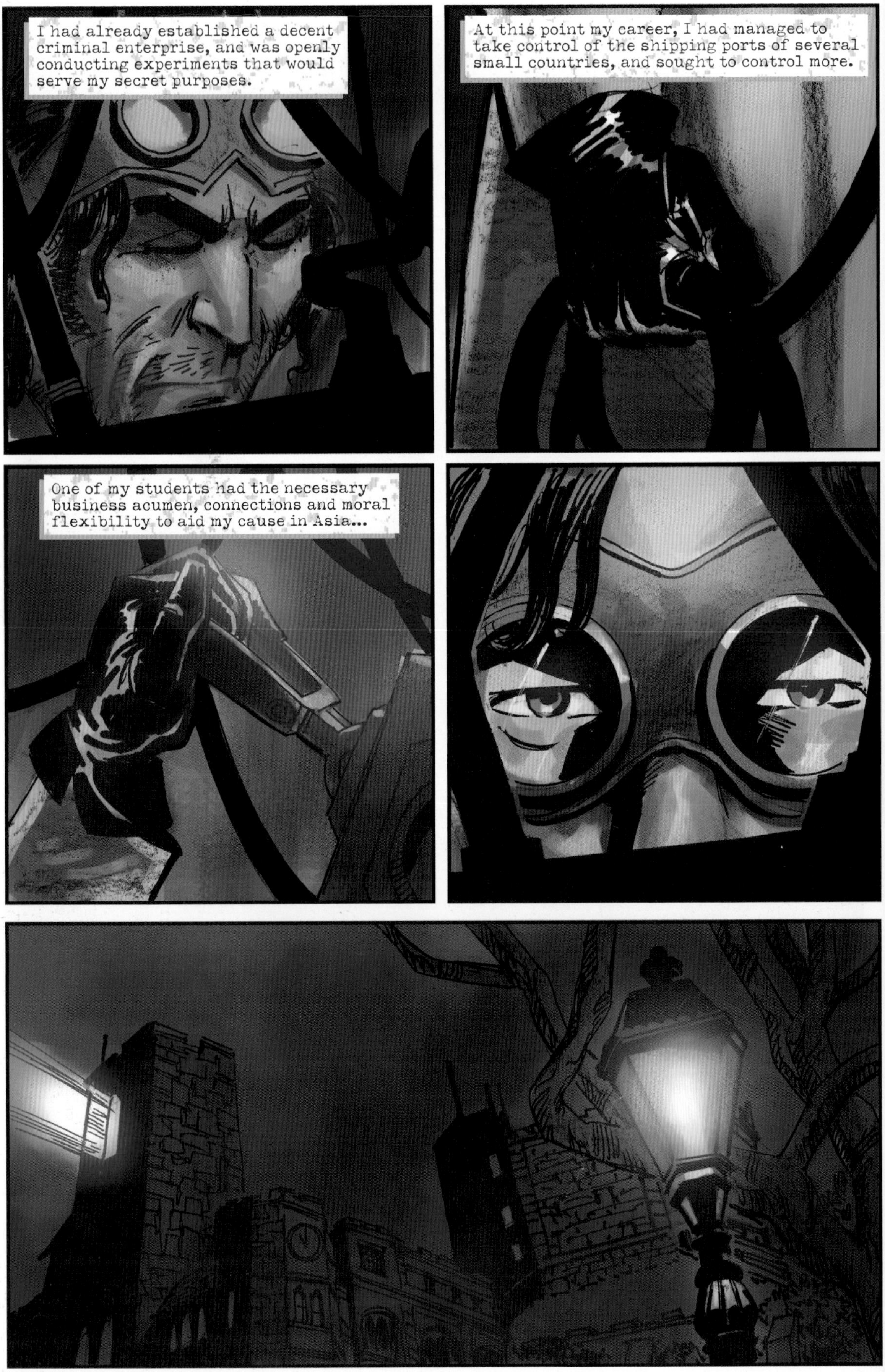
I had already established a decent criminal enterprise, and was openly conducting experiments that would serve my secret purposes.
At this point my career, I had managed to take control of the shipping ports of several small countries, and sought to control more.
One of my students had the necessary business acumen, connections and moral flexibility to aid my cause in Asia...

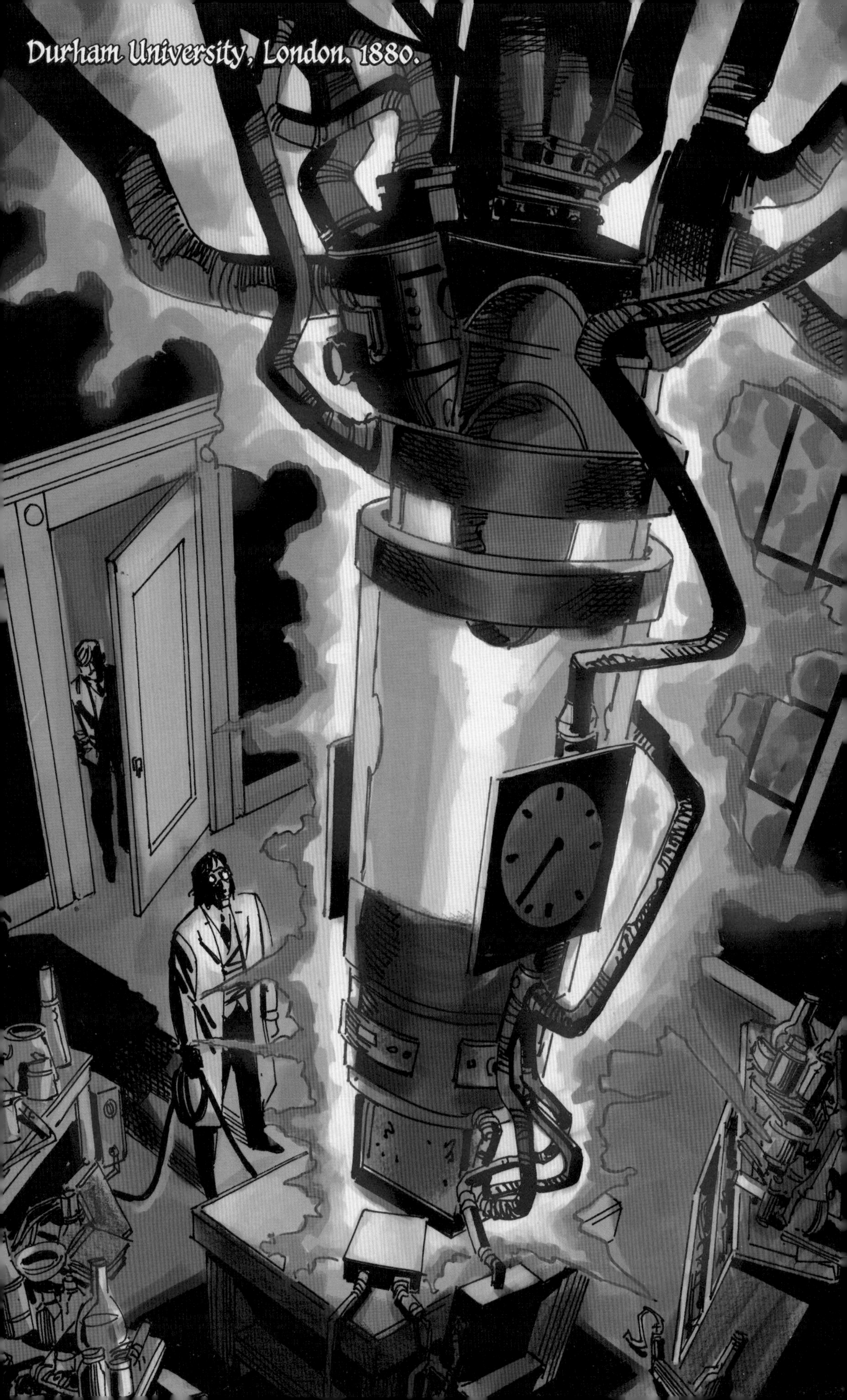
Durham University, London. 1880.

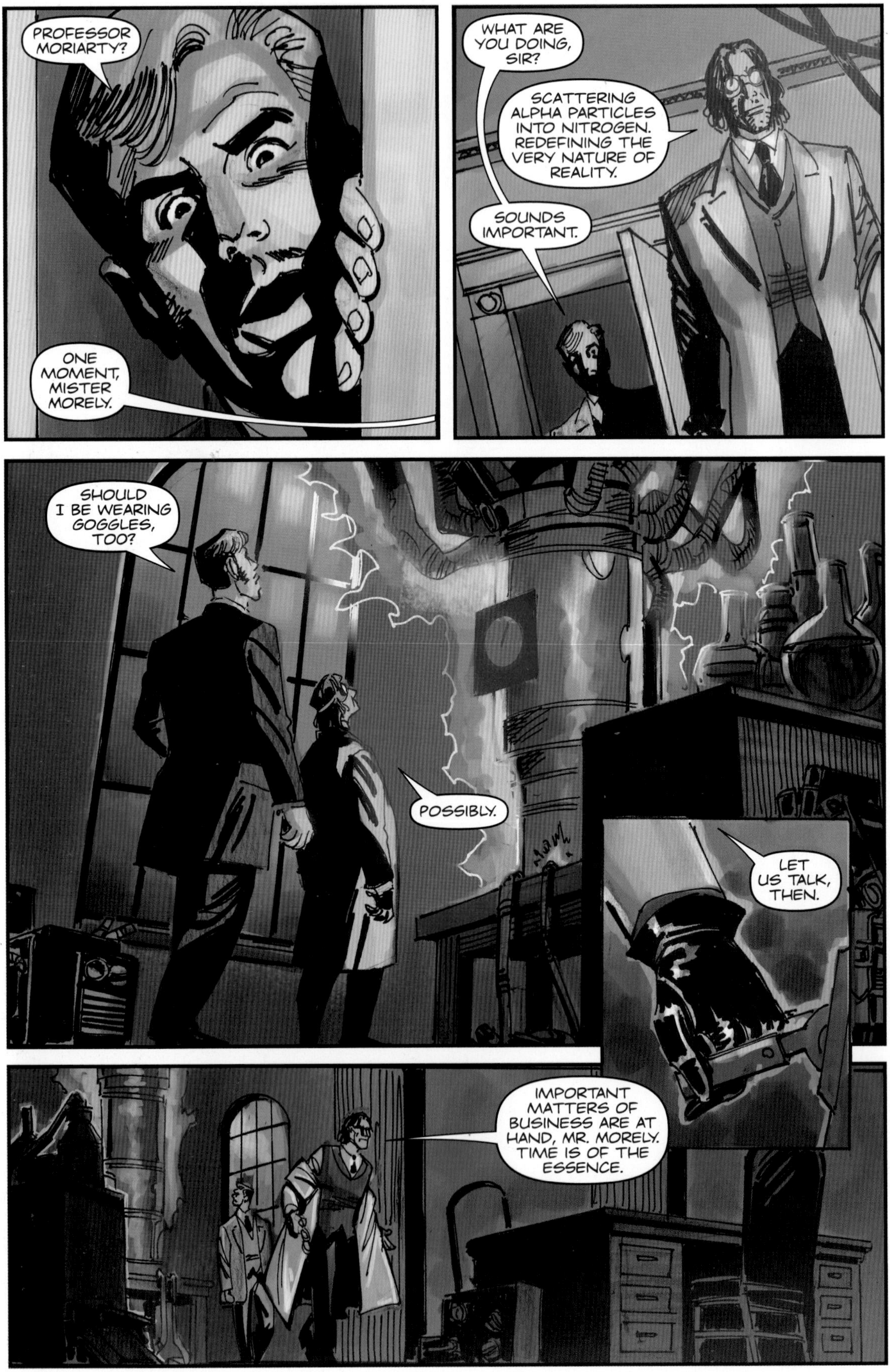
PROFESSOR MORIARTY?
ONE MOMENT, MISTER MORELY.
WHAT ARE YOU DOING, SIR?
SCATTERING ALPHA PARTICLES INTO NITROGEN. REDEFINING THE VERY NATURE OF REALITY.
SOUNDS IMPORTANT.
SHOULD I BE WEARING GOGGLES, TOO?
POSSIBLY.
LET US TALK, THEN.
IMPORTANT MATTERS OF BUSINESS ARE AT HAND, MR. MORELY. TIME IS OF THE ESSENCE.

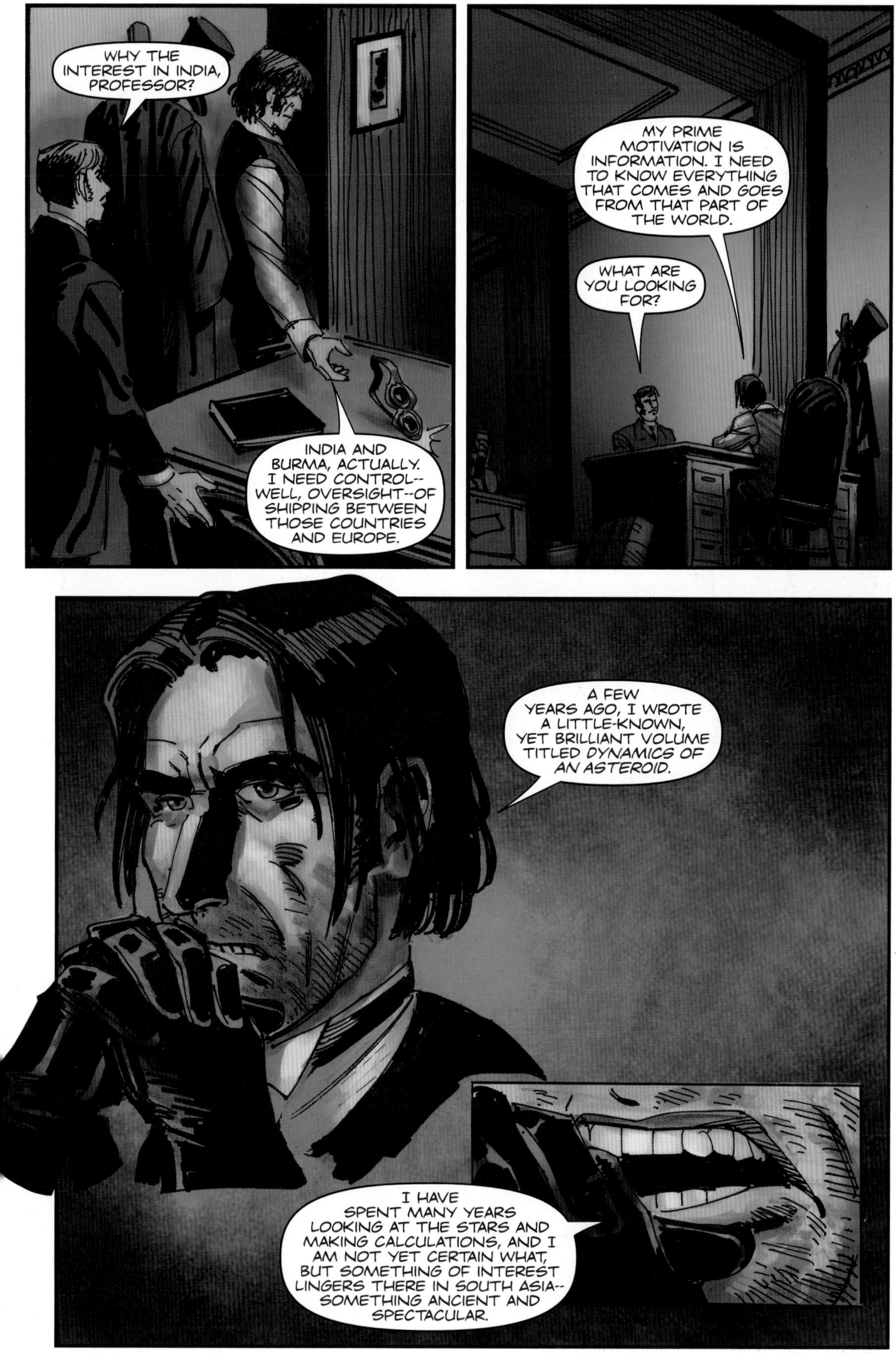
WHY THE INTEREST IN INDIA, PROFESSOR?
INDIA AND BURMA, ACTUALLY. I NEED CONTROL--WELL, OVERSIGHT--OF SHIPPING BETWEEN THOSE COUNTRIES AND EUROPE.
MY PRIME MOTIVATION IS INFORMATION. I NEED TO KNOW EVERYTHING THAT COMES AND GOES FROM THAT PART OF THE WORLD.
WHAT ARE YOU LOOKING FOR?
A FEW YEARS AGO, I WROTE A LITTLE-KNOWN, YET BRILLIANT VOLUME TITLED *DYNAMICS OF AN ASTEROID.*
I HAVE SPENT MANY YEARS LOOKING AT THE STARS AND MAKING CALCULATIONS, AND I AM NOT YET CERTAIN WHAT, BUT SOMETHING OF INTEREST LINGERS THERE IN SOUTH ASIA--SOMETHING ANCIENT AND SPECTACULAR.

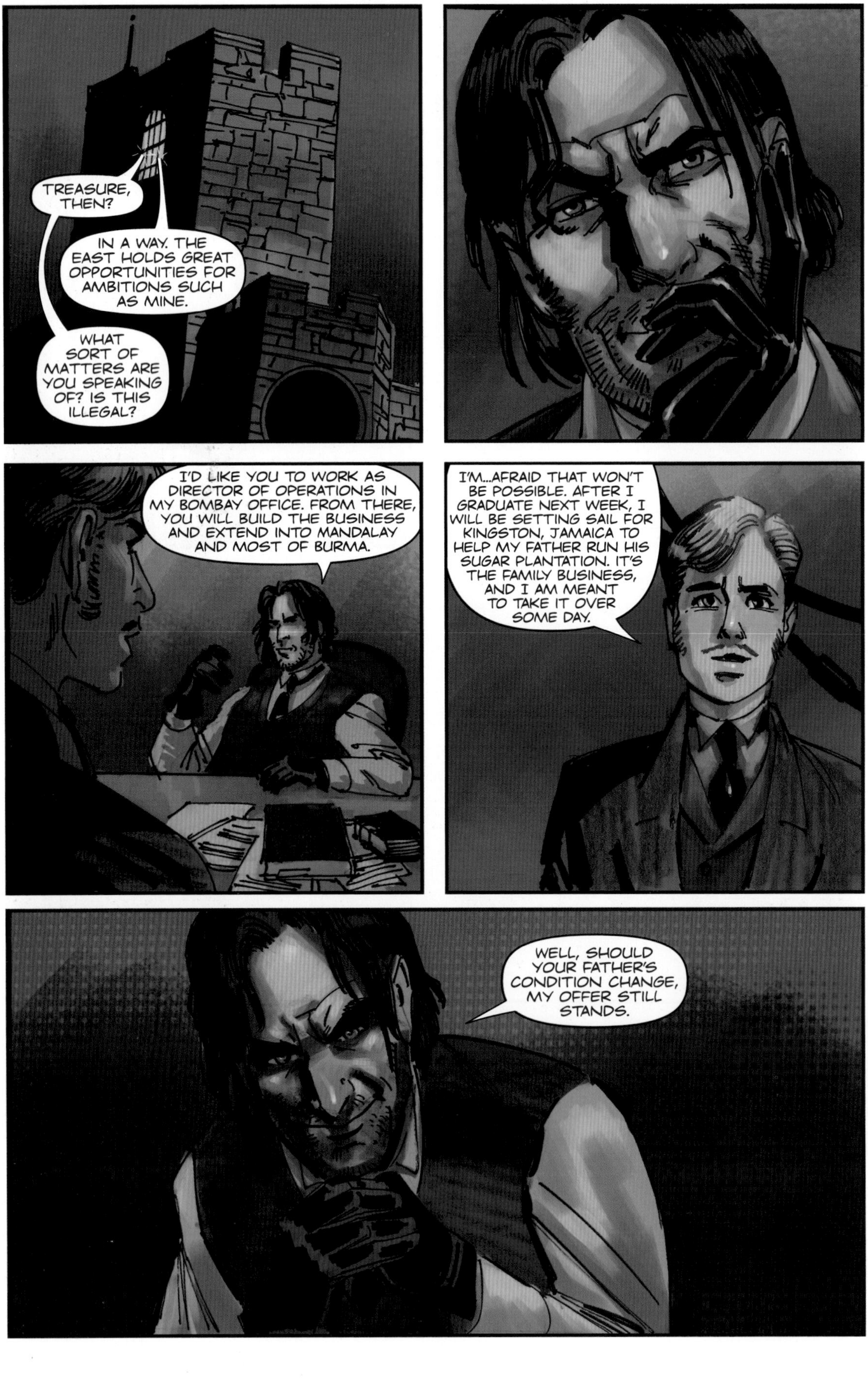
TREASURE, THEN?
IN A WAY. THE EAST HOLDS GREAT OPPORTUNITIES FOR AMBITIONS SUCH AS MINE.
WHAT SORT OF MATTERS ARE YOU SPEAKING OF? IS THIS ILLEGAL?
I'D LIKE YOU TO WORK AS DIRECTOR OF OPERATIONS IN MY BOMBAY OFFICE. FROM THERE, YOU WILL BUILD THE BUSINESS AND EXTEND INTO MANDALAY AND MOST OF BURMA.
I'M...AFRAID THAT WON'T BE POSSIBLE. AFTER I GRADUATE NEXT WEEK, I WILL BE SETTING SAIL FOR KINGSTON, JAMAICA TO HELP MY FATHER RUN HIS SUGAR PLANTATION. IT'S THE FAMILY BUSINESS, AND I AM MEANT TO TAKE IT OVER SOME DAY.
WELL, SHOULD YOUR FATHER'S CONDITION CHANGE, MY OFFER STILL STANDS.

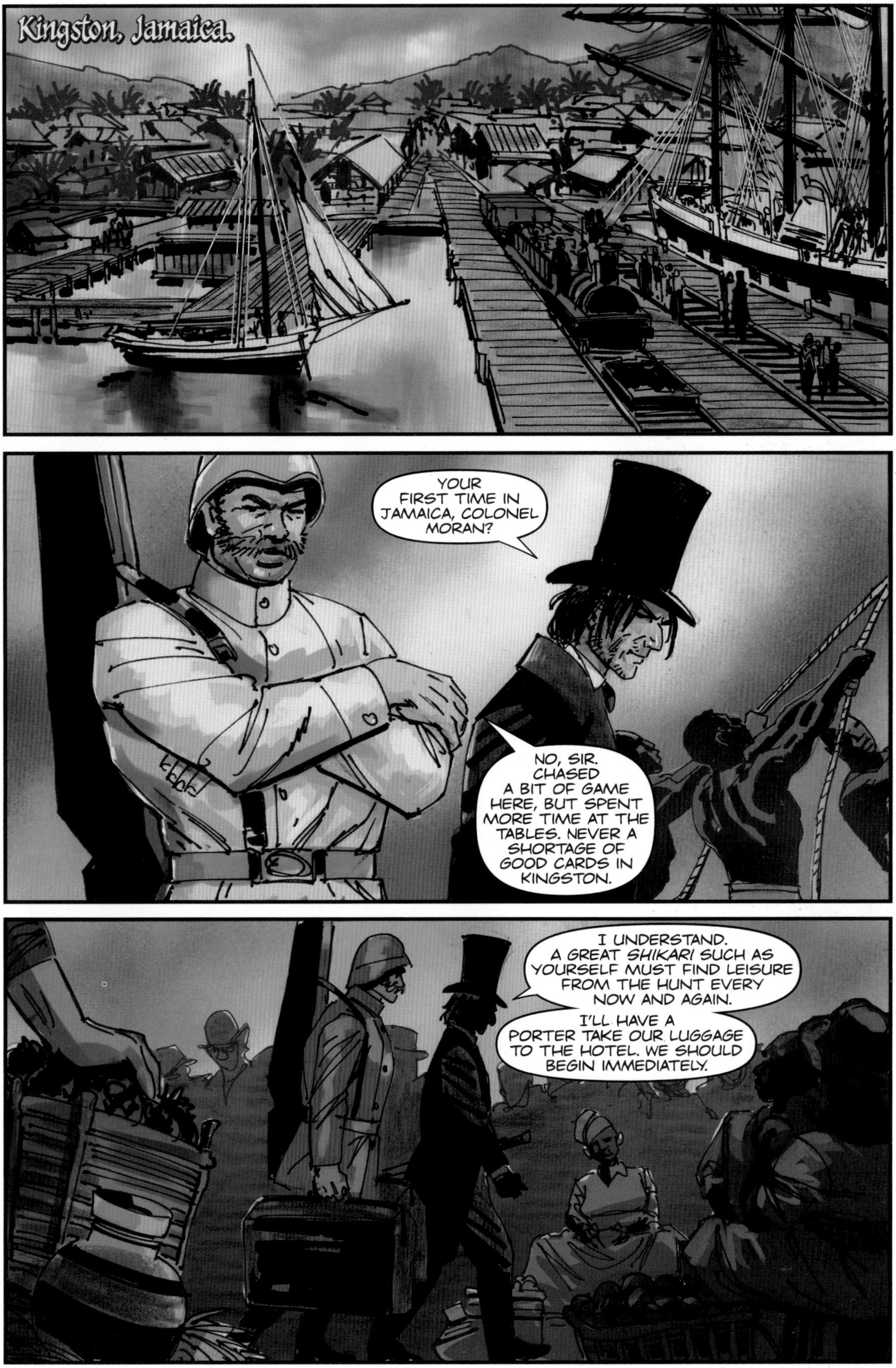
Kingston, Jamaica.
YOUR FIRST TIME IN JAMAICA, COLONEL MORAN?
NO, SIR. CHASED A BIT OF GAME HERE, BUT SPENT MORE TIME AT THE TABLES. NEVER A SHORTAGE OF GOOD CARDS IN KINGSTON.
I UNDERSTAND. A GREAT *SHIKARI* SUCH AS YOURSELF MUST FIND LEISURE FROM THE HUNT EVERY NOW AND AGAIN.
I'LL HAVE A PORTER TAKE OUR LUGGAGE TO THE HOTEL. WE SHOULD BEGIN IMMEDIATELY.

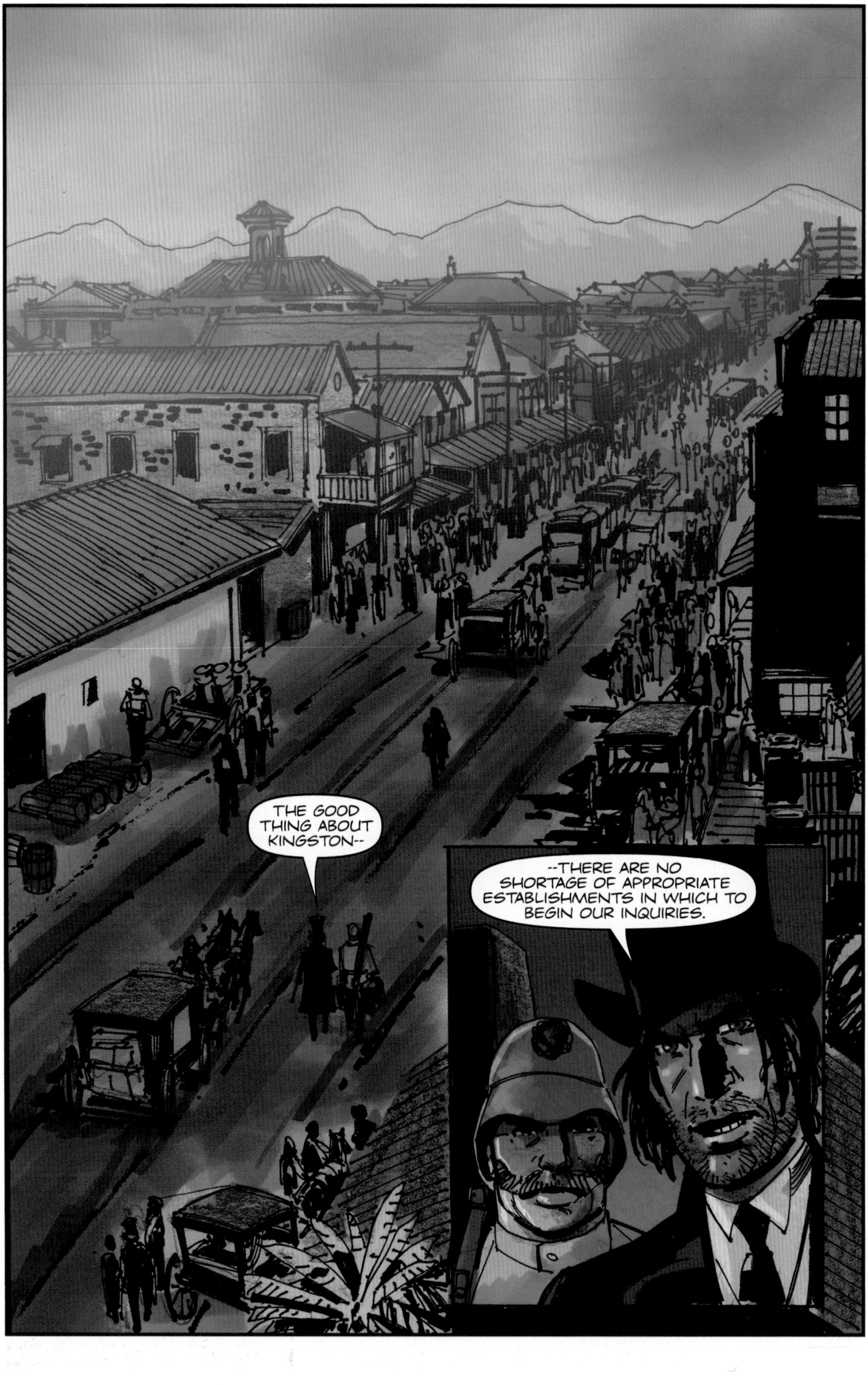
THE GOOD THING ABOUT KINGSTON--
--THERE ARE NO SHORTAGE OF APPROPRIATE ESTABLISHMENTS IN WHICH TO BEGIN OUR INQUIRIES.

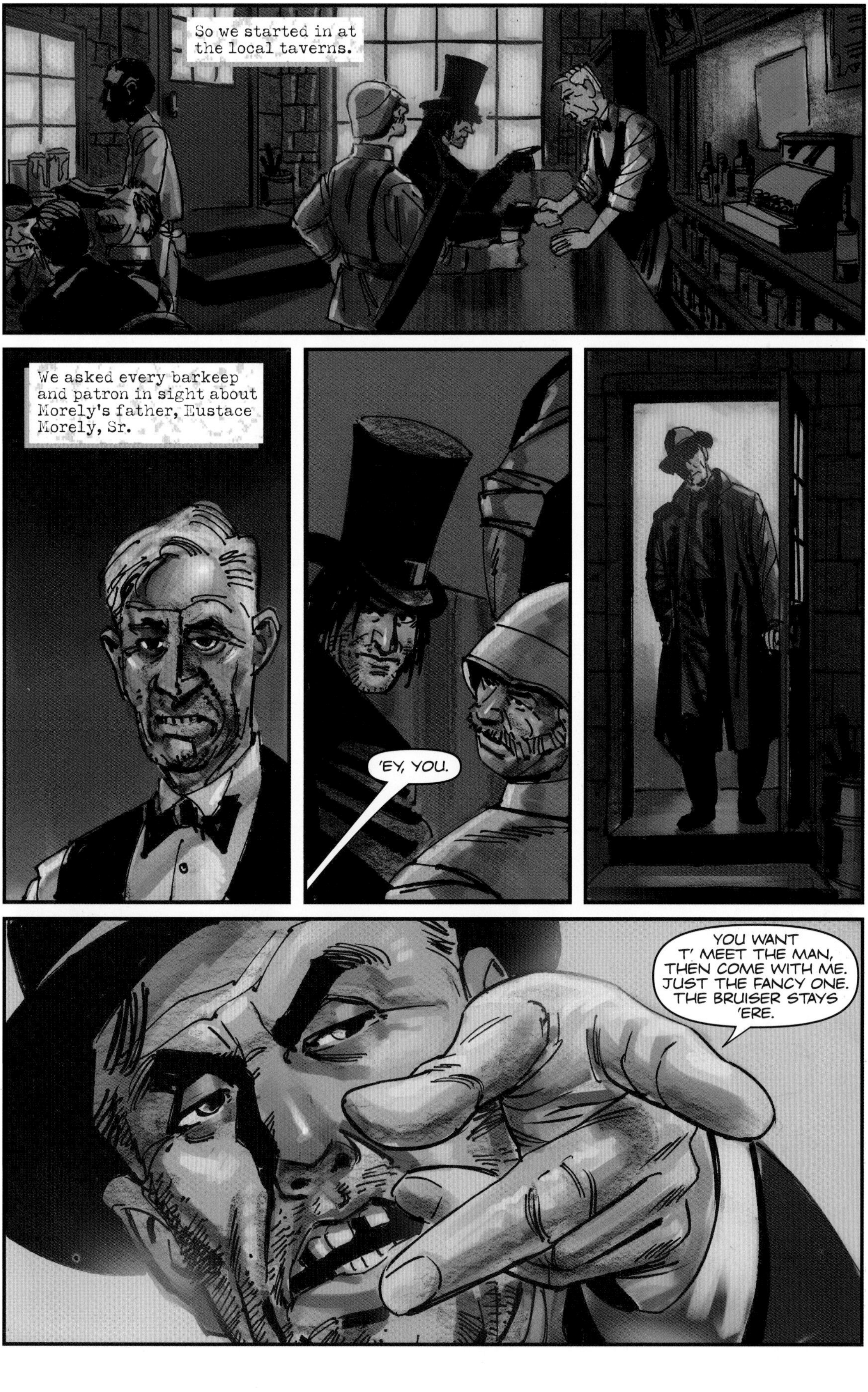
So we started in at the local taverns.
We asked every barkeep and patron in sight about Morely's father, Eustace Morely, Sr.
'EY, YOU.
YOU WANT T' MEET THE MAN, THEN COME WITH ME. JUST THE FANCY ONE. THE BRUISER STAYS 'ERE.

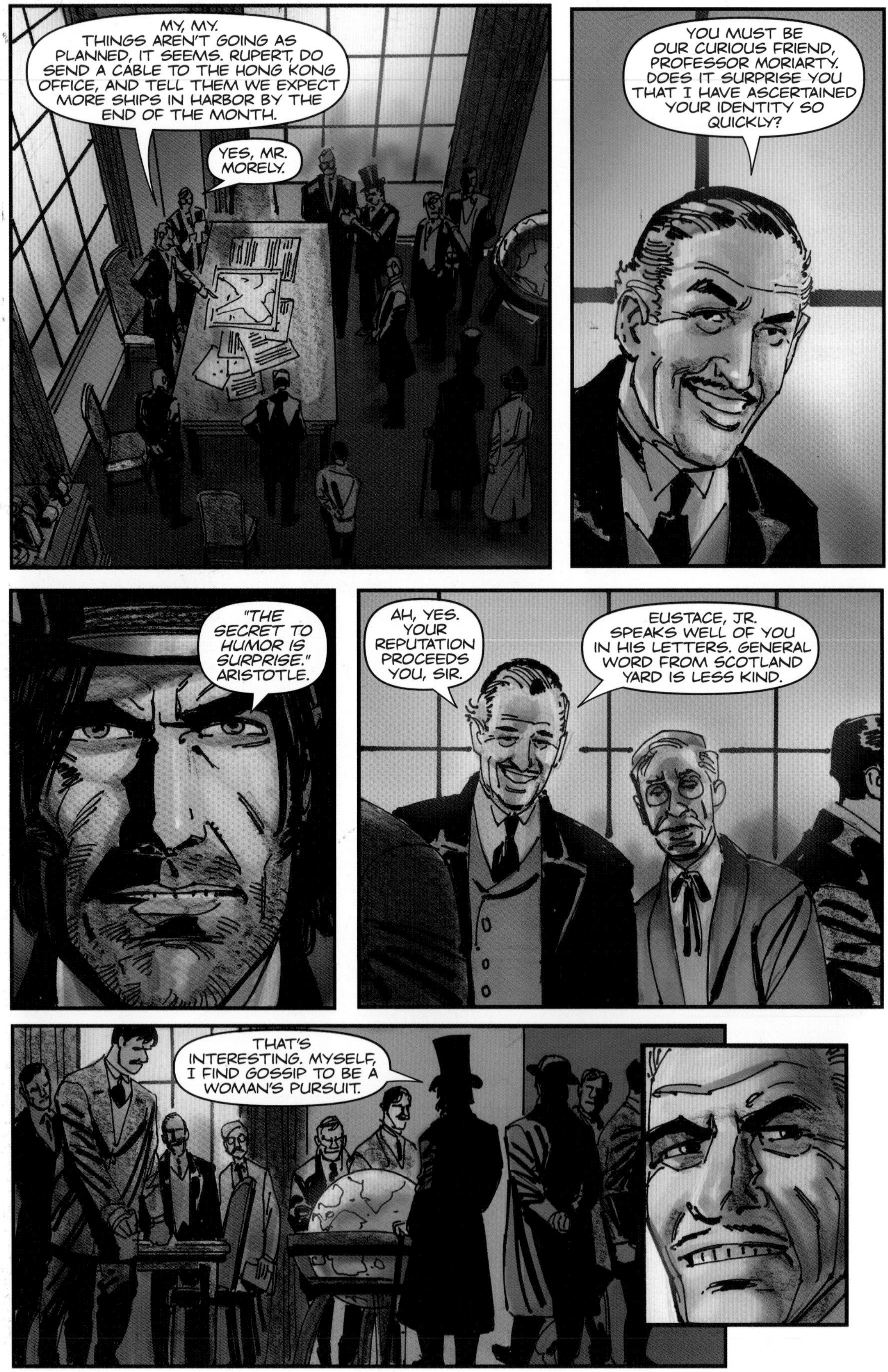
MY, MY. THINGS AREN'T GOING AS PLANNED, IT SEEMS. RUPERT, DO SEND A CABLE TO THE HONG KONG OFFICE, AND TELL THEM WE EXPECT MORE SHIPS IN HARBOR BY THE END OF THE MONTH.
YES, MR. MORELY.
YOU MUST BE OUR CURIOUS FRIEND, PROFESSOR MORIARTY. DOES IT SURPRISE YOU THAT I HAVE ASCERTAINED YOUR IDENTITY SO QUICKLY?
"THE SECRET TO HUMOR IS SURPRISE." ARISTOTLE.
AH, YES. YOUR REPUTATION PROCEEDS YOU, SIR.
EUSTACE, JR. SPEAKS WELL OF YOU IN HIS LETTERS. GENERAL WORD FROM SCOTLAND YARD IS LESS KIND.
THAT'S INTERESTING. MYSELF, I FIND GOSSIP TO BE A WOMAN'S PURSUIT.

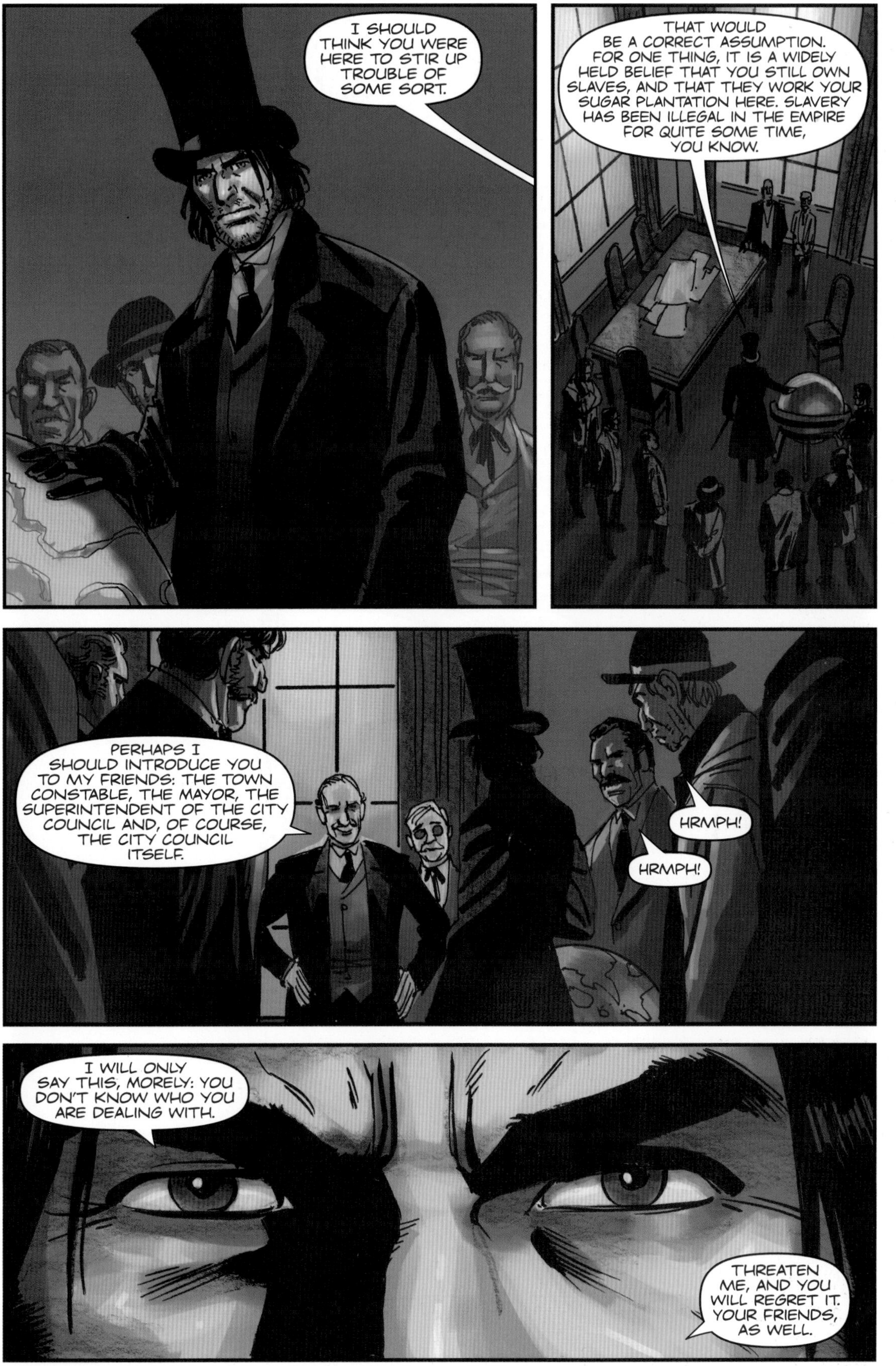
I SHOULD THINK YOU WERE HERE TO STIR UP TROUBLE OF SOME SORT.
THAT WOULD BE A CORRECT ASSUMPTION. FOR ONE THING, IT IS A WIDELY HELD BELIEF THAT YOU STILL OWN SLAVES, AND THAT THEY WORK YOUR SUGAR PLANTATION HERE. SLAVERY HAS BEEN ILLEGAL IN THE EMPIRE FOR QUITE SOME TIME, YOU KNOW.
PERHAPS I SHOULD INTRODUCE YOU TO MY FRIENDS: THE TOWN CONSTABLE, THE MAYOR, THE SUPERINTENDENT OF THE CITY COUNCIL AND, OF COURSE, THE CITY COUNCIL ITSELF.
HRMPH!
HRMPH!
I WILL ONLY SAY THIS, MORELY: YOU DON'T KNOW WHO YOU ARE DEALING WITH.
THREATEN ME, AND YOU WILL REGRET IT. YOUR FRIENDS, AS WELL.

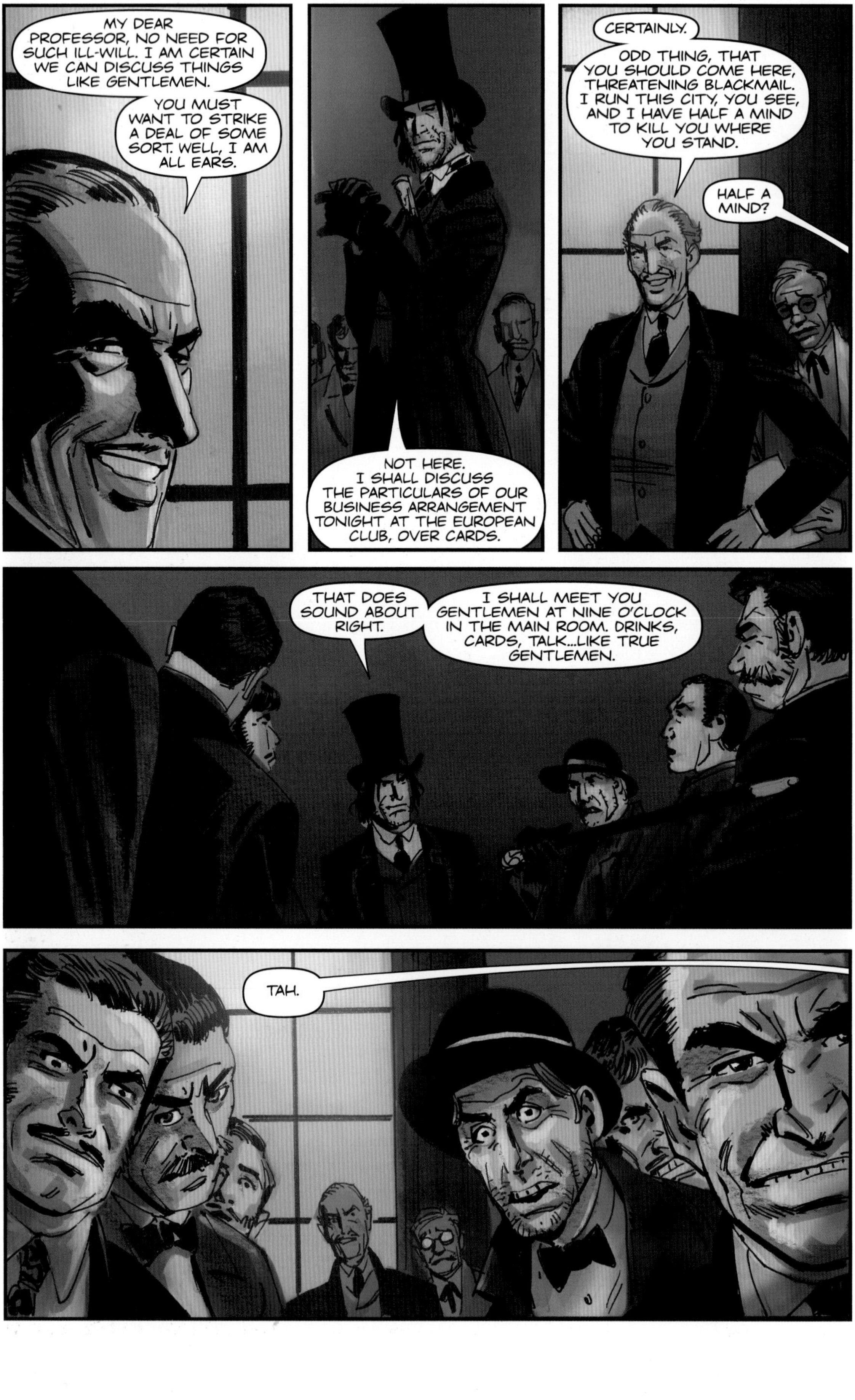
MY DEAR PROFESSOR, NO NEED FOR SUCH ILL-WILL. I AM CERTAIN WE CAN DISCUSS THINGS LIKE GENTLEMEN.
YOU MUST WANT TO STRIKE A DEAL OF SOME SORT. WELL, I AM ALL EARS.
NOT HERE. I SHALL DISCUSS THE PARTICULARS OF OUR BUSINESS ARRANGEMENT TONIGHT AT THE EUROPEAN CLUB, OVER CARDS.
CERTAINLY.
ODD THING, THAT YOU SHOULD COME HERE, THREATENING BLACKMAIL. I RUN THIS CITY, YOU SEE, AND I HAVE HALF A MIND TO KILL YOU WHERE YOU STAND.
HALF A MIND?
THAT DOES SOUND ABOUT RIGHT.
I SHALL MEET YOU GENTLEMEN AT NINE O'CLOCK IN THE MAIN ROOM. DRINKS, CARDS, TALK...LIKE TRUE GENTLEMEN.
TAH.

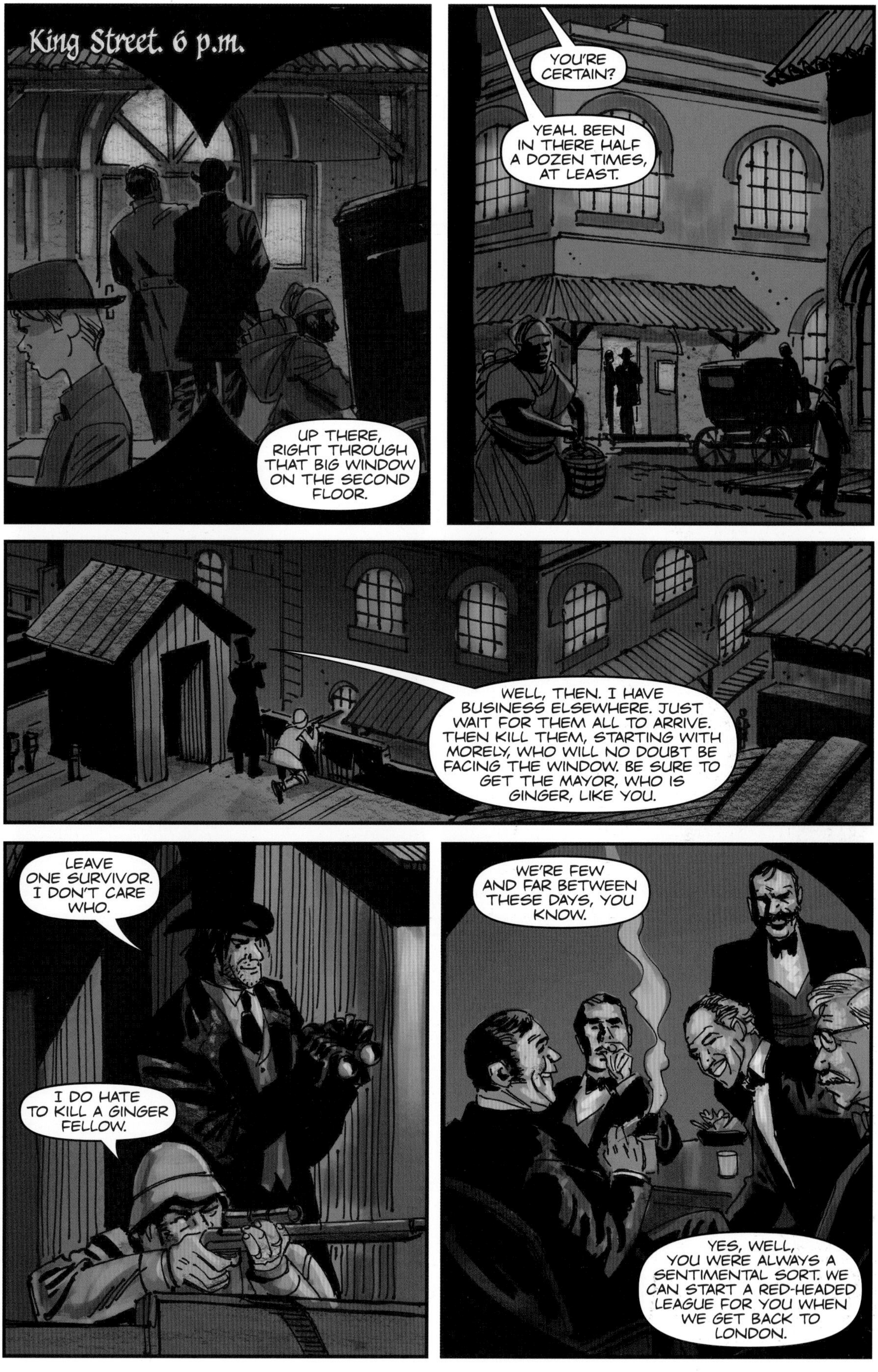
King Street. 6 p.m.
UP THERE, RIGHT THROUGH THAT BIG WINDOW ON THE SECOND FLOOR.
YOU'RE CERTAIN?
YEAH. BEEN IN THERE HALF A DOZEN TIMES, AT LEAST.
WELL, THEN. I HAVE BUSINESS ELSEWHERE. JUST WAIT FOR THEM ALL TO ARRIVE. THEN KILL THEM, STARTING WITH MORELY, WHO WILL NO DOUBT BE FACING THE WINDOW. BE SURE TO GET THE MAYOR, WHO IS GINGER, LIKE YOU.
LEAVE ONE SURVIVOR. I DON'T CARE WHO.
I DO HATE TO KILL A GINGER FELLOW.
WE'RE FEW AND FAR BETWEEN THESE DAYS, YOU KNOW.
YES, WELL, YOU WERE ALWAYS A SENTIMENTAL SORT. WE CAN START A RED-HEADED LEAGUE FOR YOU WHEN WE GET BACK TO LONDON.

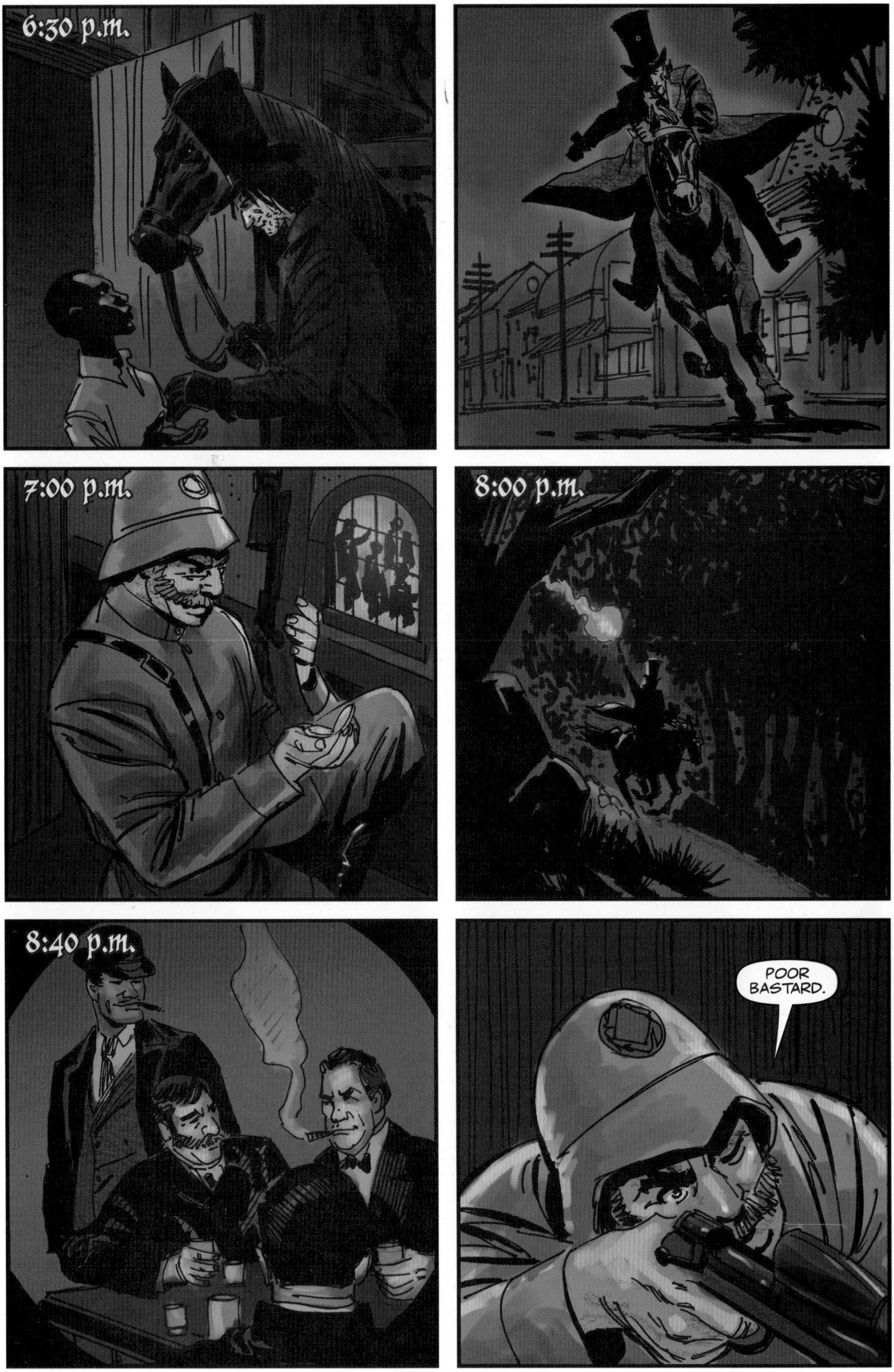
6:30 p.m.
7:00 p.m.
8:00 p.m.
8:40 p.m.
POOR BASTARD.

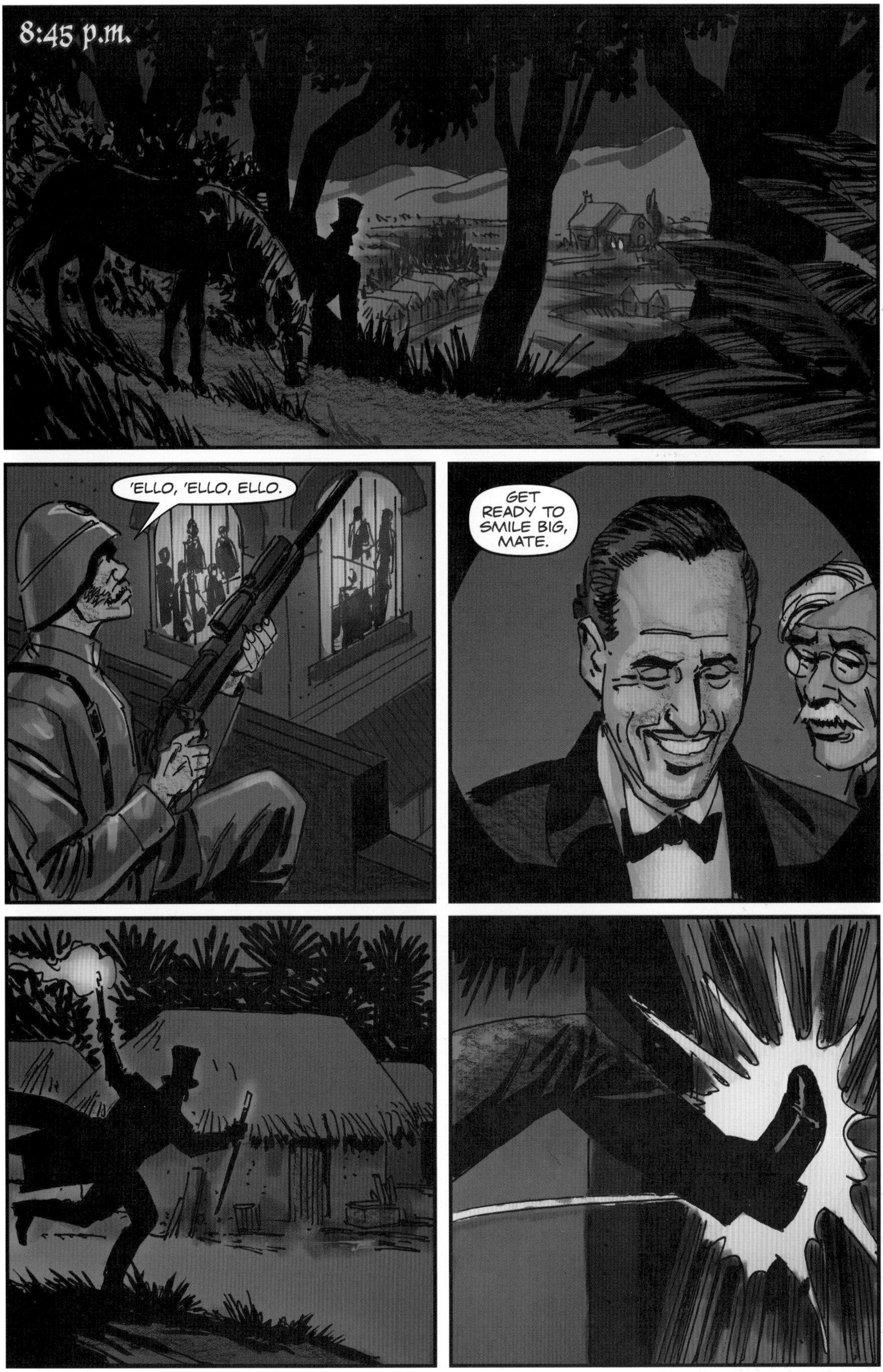
8:45 p.m.
'ELLO, 'ELLO, ELLO.
GET READY TO SMILE BIG, MATE.

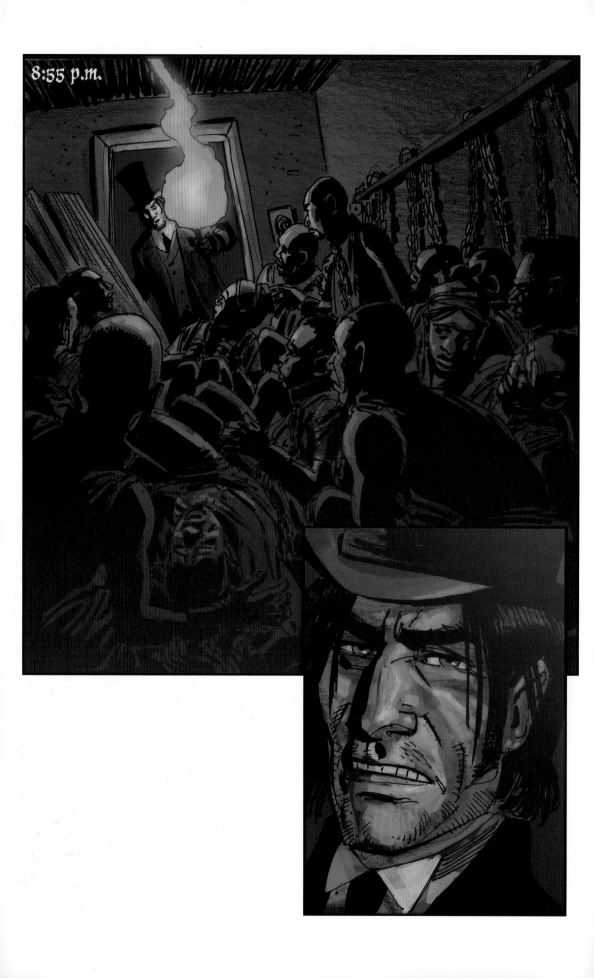

8:55 p.m.

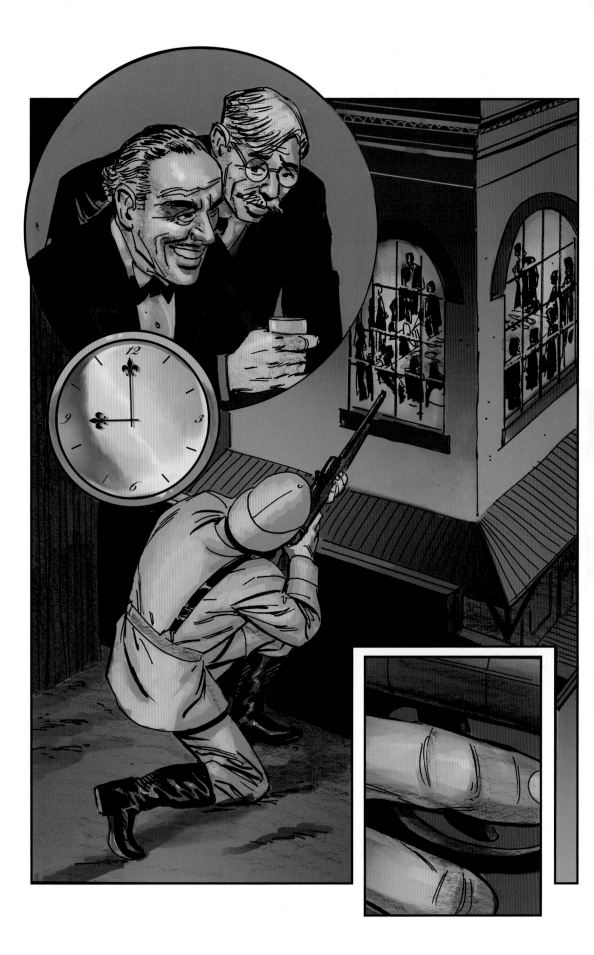

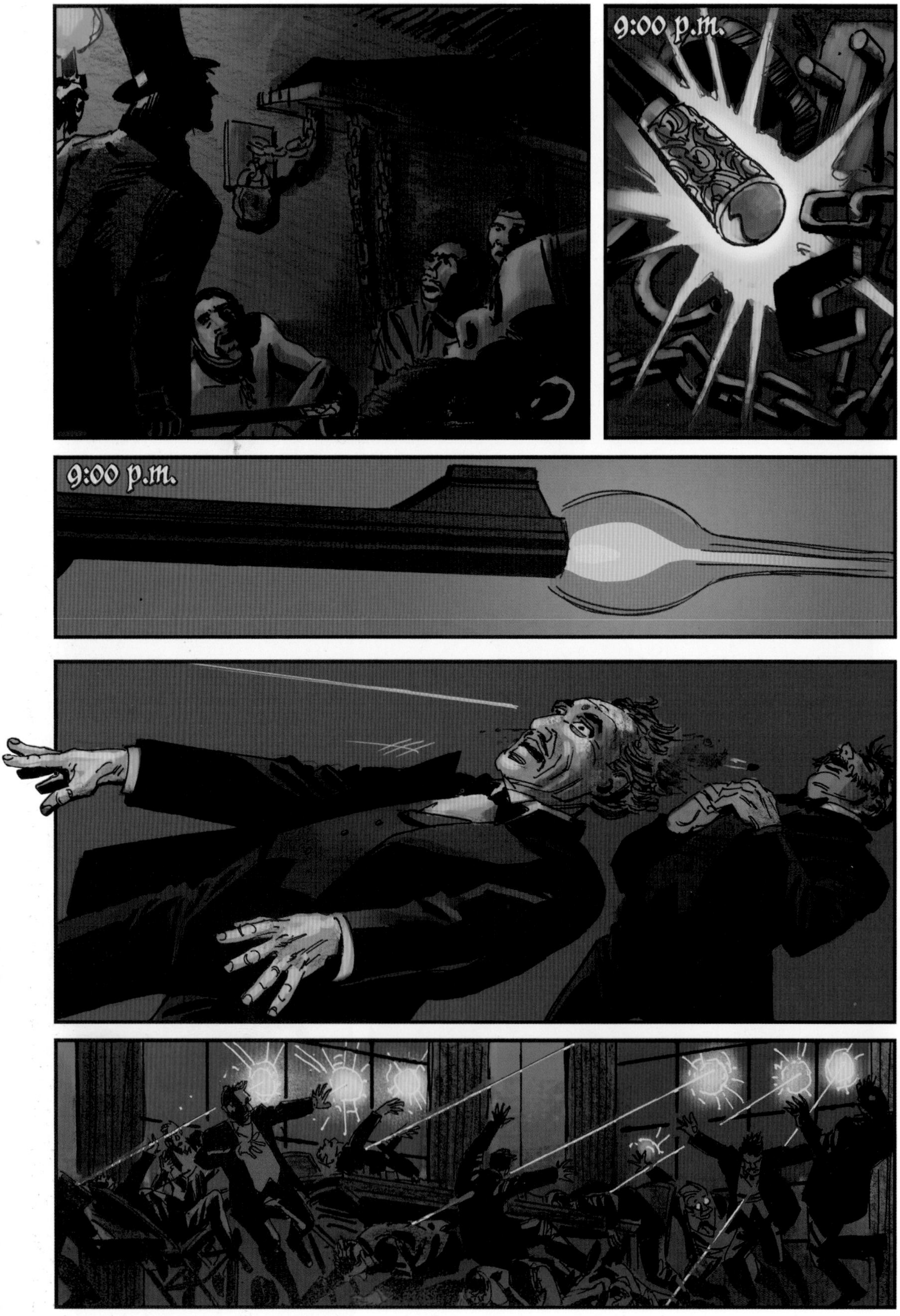
9:00 p.m.
9:00 p.m.

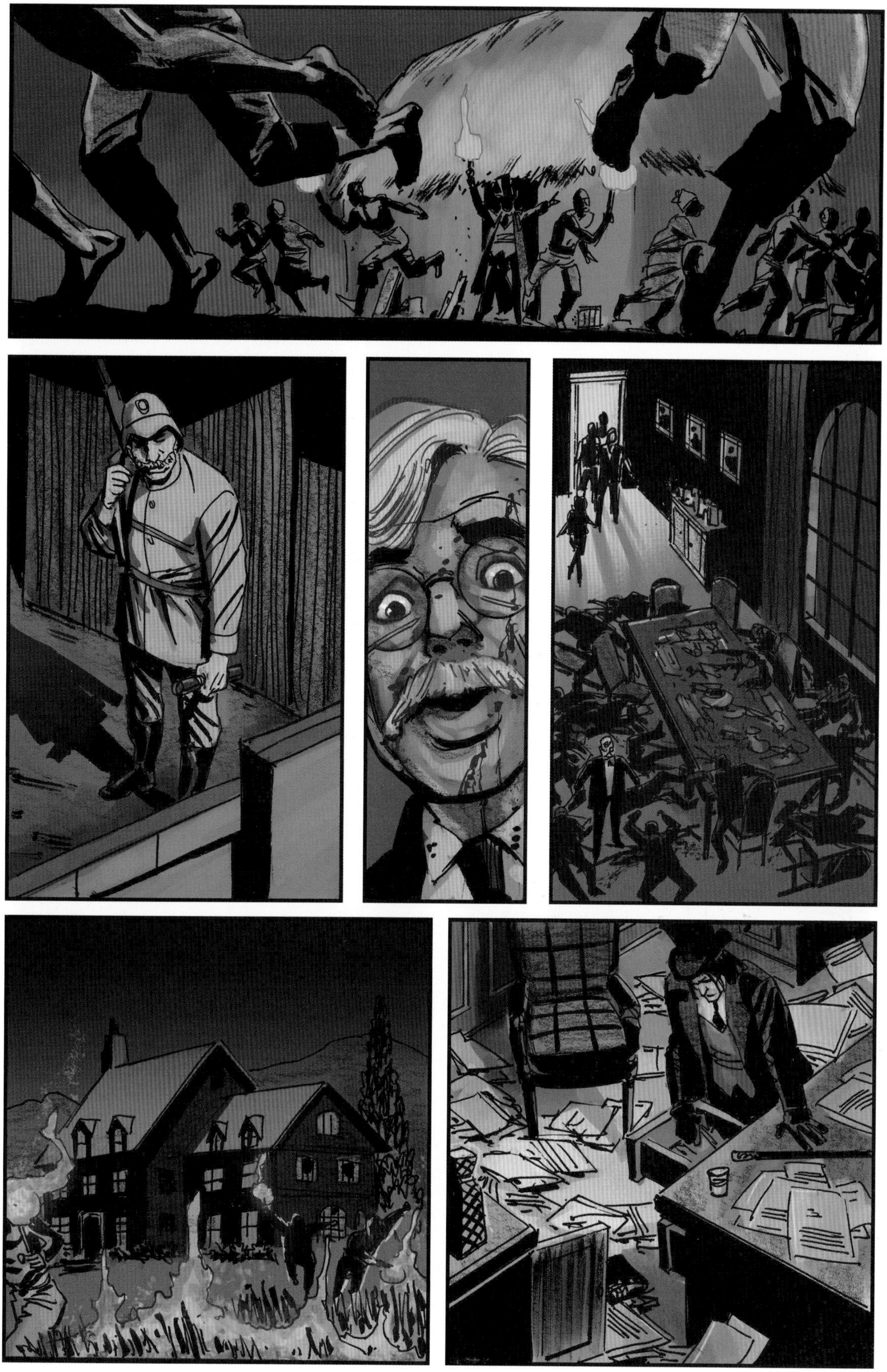

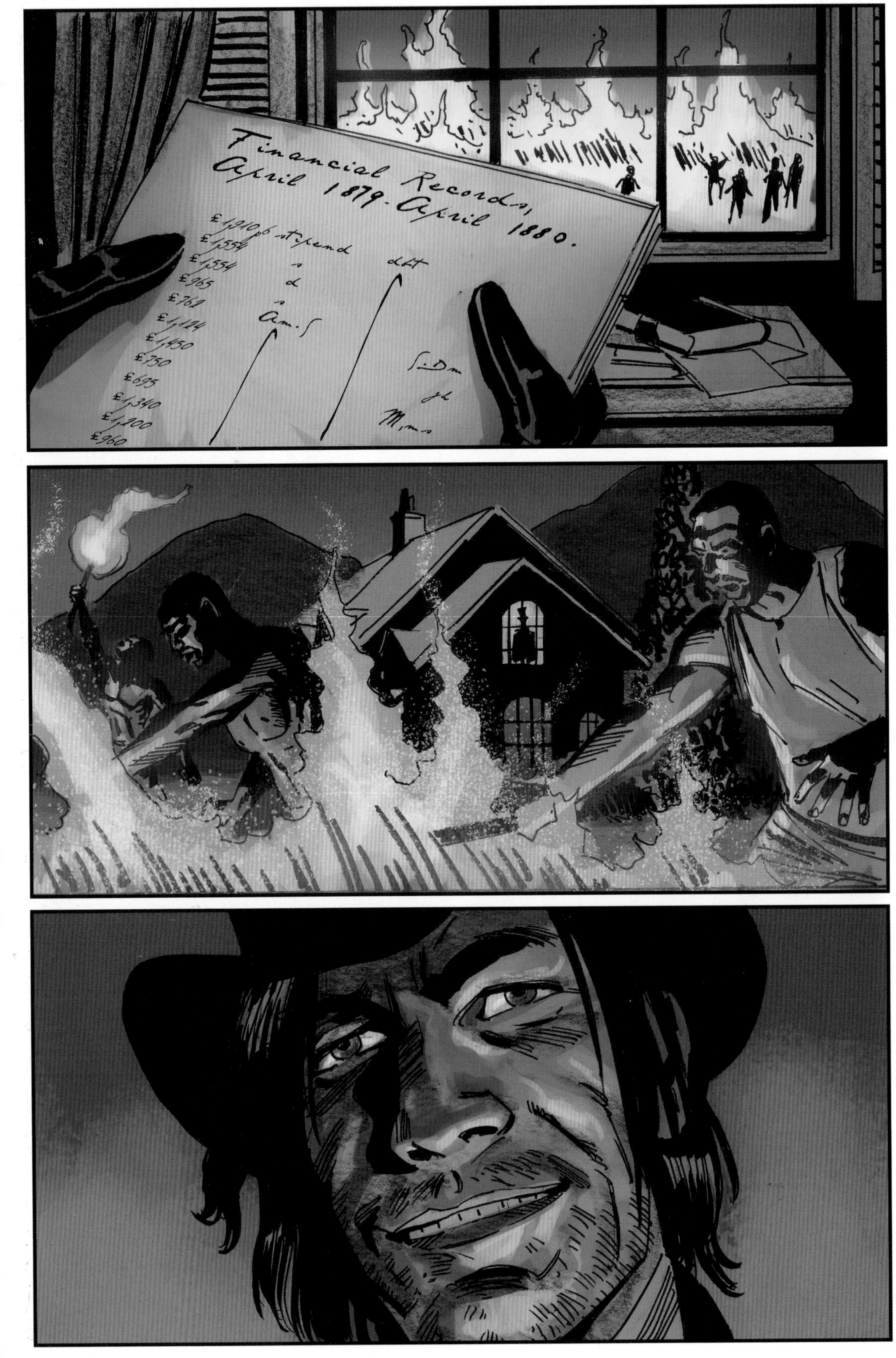
Financial Records,
April 1879-April 1880.
£1,910 p6 stipend
£1,554
£1,554
£965
£762
£1,124
£1,450
£750
£695
£1,340
£1,200
£960
debt

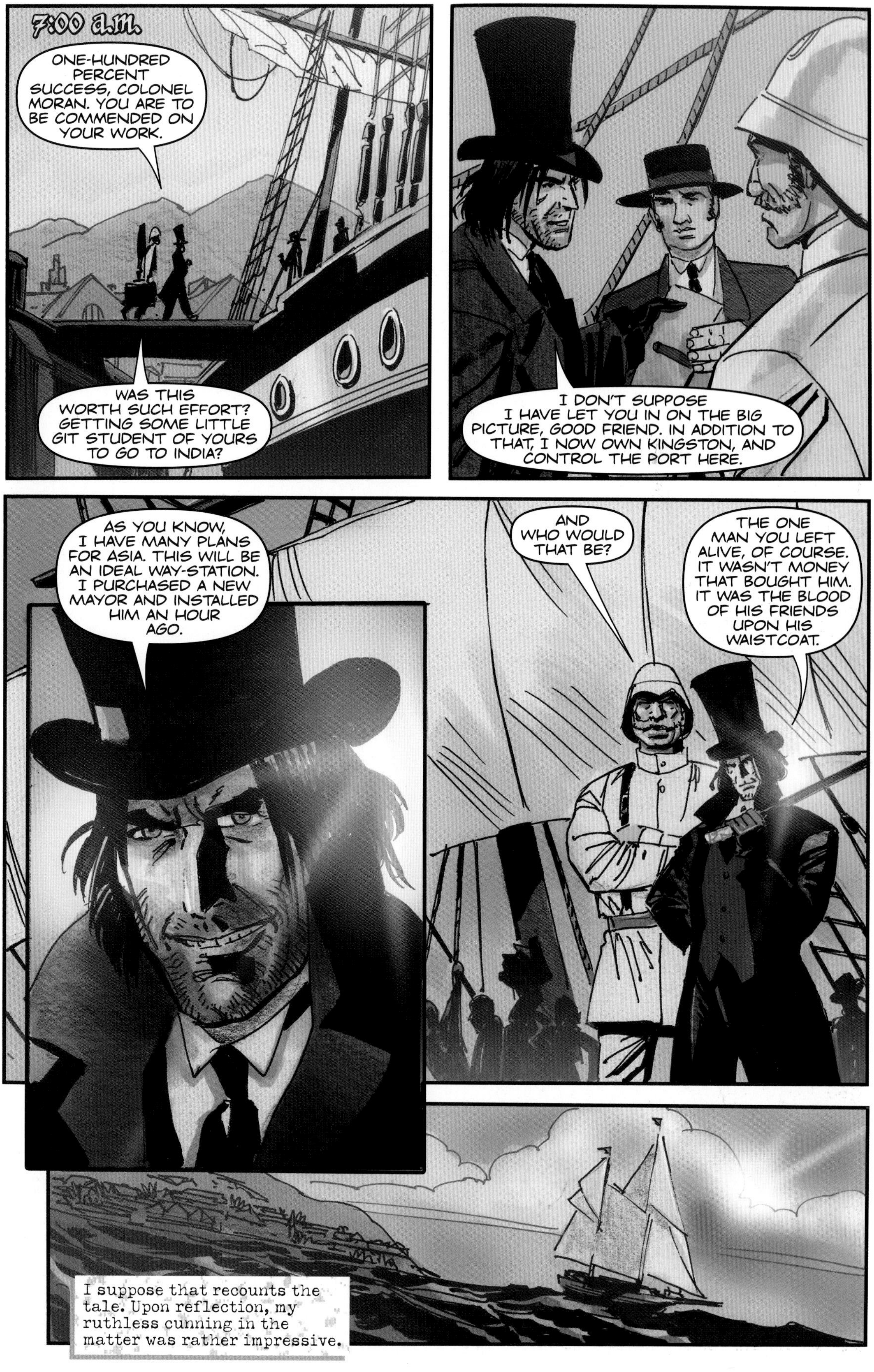
7:00 a.m.
ONE-HUNDRED PERCENT SUCCESS, COLONEL MORAN. YOU ARE TO BE COMMENDED ON YOUR WORK.
WAS THIS WORTH SUCH EFFORT? GETTING SOME LITTLE GIT STUDENT OF YOURS TO GO TO INDIA?
I DON'T SUPPOSE I HAVE LET YOU IN ON THE BIG PICTURE, GOOD FRIEND. IN ADDITION TO THAT, I NOW OWN KINGSTON, AND CONTROL THE PORT HERE.
AS YOU KNOW, I HAVE MANY PLANS FOR ASIA. THIS WILL BE AN IDEAL WAY-STATION. I PURCHASED A NEW MAYOR AND INSTALLED HIM AN HOUR AGO.
AND WHO WOULD THAT BE?
THE ONE MAN YOU LEFT ALIVE, OF COURSE. IT WASN'T MONEY THAT BOUGHT HIM. IT WAS THE BLOOD OF HIS FRIENDS UPON HIS WAISTCOAT.
I suppose that recounts the tale. Upon reflection, my ruthless cunning in the matter was rather impressive.

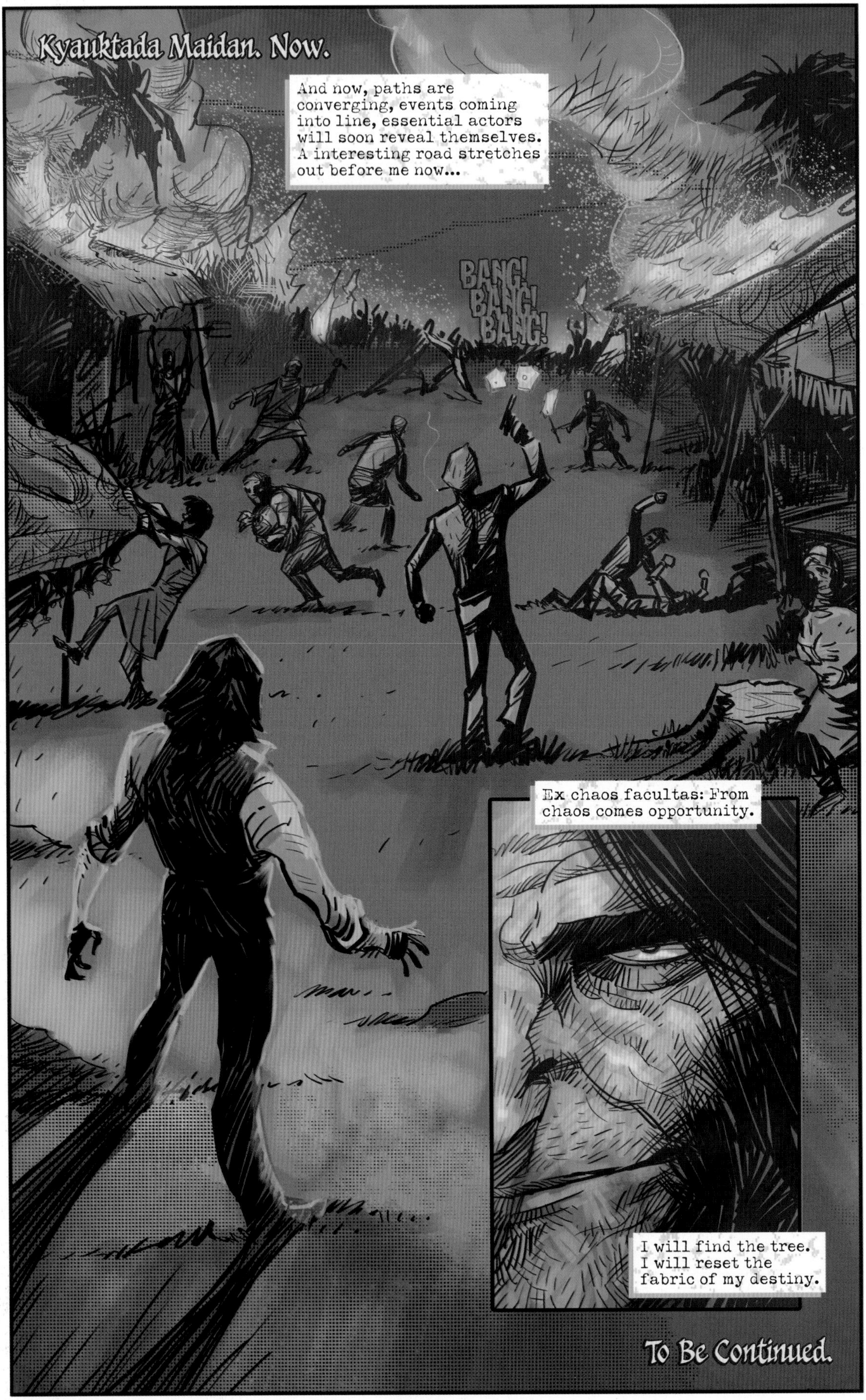
Kyauktada Maidan. Now.
And now, paths are converging, events coming into line, essential actors will soon reveal themselves. A interesting road stretches out before me now...
BANG! BANG! BANG!
Ex chaos facultas: From chaos comes opportunity.
I will find the tree. I will reset the fabric of my destiny.
To Be Continued.

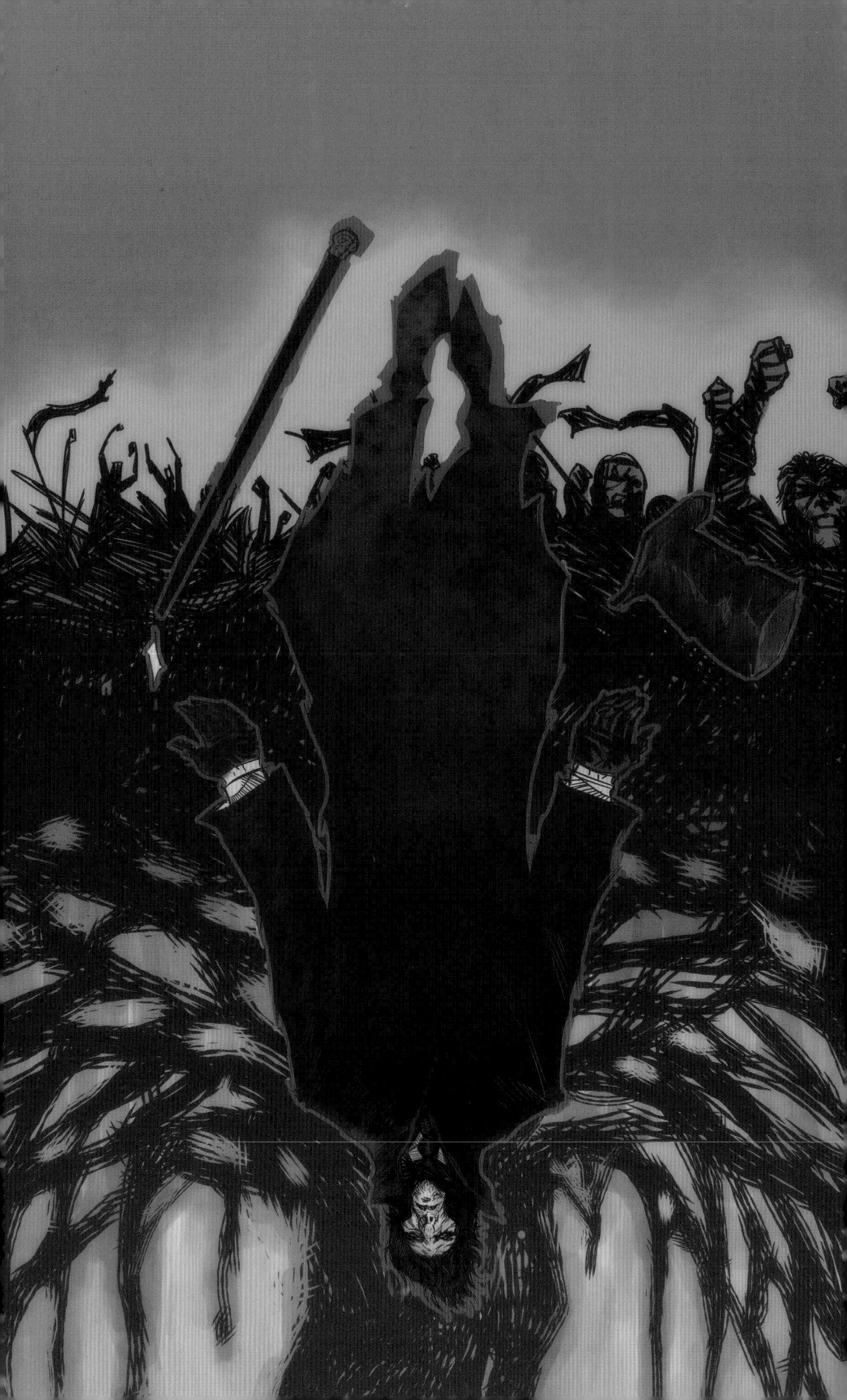

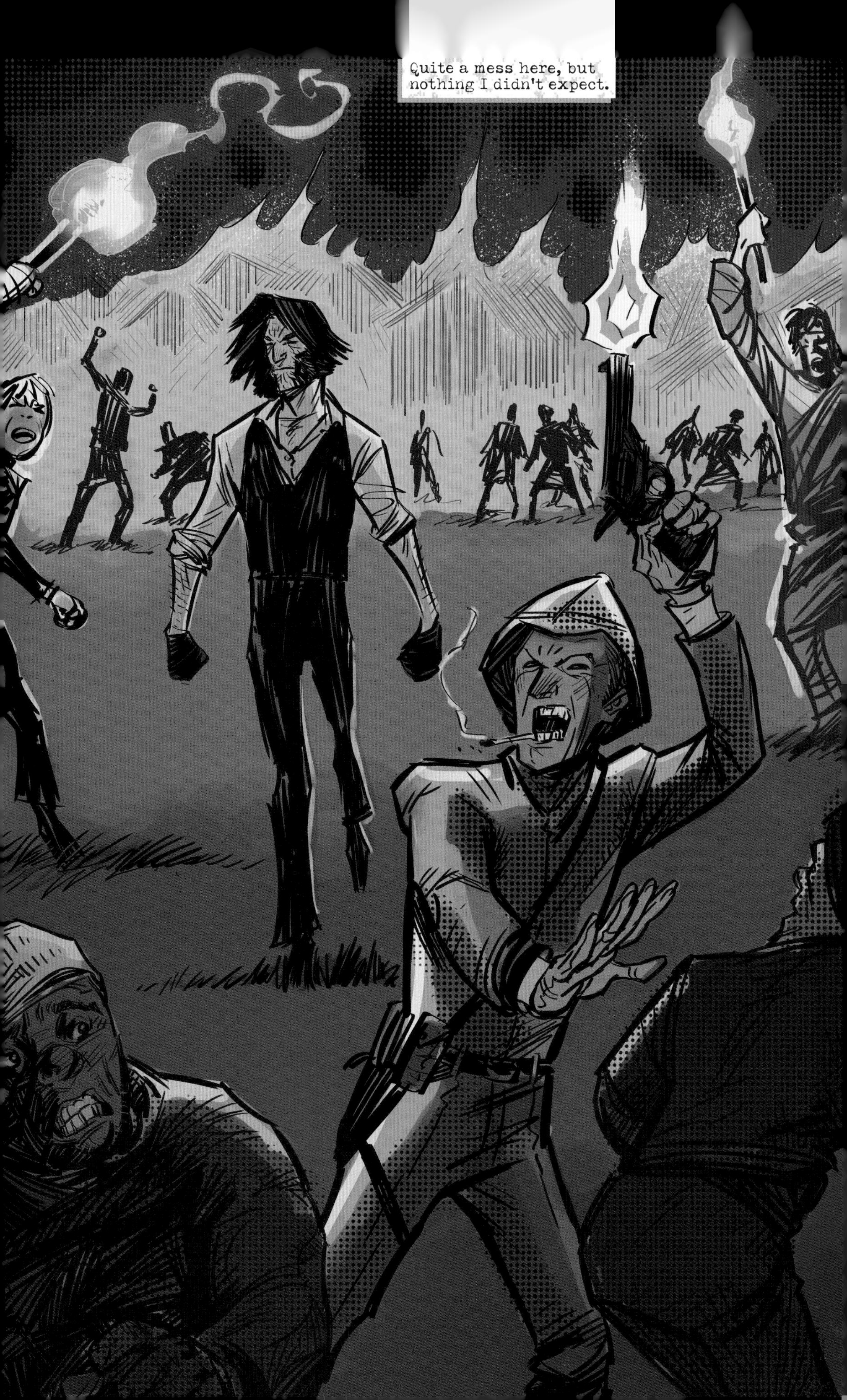
Quite a mess here, but
nothing I didn't expect.

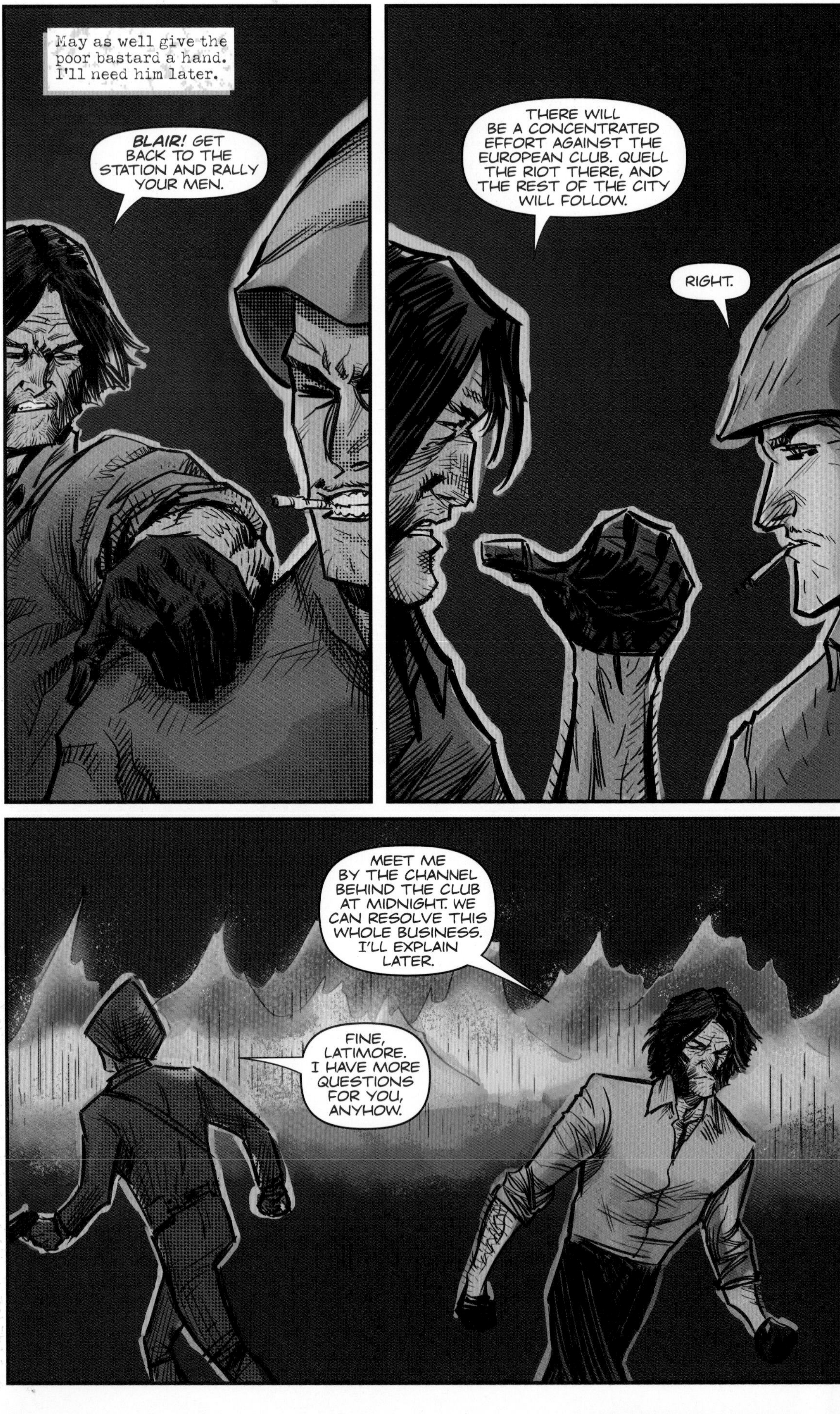
May as well give the poor bastard a hand. I'll need him later.
BLAIR! GET BACK TO THE STATION AND RALLY YOUR MEN.
THERE WILL BE A CONCENTRATED EFFORT AGAINST THE EUROPEAN CLUB. QUELL THE RIOT THERE, AND THE REST OF THE CITY WILL FOLLOW.
RIGHT.
MEET ME BY THE CHANNEL BEHIND THE CLUB AT MIDNIGHT. WE CAN RESOLVE THIS WHOLE BUSINESS. I'LL EXPLAIN LATER.
FINE, LATIMORE. I HAVE MORE QUESTIONS FOR YOU, ANYHOW.

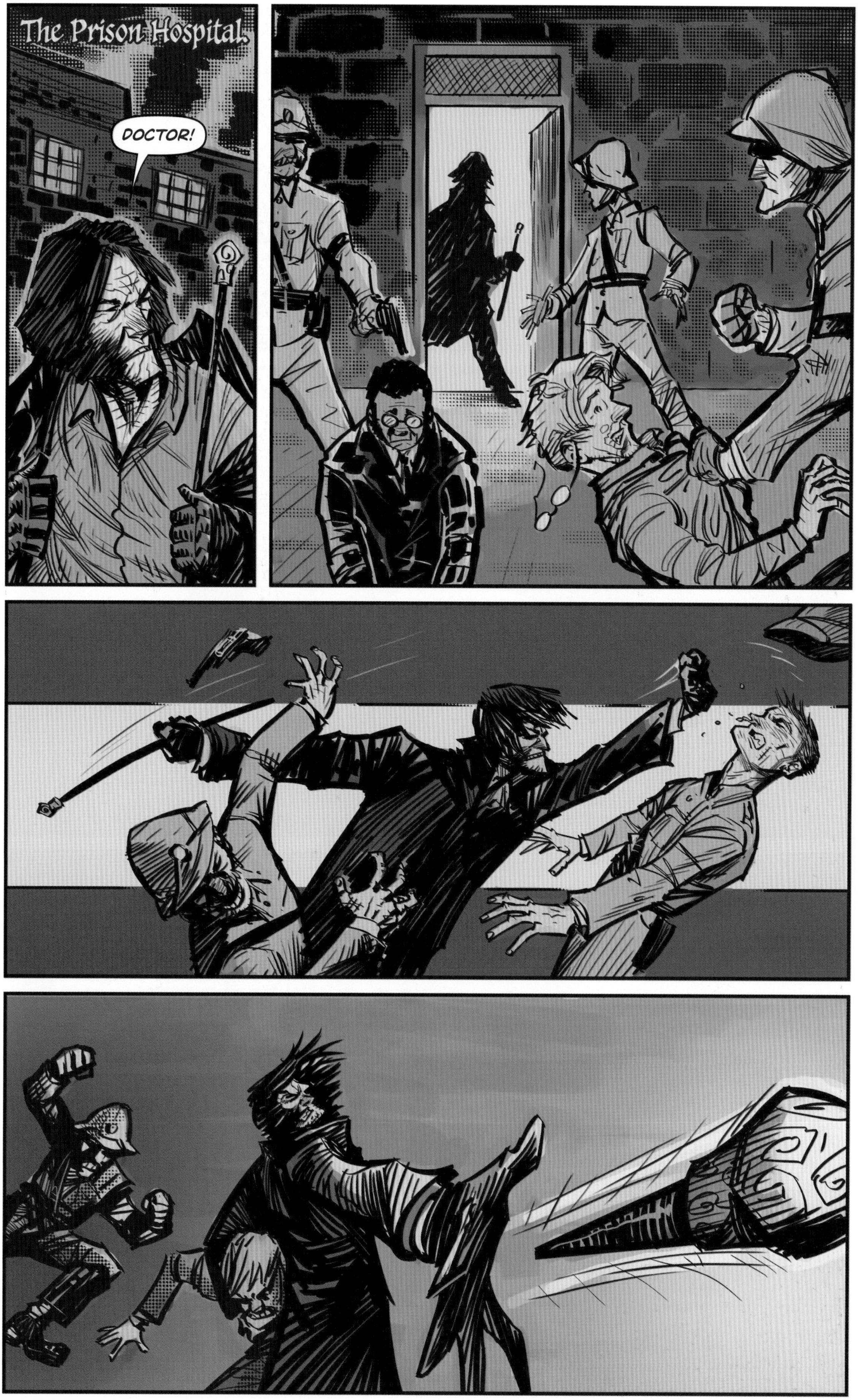
The Prison Hospital.
DOCTOR!

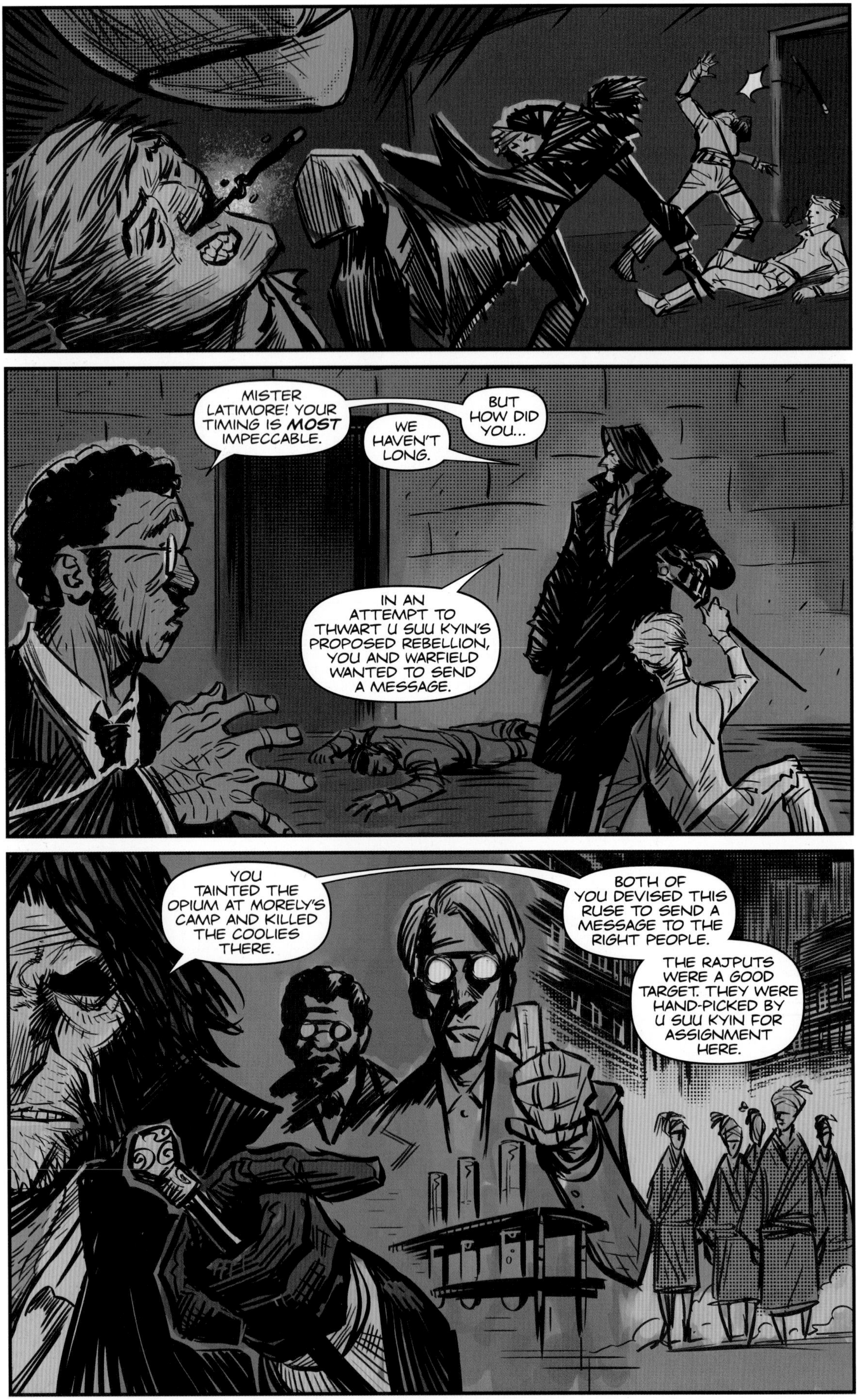
MISTER LATIMORE! YOUR TIMING IS **MOST** IMPECCABLE.
WE HAVEN'T LONG.
BUT HOW DID YOU...
IN AN ATTEMPT TO THWART U SUU KYIN'S PROPOSED REBELLION, YOU AND WARFIELD WANTED TO SEND A MESSAGE.
YOU TAINTED THE OPIUM AT MORELY'S CAMP AND KILLED THE COOLIES THERE.
BOTH OF YOU DEVISED THIS RUSE TO SEND A MESSAGE TO THE RIGHT PEOPLE.
THE RAJPUTS WERE A GOOD TARGET. THEY WERE HAND-PICKED BY U SUU KYIN FOR ASSIGNMENT HERE.

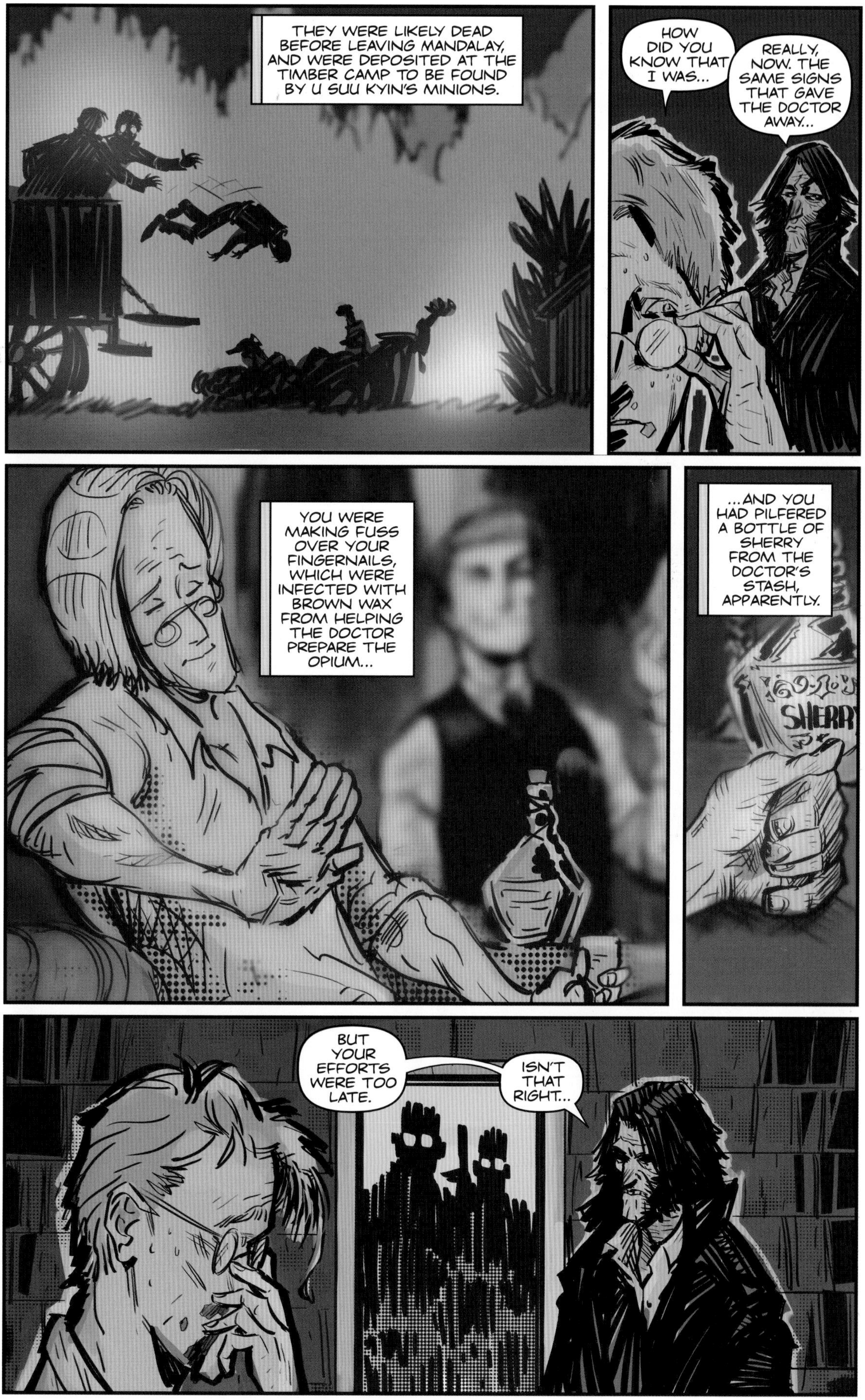
THEY WERE LIKELY DEAD BEFORE LEAVING MANDALAY, AND WERE DEPOSITED AT THE TIMBER CAMP TO BE FOUND BY U SUU KYIN'S MINIONS.
HOW DID YOU KNOW THAT I WAS...
REALLY, NOW. THE SAME SIGNS THAT GAVE THE DOCTOR AWAY...
YOU WERE MAKING FUSS OVER YOUR FINGERNAILS, WHICH WERE INFECTED WITH BROWN WAX FROM HELPING THE DOCTOR PREPARE THE OPIUM...
...AND YOU HAD PILFERED A BOTTLE OF SHERRY FROM THE DOCTOR'S STASH, APPARENTLY.
BUT YOUR EFFORTS WERE TOO LATE.
ISN'T THAT RIGHT...

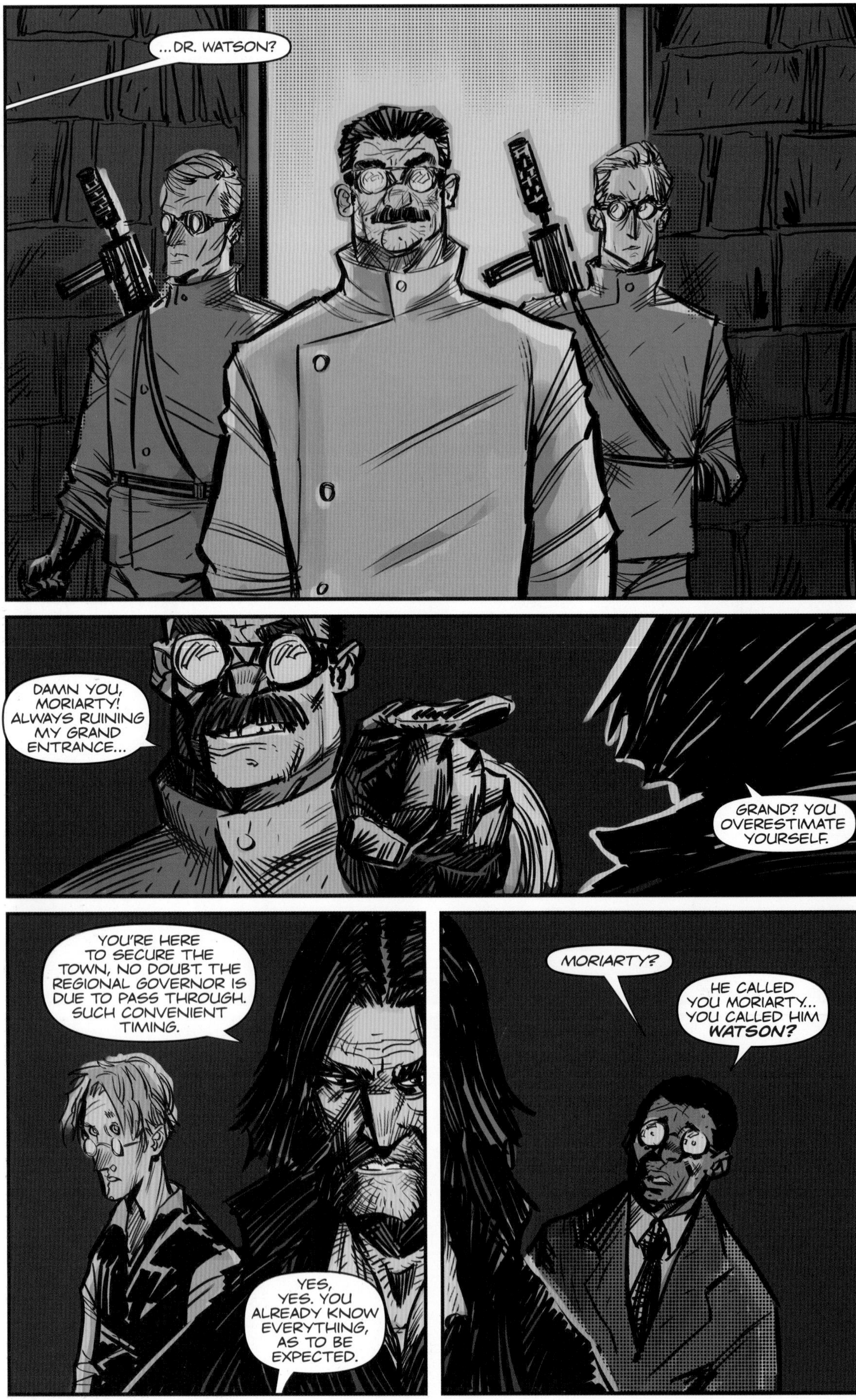
...DR. WATSON?
DAMN YOU, MORIARTY! ALWAYS RUINING MY GRAND ENTRANCE...
GRAND? YOU OVERESTIMATE YOURSELF.
YOU'RE HERE TO SECURE THE TOWN, NO DOUBT. THE REGIONAL GOVERNOR IS DUE TO PASS THROUGH. SUCH CONVENIENT TIMING.
YES, YES. YOU ALREADY KNOW EVERYTHING, AS TO BE EXPECTED.
MORIARTY?
HE CALLED YOU MORIARTY... YOU CALLED HIM WATSON?

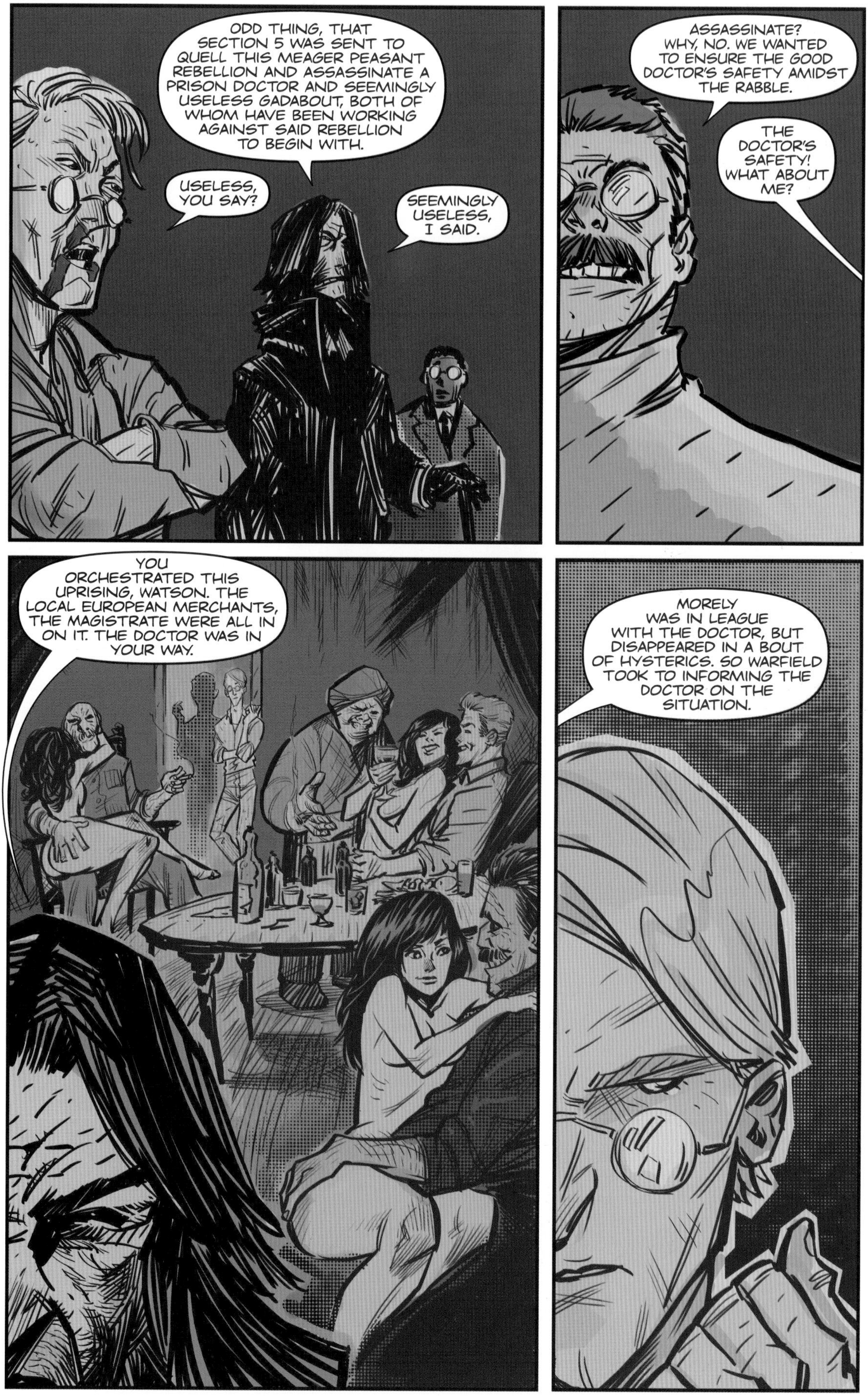
ODD THING, THAT SECTION 5 WAS SENT TO QUELL THIS MEAGER PEASANT REBELLION AND ASSASSINATE A PRISON DOCTOR AND SEEMINGLY USELESS GADABOUT, BOTH OF WHOM HAVE BEEN WORKING AGAINST SAID REBELLION TO BEGIN WITH.
USELESS, YOU SAY?
SEEMINGLY USELESS, I SAID.
ASSASSINATE? WHY, NO. WE WANTED TO ENSURE THE GOOD DOCTOR'S SAFETY AMIDST THE RABBLE.
THE DOCTOR'S SAFETY! WHAT ABOUT ME?
YOU ORCHESTRATED THIS UPRISING, WATSON. THE LOCAL EUROPEAN MERCHANTS, THE MAGISTRATE WERE ALL IN ON IT. THE DOCTOR WAS IN YOUR WAY.
MORELY WAS IN LEAGUE WITH THE DOCTOR, BUT DISAPPEARED IN A BOUT OF HYSTERICS. SO WARFIELD TOOK TO INFORMING THE DOCTOR ON THE SITUATION.

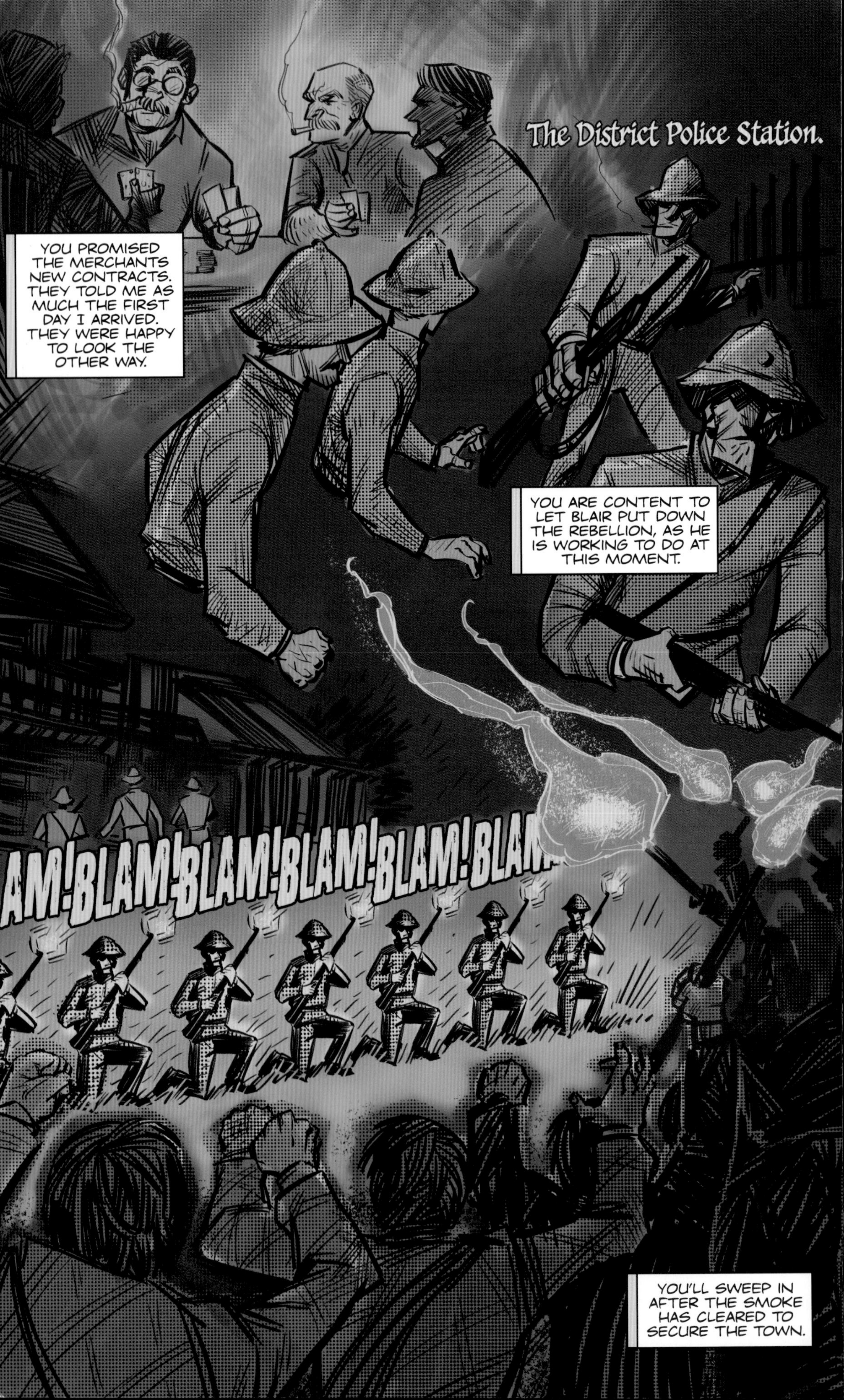
The District Police Station.
YOU PROMISED THE MERCHANTS NEW CONTRACTS. THEY TOLD ME AS MUCH THE FIRST DAY I ARRIVED. THEY WERE HAPPY TO LOOK THE OTHER WAY.
YOU ARE CONTENT TO LET BLAIR PUT DOWN THE REBELLION, AS HE IS WORKING TO DO AT THIS MOMENT.
AM! BLAM! BLAM! BLAM! BLAM! BLAM
YOU'LL SWEEP IN AFTER THE SMOKE HAS CLEARED TO SECURE THE TOWN.

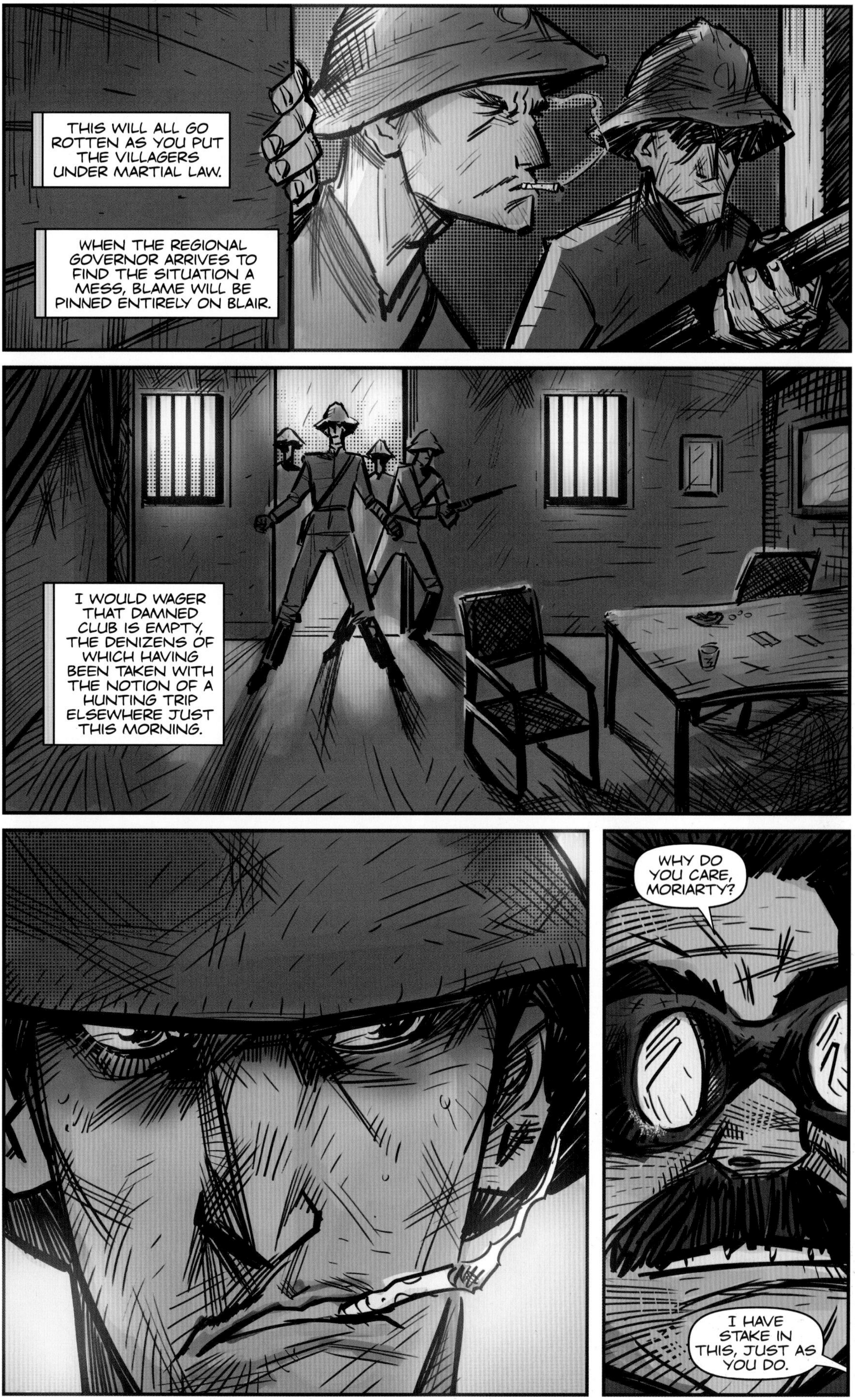

THIS WILL ALL GO ROTTEN AS YOU PUT THE VILLAGERS UNDER MARTIAL LAW.
WHEN THE REGIONAL GOVERNOR ARRIVES TO FIND THE SITUATION A MESS, BLAME WILL BE PINNED ENTIRELY ON BLAIR.
I WOULD WAGER THAT DAMNED CLUB IS EMPTY, THE DENIZENS OF WHICH HAVING BEEN TAKEN WITH THE NOTION OF A HUNTING TRIP ELSEWHERE JUST THIS MORNING.
WHY DO YOU CARE, MORIARTY?
I HAVE STAKE IN THIS, JUST AS YOU DO.

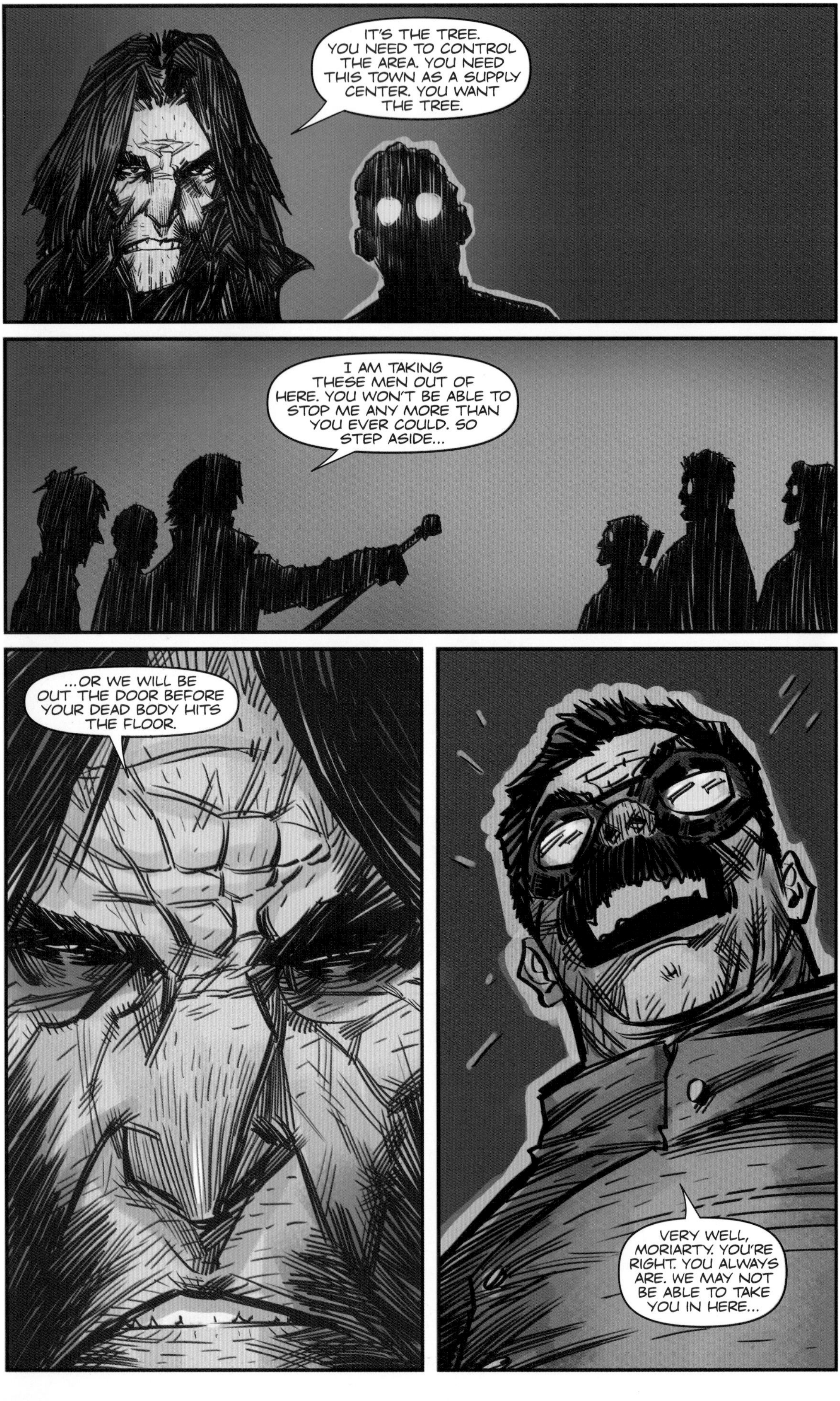
IT'S THE TREE. YOU NEED TO CONTROL THE AREA. YOU NEED THIS TOWN AS A SUPPLY CENTER. YOU WANT THE TREE.
I AM TAKING THESE MEN OUT OF HERE. YOU WON'T BE ABLE TO STOP ME ANY MORE THAN YOU EVER COULD. SO STEP ASIDE...
...OR WE WILL BE OUT THE DOOR BEFORE YOUR DEAD BODY HITS THE FLOOR.
VERY WELL, MORIARTY. YOU'RE RIGHT. YOU ALWAYS ARE. WE MAY NOT BE ABLE TO TAKE YOU IN HERE...

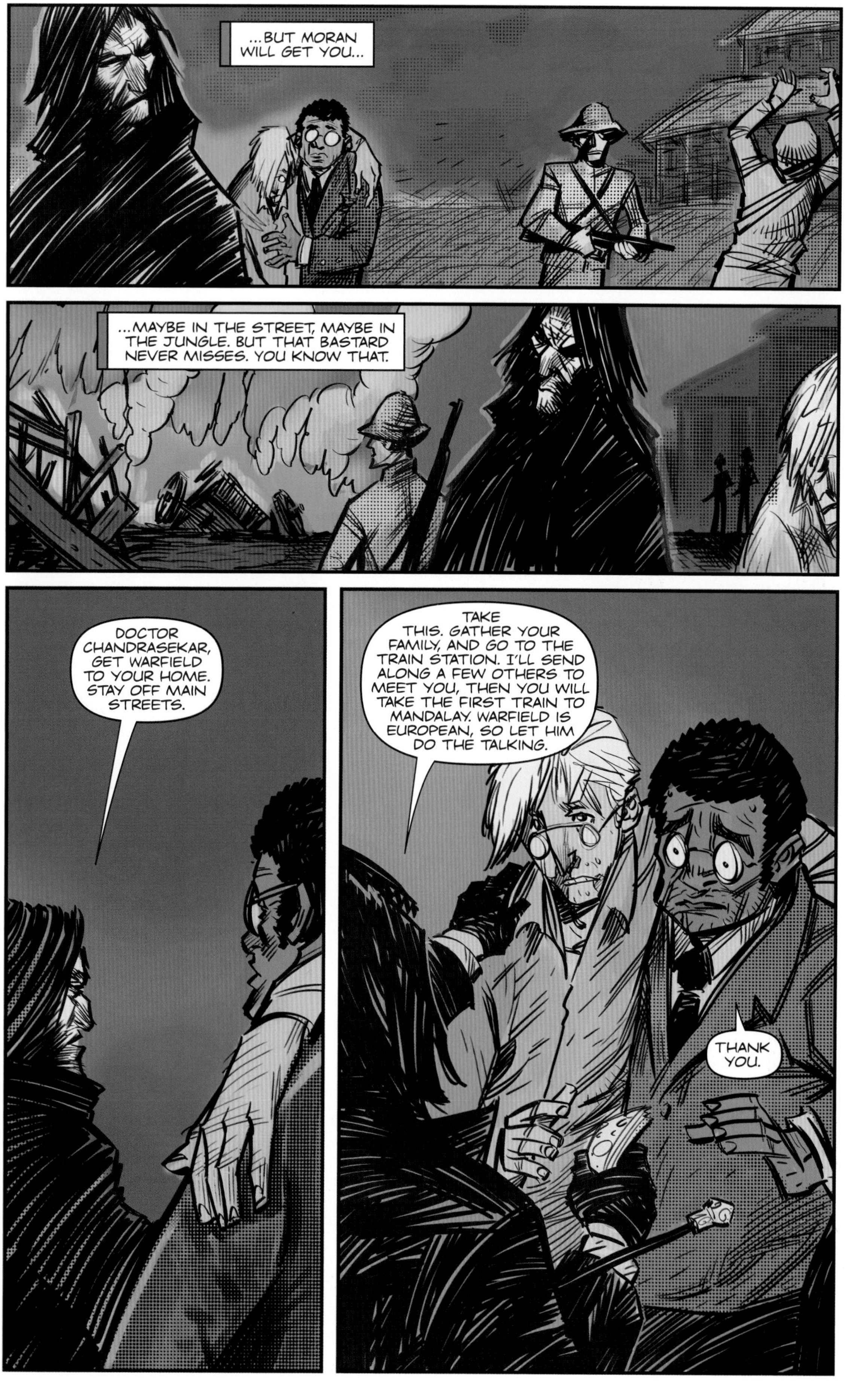
...BUT MORAN WILL GET YOU...
...MAYBE IN THE STREET, MAYBE IN THE JUNGLE. BUT THAT BASTARD NEVER MISSES. YOU KNOW THAT.
DOCTOR CHANDRASEKAR, GET WARFIELD TO YOUR HOME. STAY OFF MAIN STREETS.
TAKE THIS. GATHER YOUR FAMILY, AND GO TO THE TRAIN STATION. I'LL SEND ALONG A FEW OTHERS TO MEET YOU, THEN YOU WILL TAKE THE FIRST TRAIN TO MANDALAY. WARFIELD IS EUROPEAN, SO LET HIM DO THE TALKING.
THANK YOU.

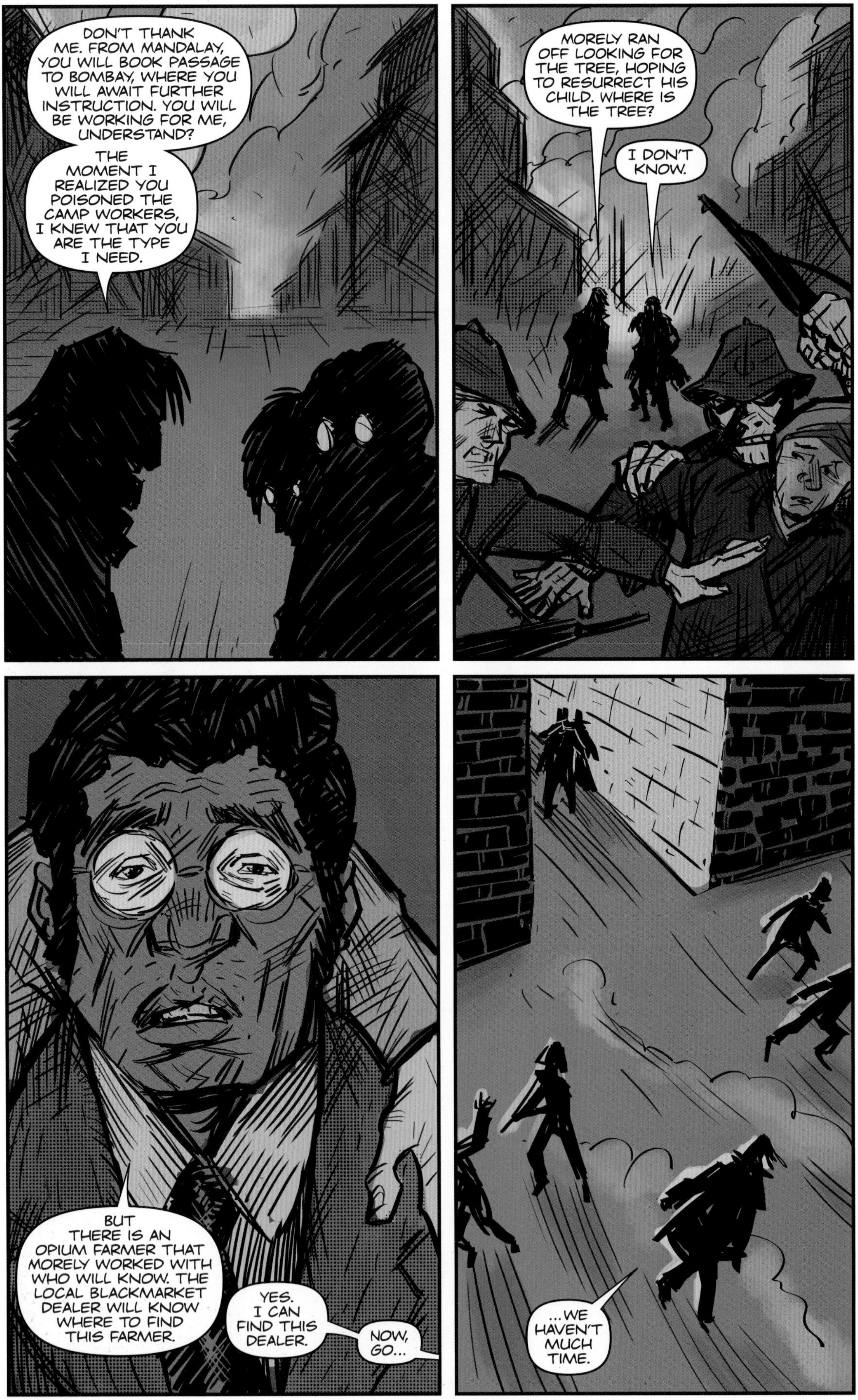
DON'T THANK ME. FROM MANDALAY, YOU WILL BOOK PASSAGE TO BOMBAY, WHERE YOU WILL AWAIT FURTHER INSTRUCTION. YOU WILL BE WORKING FOR ME, UNDERSTAND?
THE MOMENT I REALIZED YOU POISONED THE CAMP WORKERS, I KNEW THAT YOU ARE THE TYPE I NEED.
MORELY RAN OFF LOOKING FOR THE TREE, HOPING TO RESURRECT HIS CHILD. WHERE IS THE TREE?
I DON'T KNOW.
BUT THERE IS AN OPIUM FARMER THAT MORELY WORKED WITH WHO WILL KNOW. THE LOCAL BLACKMARKET DEALER WILL KNOW WHERE TO FIND THIS FARMER.
YES. I CAN FIND THIS DEALER.
NOW, GO...
...WE HAVEN'T MUCH TIME.

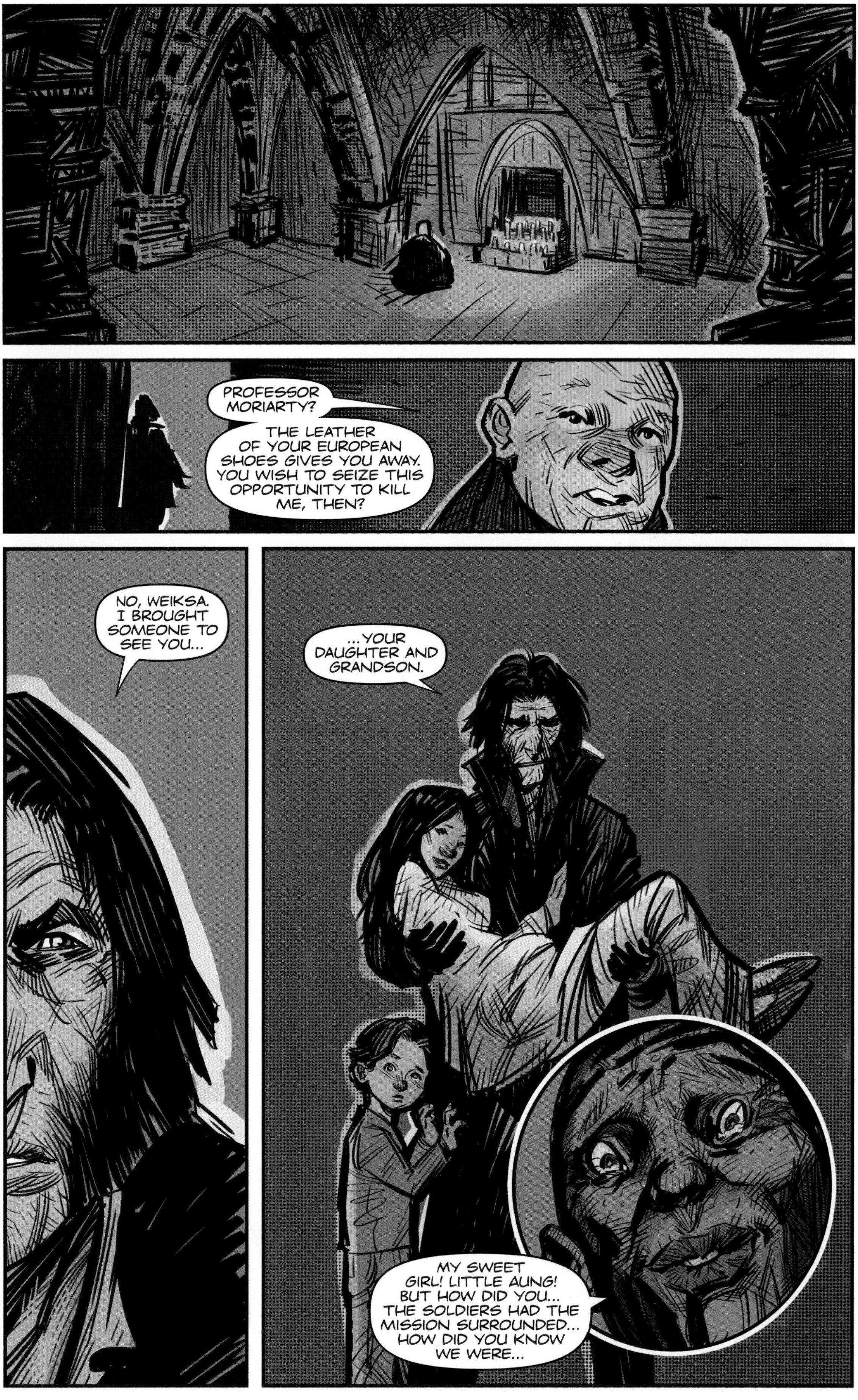
PROFESSOR MORIARTY?
THE LEATHER OF YOUR EUROPEAN SHOES GIVES YOU AWAY. YOU WISH TO SEIZE THIS OPPORTUNITY TO KILL ME, THEN?
NO, WEIKSA. I BROUGHT SOMEONE TO SEE YOU...
...YOUR DAUGHTER AND GRANDSON.
MY SWEET GIRL! LITTLE AUNG! BUT HOW DID YOU... THE SOLDIERS HAD THE MISSION SURROUNDED... HOW DID YOU KNOW WE WERE...

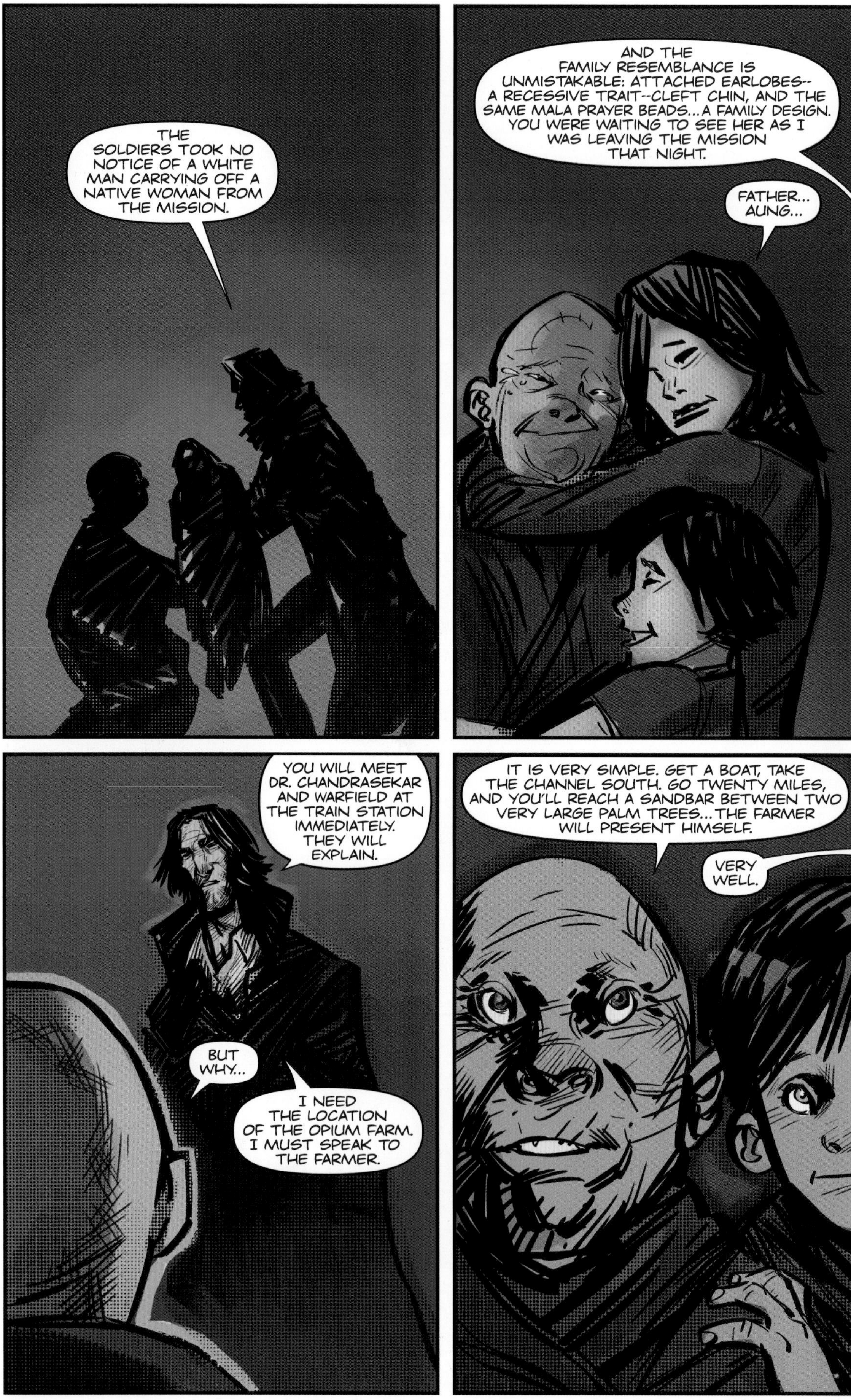
THE SOLDIERS TOOK NO NOTICE OF A WHITE MAN CARRYING OFF A NATIVE WOMAN FROM THE MISSION.
AND THE FAMILY RESEMBLANCE IS UNMISTAKABLE: ATTACHED EARLOBES--A RECESSIVE TRAIT--CLEFT CHIN, AND THE SAME MALA PRAYER BEADS...A FAMILY DESIGN. YOU WERE WAITING TO SEE HER AS I WAS LEAVING THE MISSION THAT NIGHT.
FATHER... AUNG...
YOU WILL MEET DR. CHANDRASEKAR AND WARFIELD AT THE TRAIN STATION IMMEDIATELY. THEY WILL EXPLAIN.
BUT WHY...
I NEED THE LOCATION OF THE OPIUM FARM. I MUST SPEAK TO THE FARMER.
IT IS VERY SIMPLE. GET A BOAT, TAKE THE CHANNEL SOUTH. GO TWENTY MILES, AND YOU'LL REACH A SANDBAR BETWEEN TWO VERY LARGE PALM TREES...THE FARMER WILL PRESENT HIMSELF.
VERY WELL.

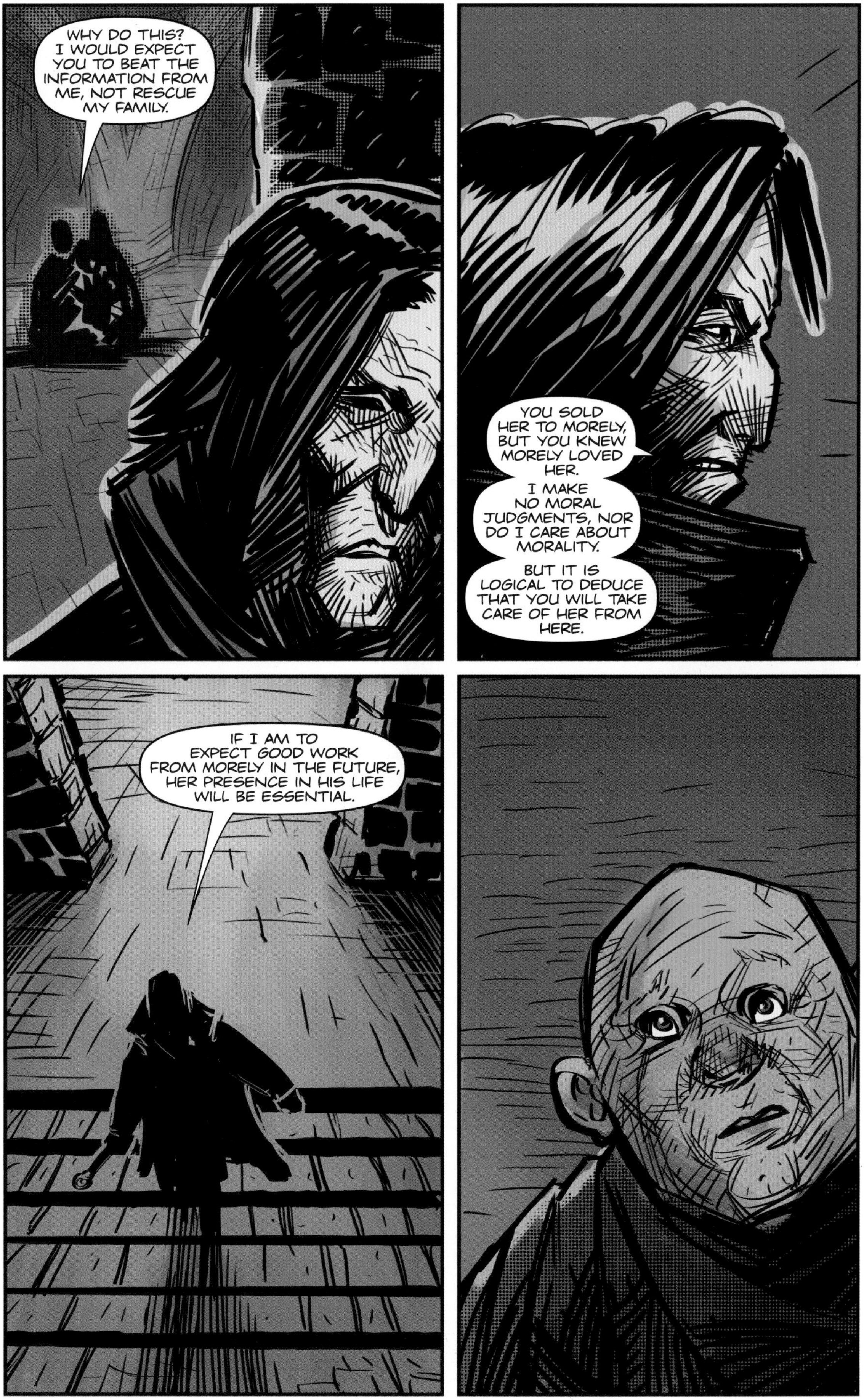
WHY DO THIS? I WOULD EXPECT YOU TO BEAT THE INFORMATION FROM ME, NOT RESCUE MY FAMILY.
YOU SOLD HER TO MORELY, BUT YOU KNEW MORELY LOVED HER.
I MAKE NO MORAL JUDGMENTS, NOR DO I CARE ABOUT MORALITY.
BUT IT IS LOGICAL TO DEDUCE THAT YOU WILL TAKE CARE OF HER FROM HERE.
IF I AM TO EXPECT GOOD WORK FROM MORELY IN THE FUTURE, HER PRESENCE IN HIS LIFE WILL BE ESSENTIAL.

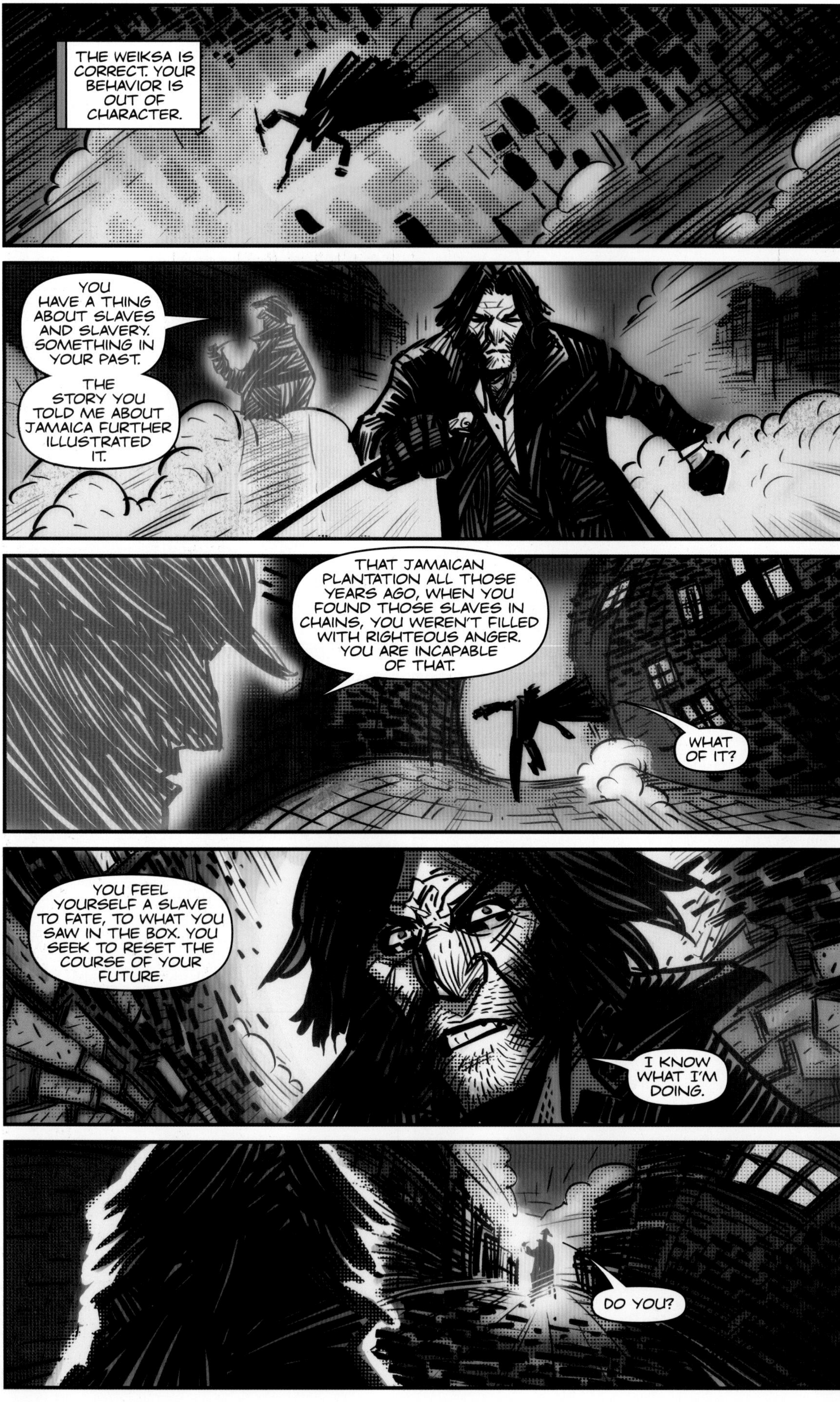
THE WEIKSA IS CORRECT. YOUR BEHAVIOR IS OUT OF CHARACTER.
YOU HAVE A THING ABOUT SLAVES AND SLAVERY. SOMETHING IN YOUR PAST.
THE STORY YOU TOLD ME ABOUT JAMAICA FURTHER ILLUSTRATED IT.
THAT JAMAICAN PLANTATION ALL THOSE YEARS AGO, WHEN YOU FOUND THOSE SLAVES IN CHAINS, YOU WEREN'T FILLED WITH RIGHTEOUS ANGER. YOU ARE INCAPABLE OF THAT.
WHAT OF IT?
YOU FEEL YOURSELF A SLAVE TO FATE, TO WHAT YOU SAW IN THE BOX. YOU SEEK TO RESET THE COURSE OF YOUR FUTURE.
I KNOW WHAT I'M DOING.
DO YOU?

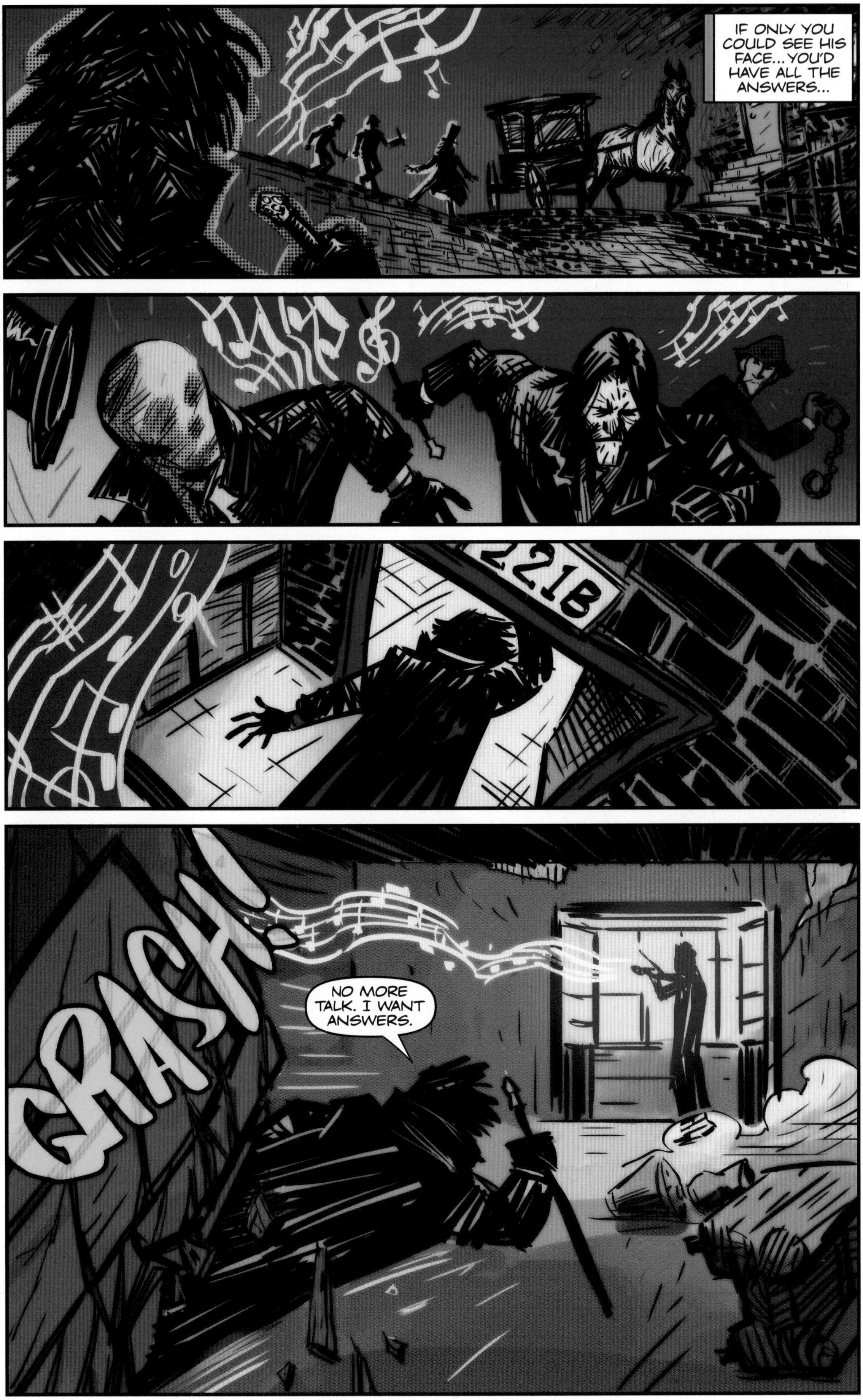
IF ONLY YOU COULD SEE HIS FACE...YOU'D HAVE ALL THE ANSWERS...
221B
CRASH!
NO MORE TALK. I WANT ANSWERS.

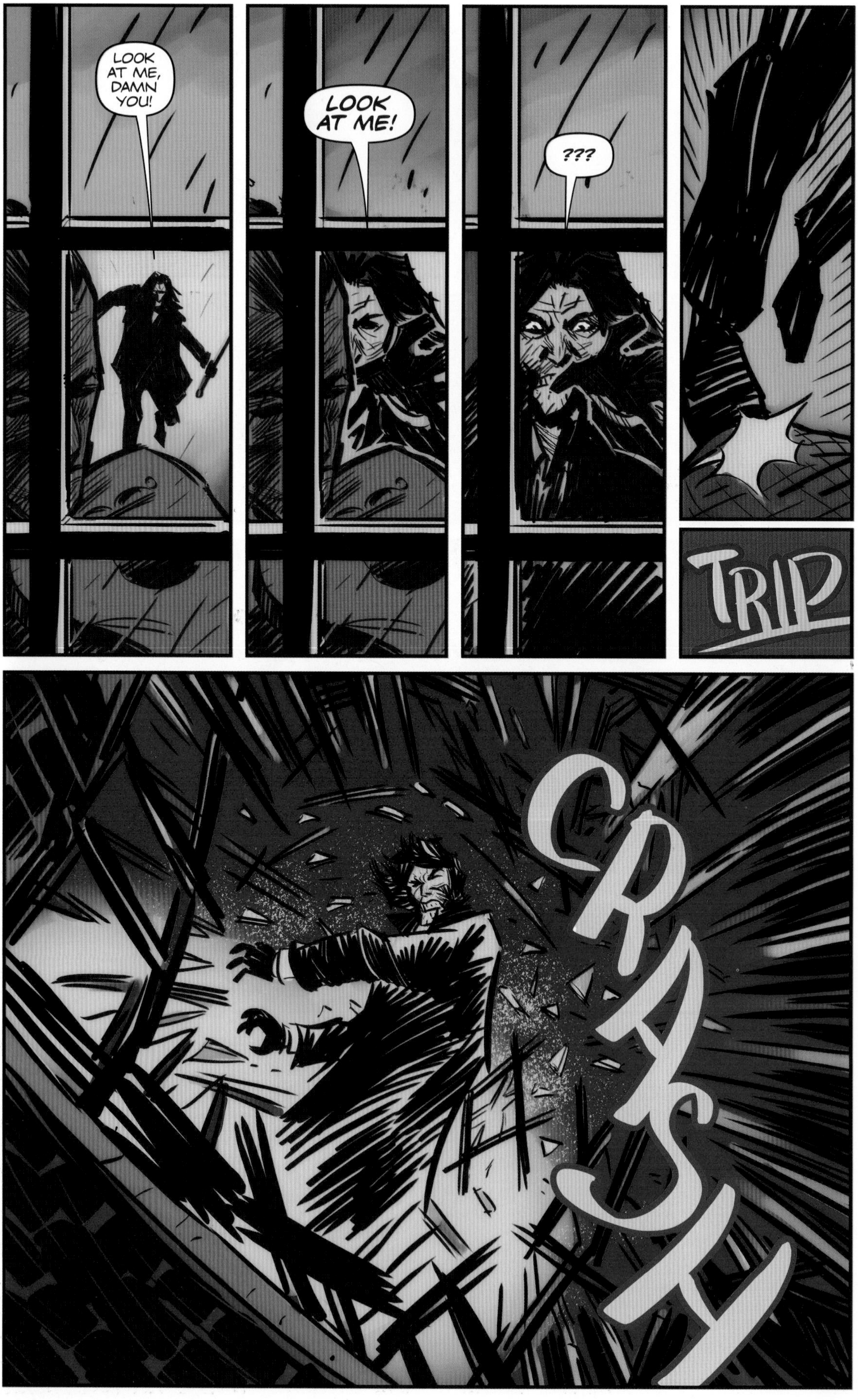

LOOK AT ME, DAMN YOU!
LOOK AT ME!
???
TRIP
CRASH

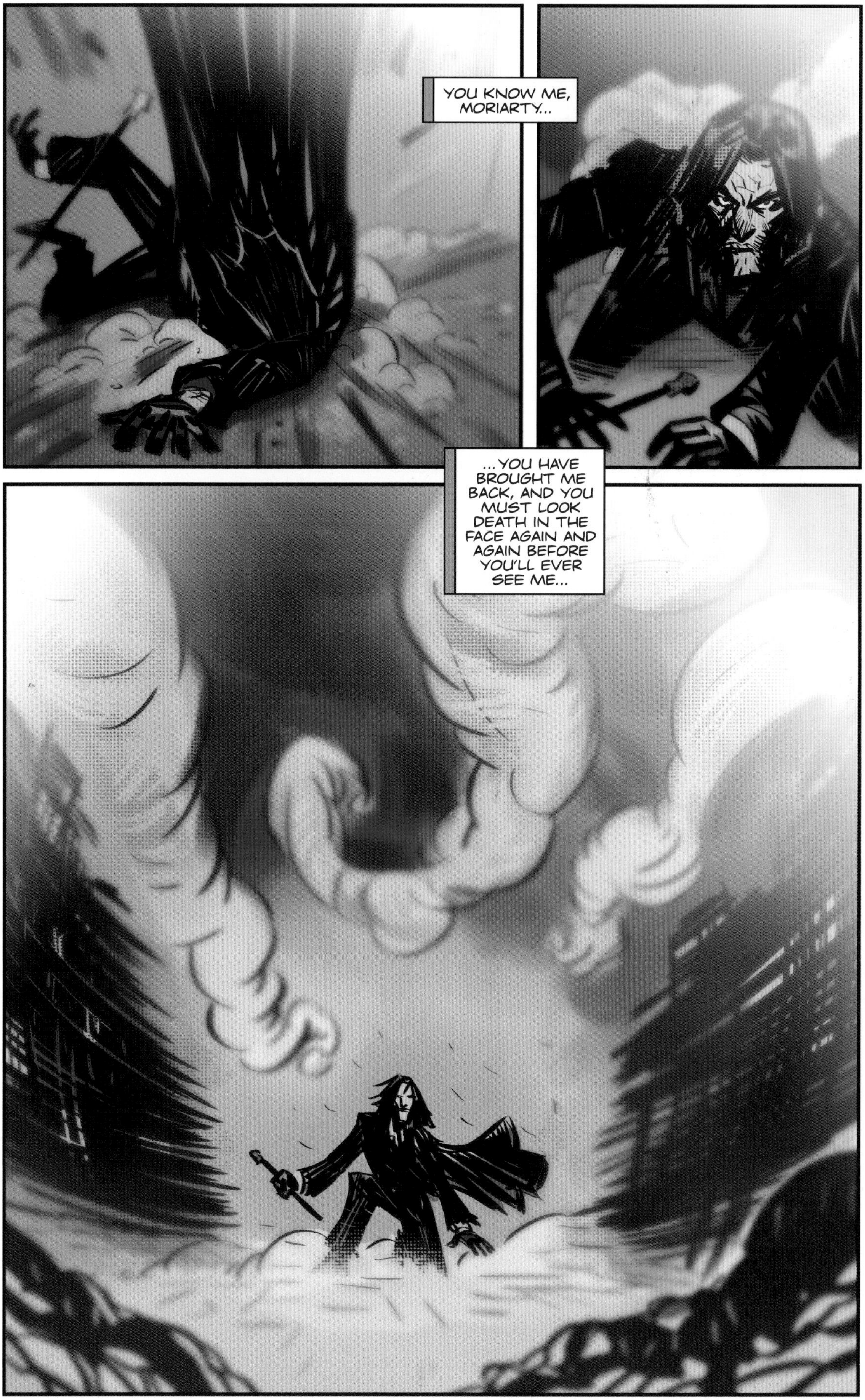
YOU KNOW ME, MORIARTY...
...YOU HAVE BROUGHT ME BACK, AND YOU MUST LOOK DEATH IN THE FACE AGAIN AND AGAIN BEFORE YOU'LL EVER SEE ME...

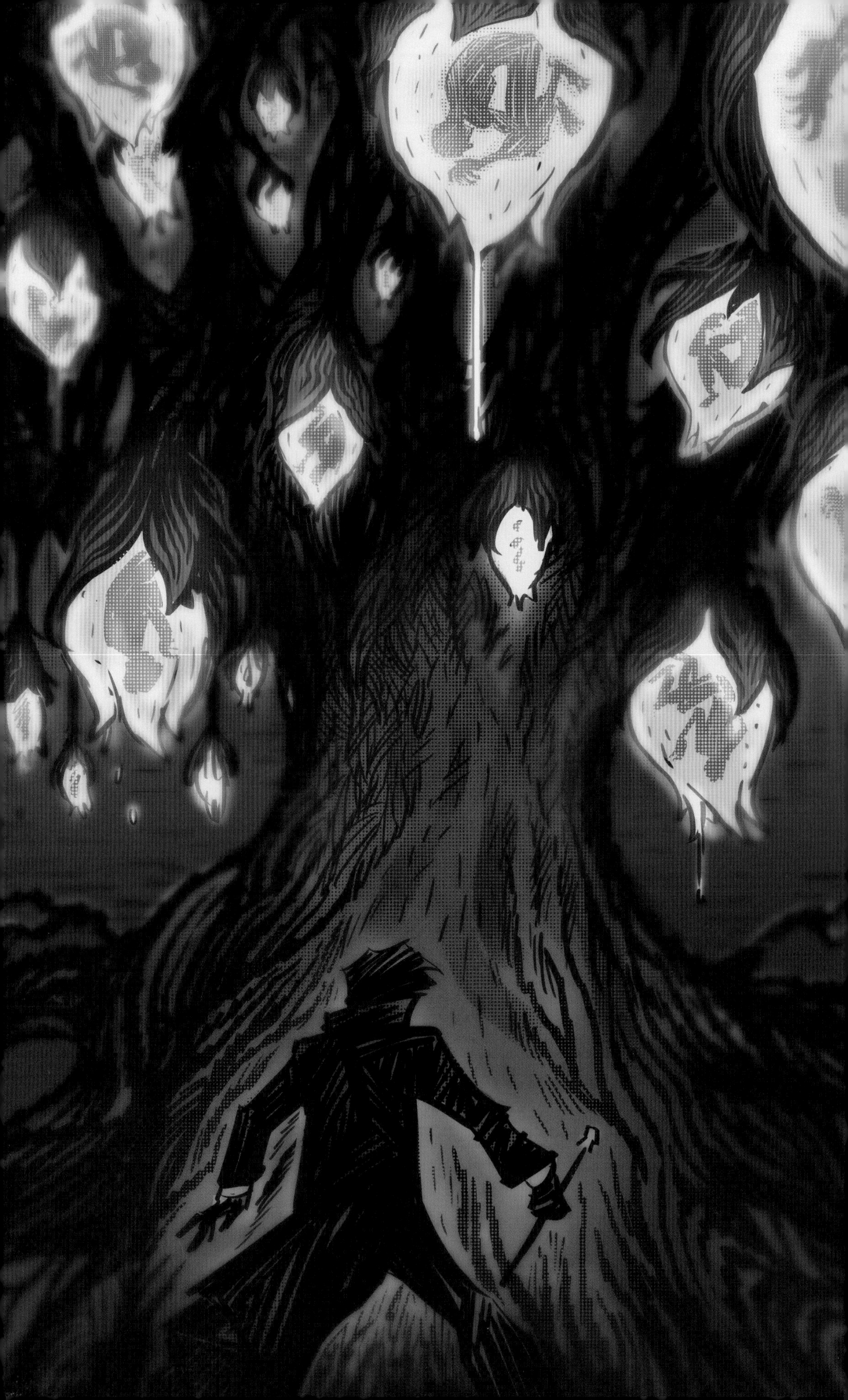

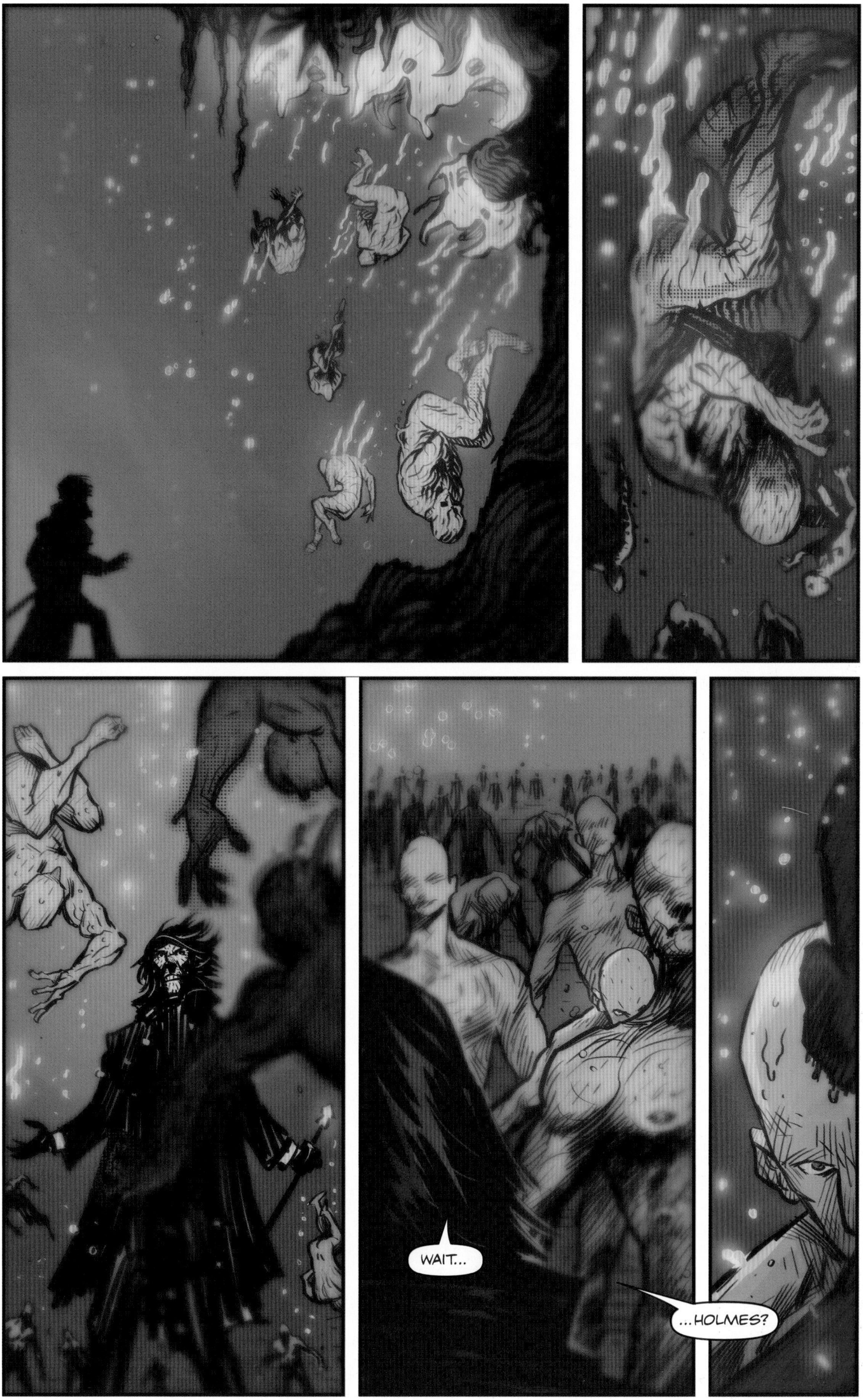
WAIT...
...HOLMES?

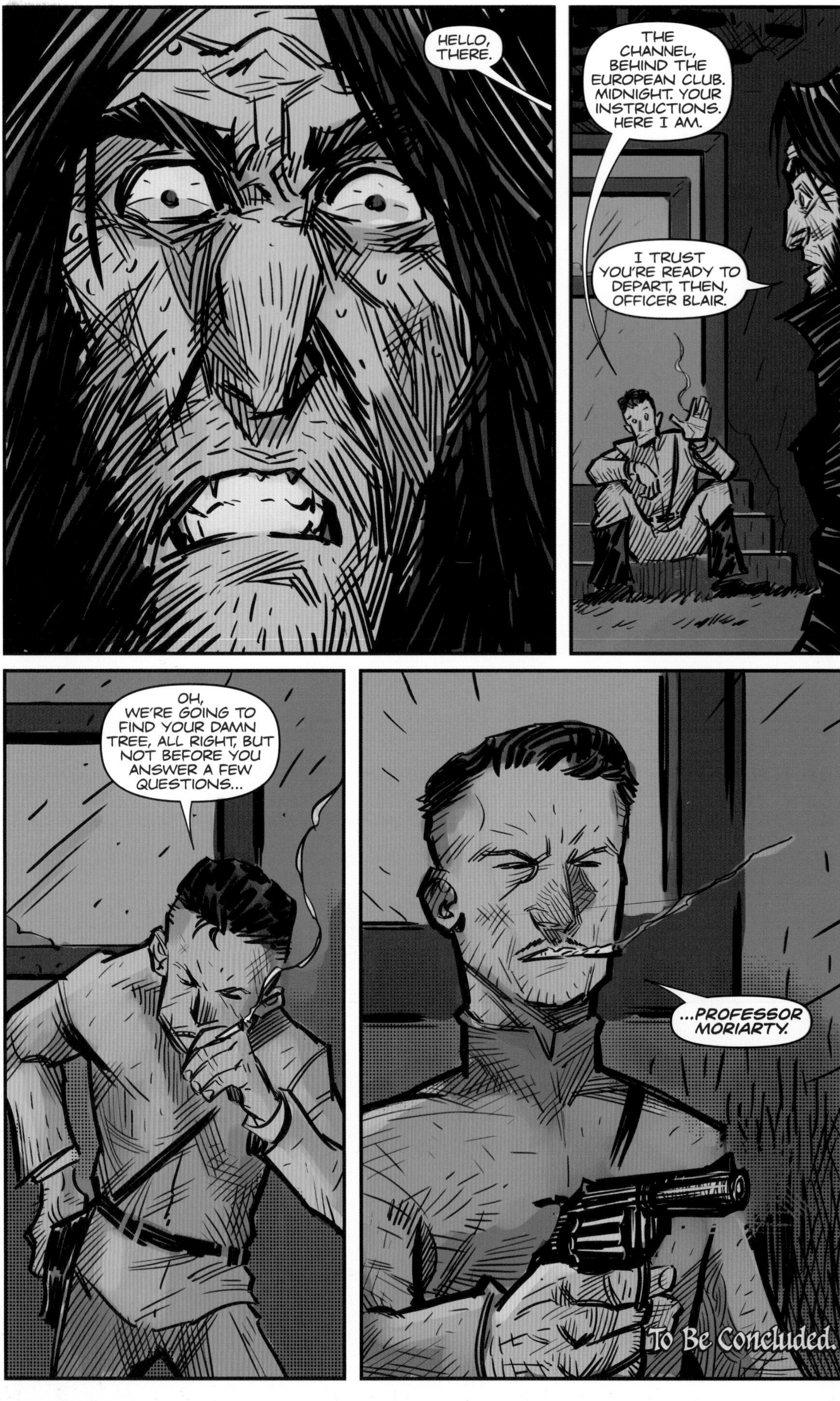
HELLO, THERE.
THE CHANNEL, BEHIND THE EUROPEAN CLUB. MIDNIGHT. YOUR INSTRUCTIONS. HERE I AM.
I TRUST YOU'RE READY TO DEPART, THEN, OFFICER BLAIR.
OH, WE'RE GOING TO FIND YOUR DAMN TREE, ALL RIGHT, BUT NOT BEFORE YOU ANSWER A FEW QUESTIONS...
...PROFESSOR MORIARTY.
To Be Concluded.

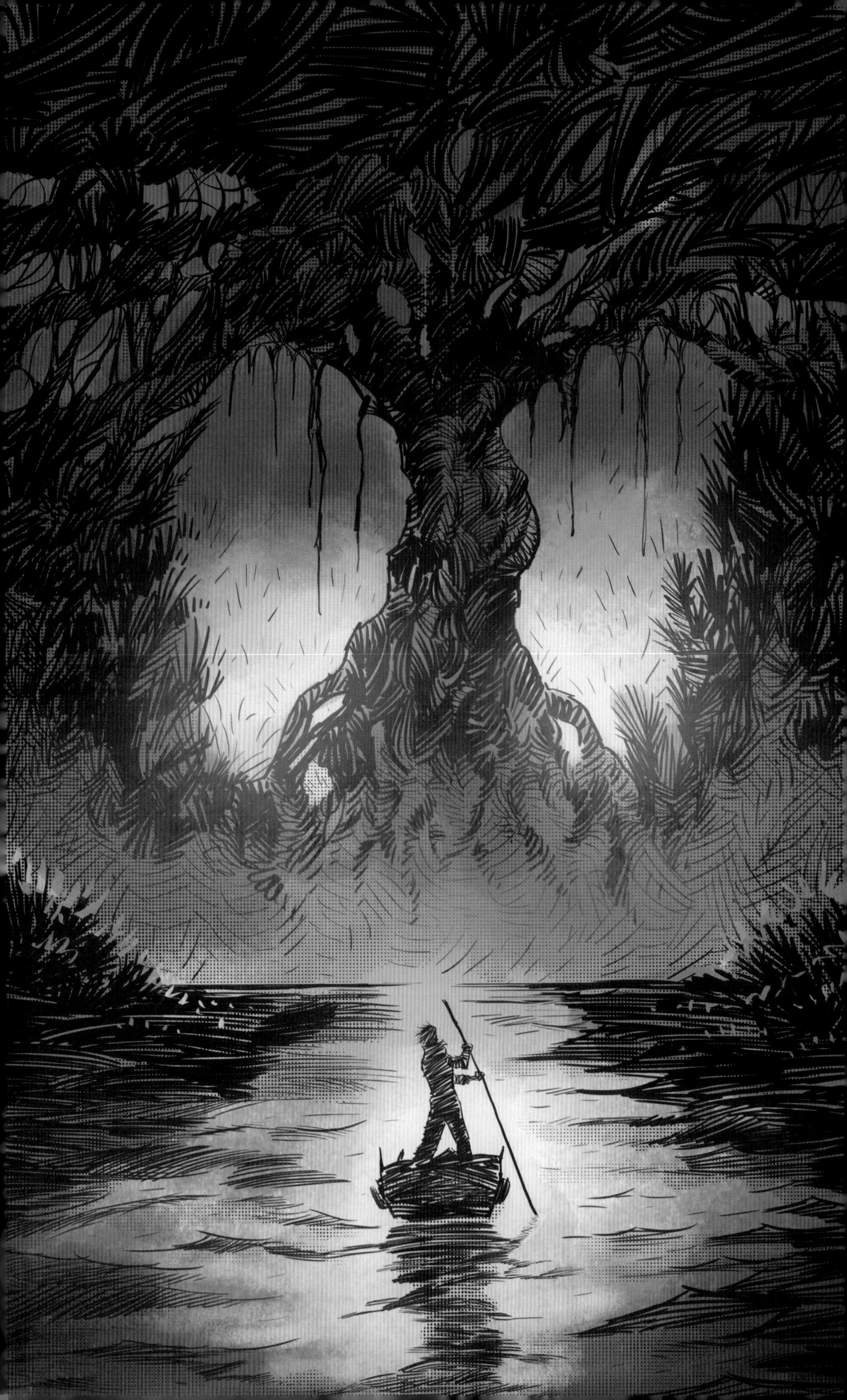

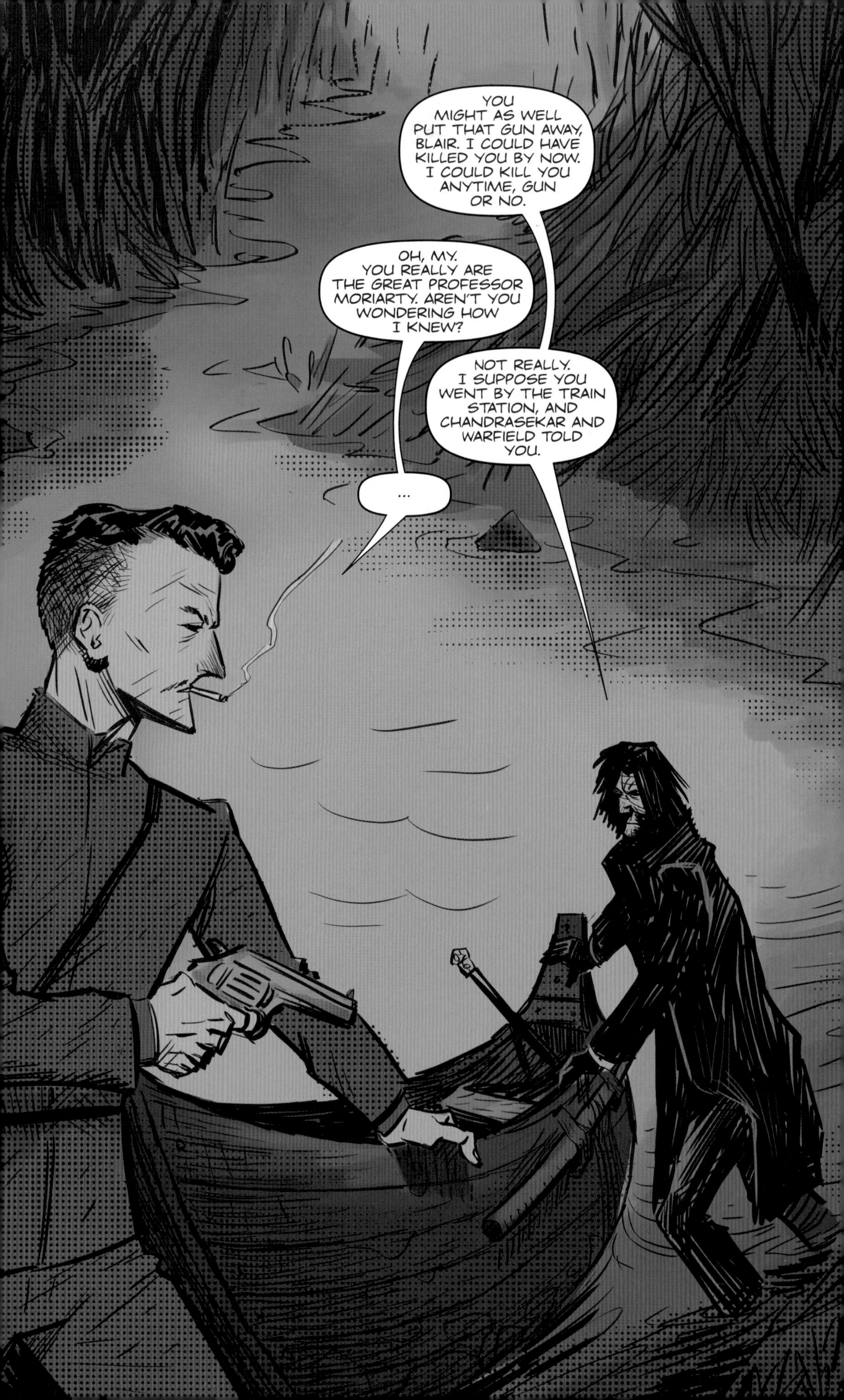

YOU MIGHT AS WELL PUT THAT GUN AWAY, BLAIR. I COULD HAVE KILLED YOU BY NOW. I COULD KILL YOU ANYTIME, GUN OR NO.
OH, MY. YOU REALLY ARE THE GREAT PROFESSOR MORIARTY. AREN'T YOU WONDERING HOW I KNEW?
NOT REALLY. I SUPPOSE YOU WENT BY THE TRAIN STATION, AND CHANDRASEKAR AND WARFIELD TOLD YOU.
...

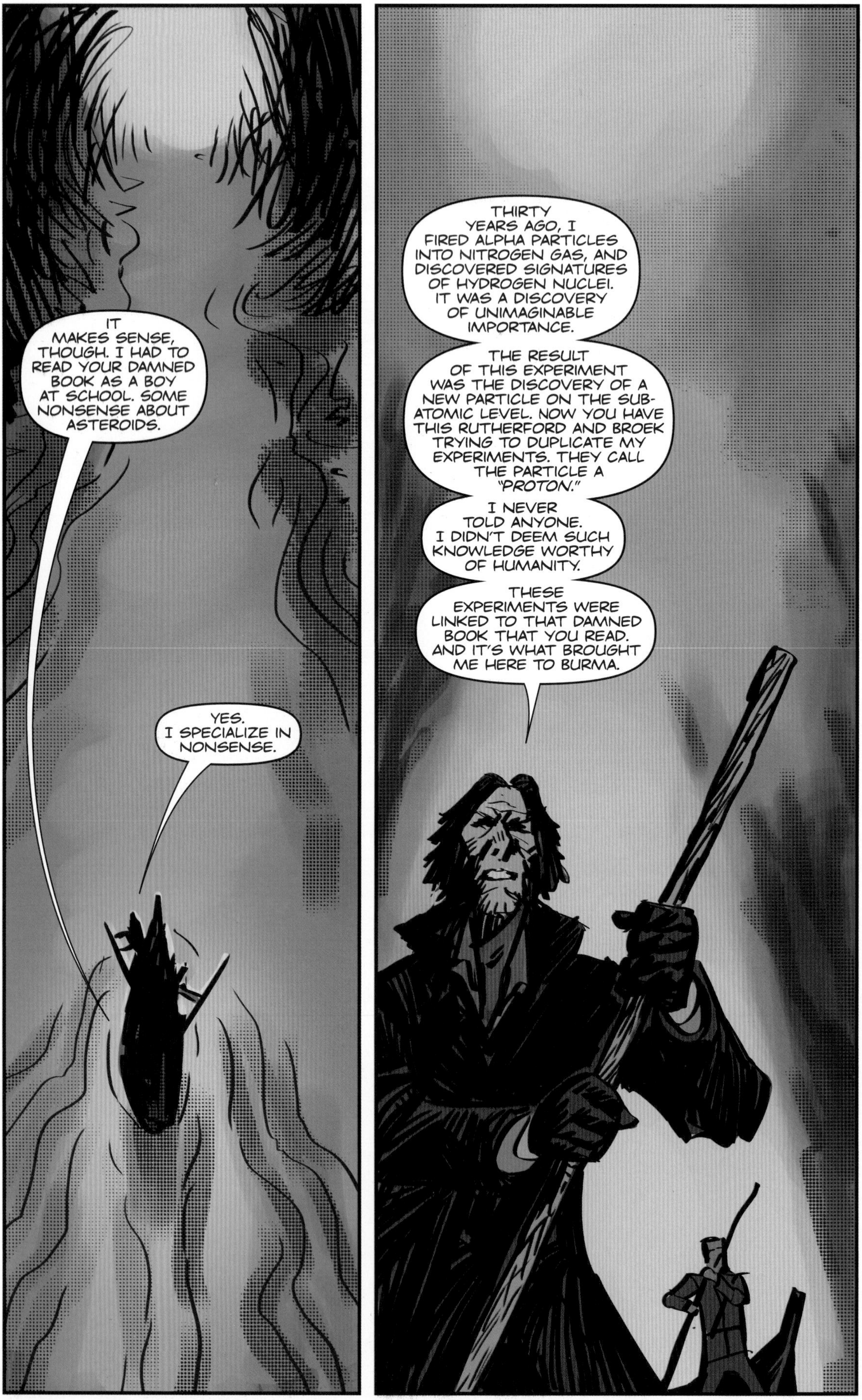
IT MAKES SENSE, THOUGH. I HAD TO READ YOUR DAMNED BOOK AS A BOY AT SCHOOL. SOME NONSENSE ABOUT ASTEROIDS.
YES. I SPECIALIZE IN NONSENSE.
THIRTY YEARS AGO, I FIRED ALPHA PARTICLES INTO NITROGEN GAS, AND DISCOVERED SIGNATURES OF HYDROGEN NUCLEI. IT WAS A DISCOVERY OF UNIMAGINABLE IMPORTANCE.
THE RESULT OF THIS EXPERIMENT WAS THE DISCOVERY OF A NEW PARTICLE ON THE SUB-ATOMIC LEVEL. NOW YOU HAVE THIS RUTHERFORD AND BROEK TRYING TO DUPLICATE MY EXPERIMENTS. THEY CALL THE PARTICLE A "PROTON."
I NEVER TOLD ANYONE. I DIDN'T DEEM SUCH KNOWLEDGE WORTHY OF HUMANITY.
THESE EXPERIMENTS WERE LINKED TO THAT DAMNED BOOK THAT YOU READ. AND IT'S WHAT BROUGHT ME HERE TO BURMA.

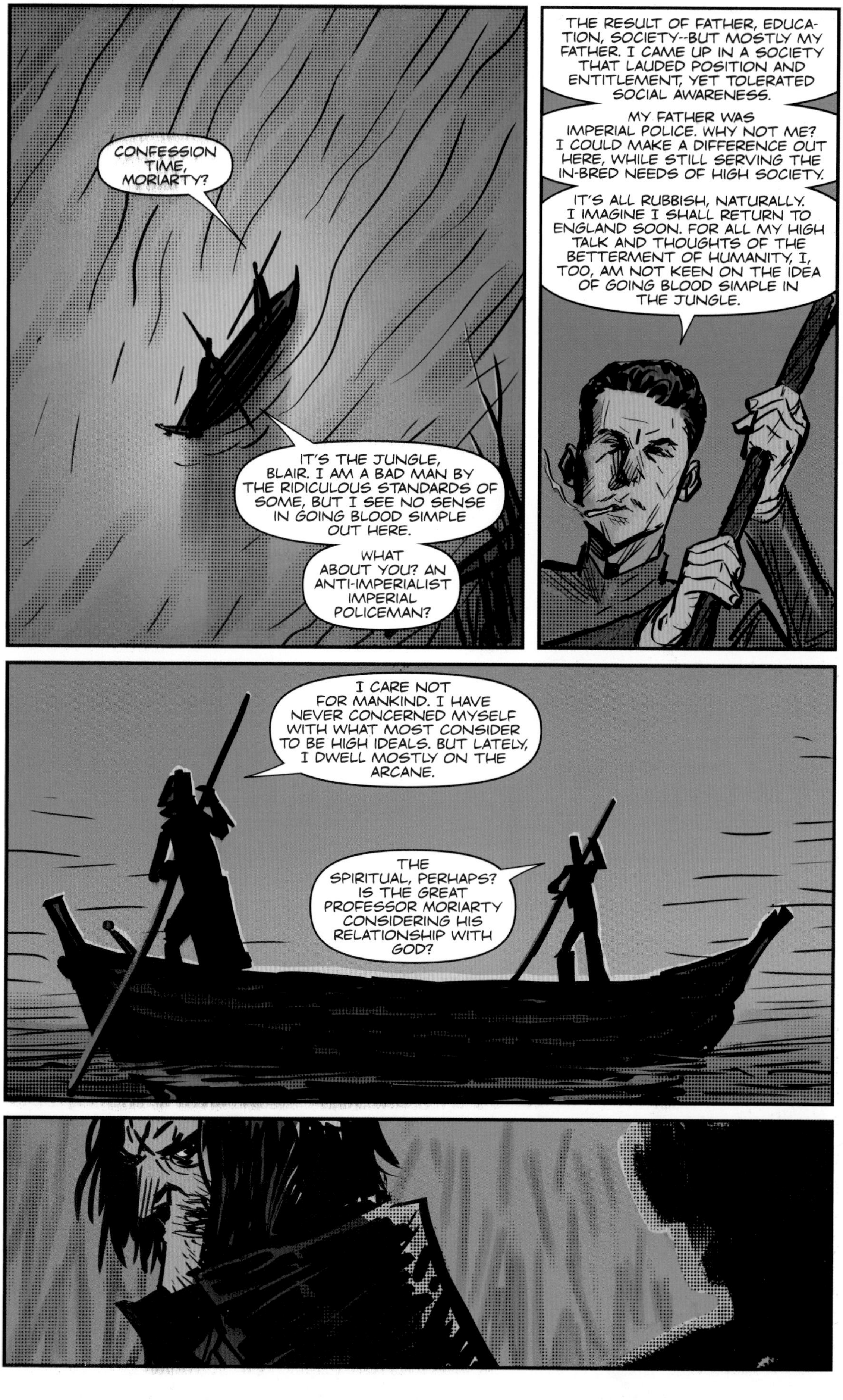
CONFESSION TIME, MORIARTY?
IT'S THE JUNGLE, BLAIR. I AM A BAD MAN BY THE RIDICULOUS STANDARDS OF SOME, BUT I SEE NO SENSE IN GOING BLOOD SIMPLE OUT HERE.
WHAT ABOUT YOU? AN ANTI-IMPERIALIST IMPERIAL POLICEMAN?
THE RESULT OF FATHER, EDUCATION, SOCIETY--BUT MOSTLY MY FATHER. I CAME UP IN A SOCIETY THAT LAUDED POSITION AND ENTITLEMENT, YET TOLERATED SOCIAL AWARENESS.
MY FATHER WAS IMPERIAL POLICE. WHY NOT ME? I COULD MAKE A DIFFERENCE OUT HERE, WHILE STILL SERVING THE IN-BRED NEEDS OF HIGH SOCIETY.
IT'S ALL RUBBISH, NATURALLY. I IMAGINE I SHALL RETURN TO ENGLAND SOON. FOR ALL MY HIGH TALK AND THOUGHTS OF THE BETTERMENT OF HUMANITY, I, TOO, AM NOT KEEN ON THE IDEA OF GOING BLOOD SIMPLE IN THE JUNGLE.
I CARE NOT FOR MANKIND. I HAVE NEVER CONCERNED MYSELF WITH WHAT MOST CONSIDER TO BE HIGH IDEALS. BUT LATELY, I DWELL MOSTLY ON THE ARCANE.
THE SPIRITUAL, PERHAPS? IS THE GREAT PROFESSOR MORIARTY CONSIDERING HIS RELATIONSHIP WITH GOD?

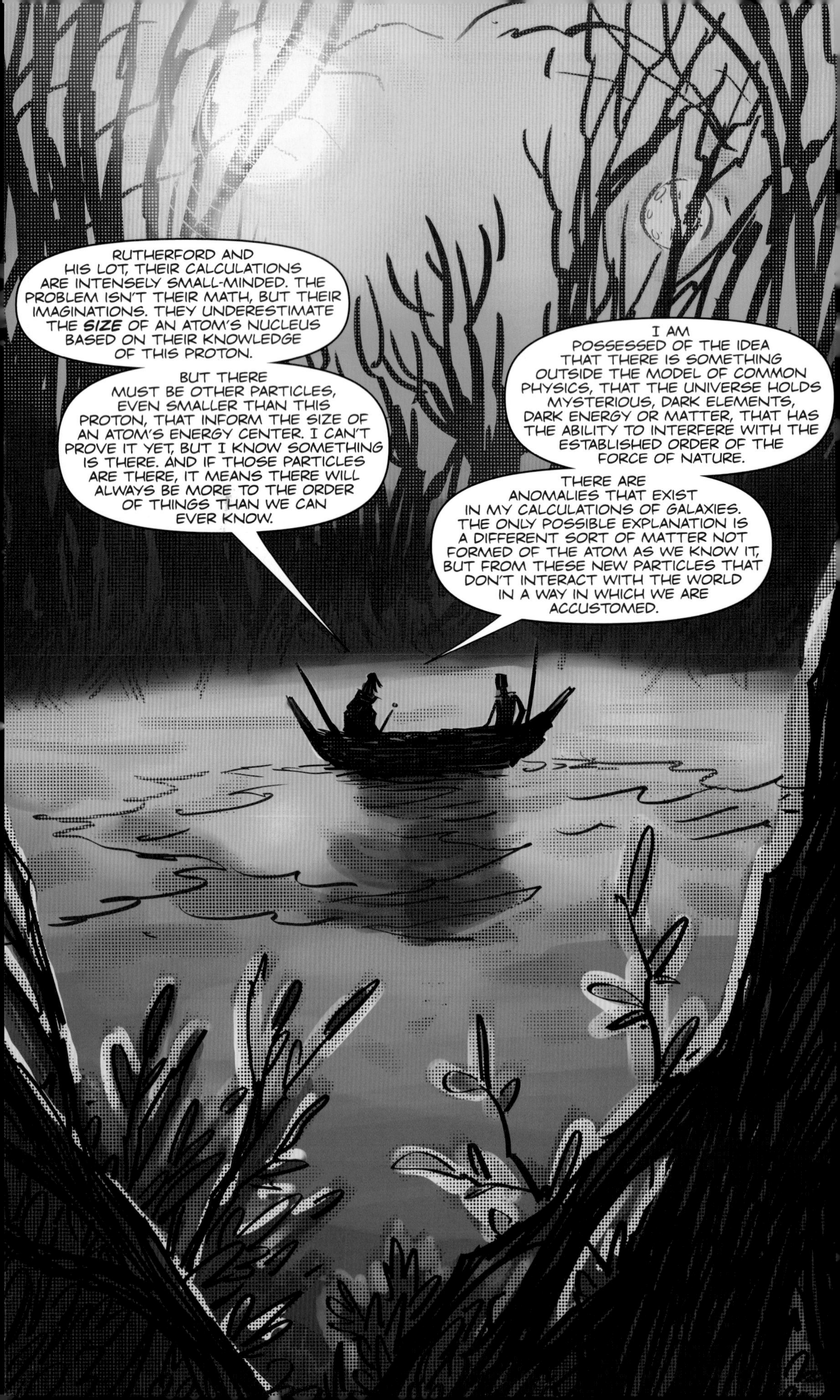
RUTHERFORD AND HIS LOT, THEIR CALCULATIONS ARE INTENSELY SMALL-MINDED. THE PROBLEM ISN'T THEIR MATH, BUT THEIR IMAGINATIONS. THEY UNDERESTIMATE THE *SIZE* OF AN ATOM'S NUCLEUS BASED ON THEIR KNOWLEDGE OF THIS PROTON.
BUT THERE MUST BE OTHER PARTICLES, EVEN SMALLER THAN THIS PROTON, THAT INFORM THE SIZE OF AN ATOM'S ENERGY CENTER. I CAN'T PROVE IT YET, BUT I KNOW SOMETHING IS THERE. AND IF THOSE PARTICLES ARE THERE, IT MEANS THERE WILL ALWAYS BE MORE TO THE ORDER OF THINGS THAN WE CAN EVER KNOW.
I AM POSSESSED OF THE IDEA THAT THERE IS SOMETHING OUTSIDE THE MODEL OF COMMON PHYSICS, THAT THE UNIVERSE HOLDS MYSTERIOUS, DARK ELEMENTS, DARK ENERGY OR MATTER, THAT HAS THE ABILITY TO INTERFERE WITH THE ESTABLISHED ORDER OF THE FORCE OF NATURE.
THERE ARE ANOMALIES THAT EXIST IN MY CALCULATIONS OF GALAXIES. THE ONLY POSSIBLE EXPLANATION IS A DIFFERENT SORT OF MATTER NOT FORMED OF THE ATOM AS WE KNOW IT, BUT FROM THESE NEW PARTICLES THAT DON'T INTERACT WITH THE WORLD IN A WAY IN WHICH WE ARE ACCUSTOMED.

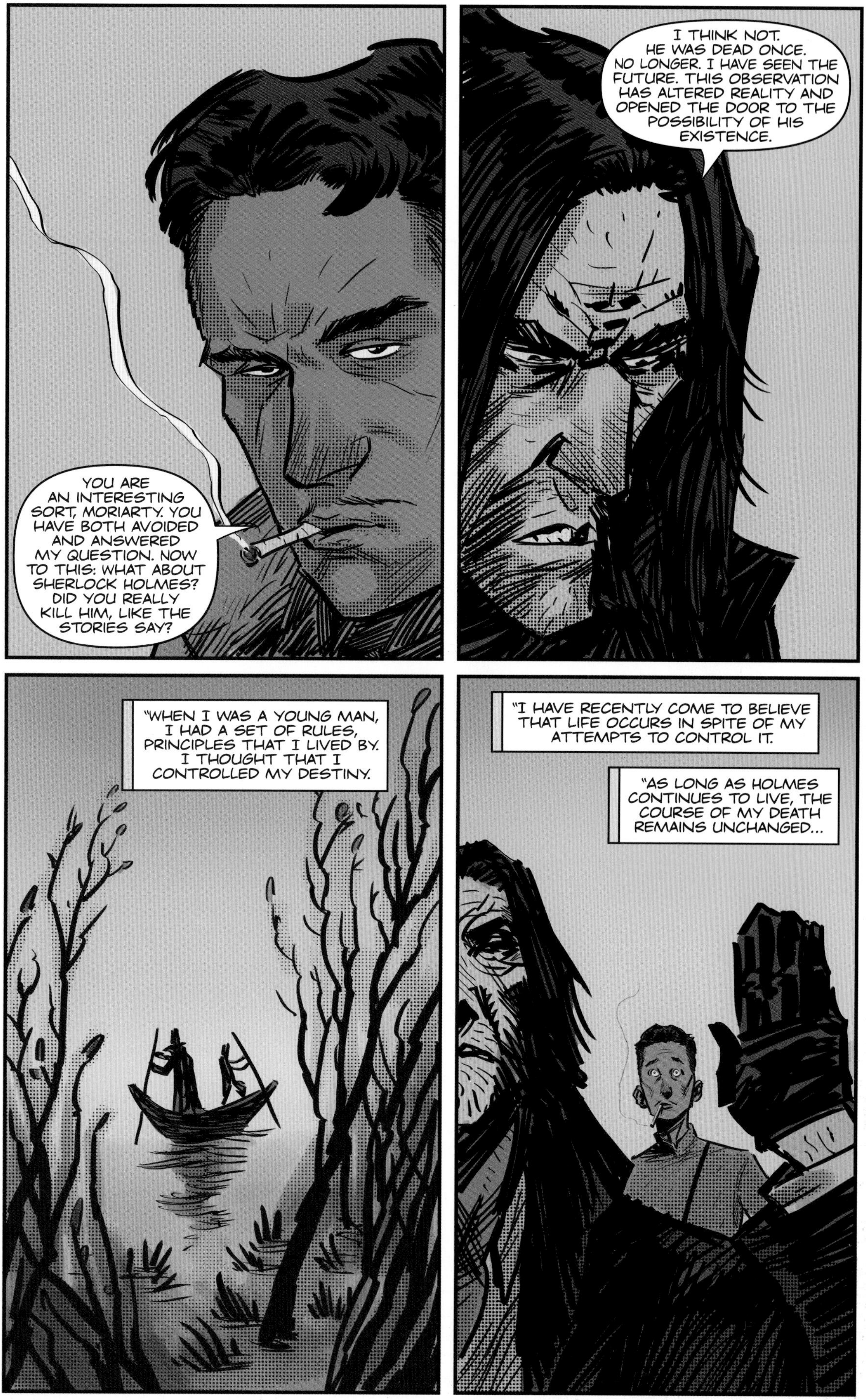
YOU ARE AN INTERESTING SORT, MORIARTY. YOU HAVE BOTH AVOIDED AND ANSWERED MY QUESTION. NOW TO THIS: WHAT ABOUT SHERLOCK HOLMES? DID YOU REALLY KILL HIM, LIKE THE STORIES SAY?
I THINK NOT. HE WAS DEAD ONCE. NO LONGER. I HAVE SEEN THE FUTURE. THIS OBSERVATION HAS ALTERED REALITY AND OPENED THE DOOR TO THE POSSIBILITY OF HIS EXISTENCE.
"WHEN I WAS A YOUNG MAN, I HAD A SET OF RULES, PRINCIPLES THAT I LIVED BY. I THOUGHT THAT I CONTROLLED MY DESTINY.
"I HAVE RECENTLY COME TO BELIEVE THAT LIFE OCCURS IN SPITE OF MY ATTEMPTS TO CONTROL IT.
"AS LONG AS HOLMES CONTINUES TO LIVE, THE COURSE OF MY DEATH REMAINS UNCHANGED...

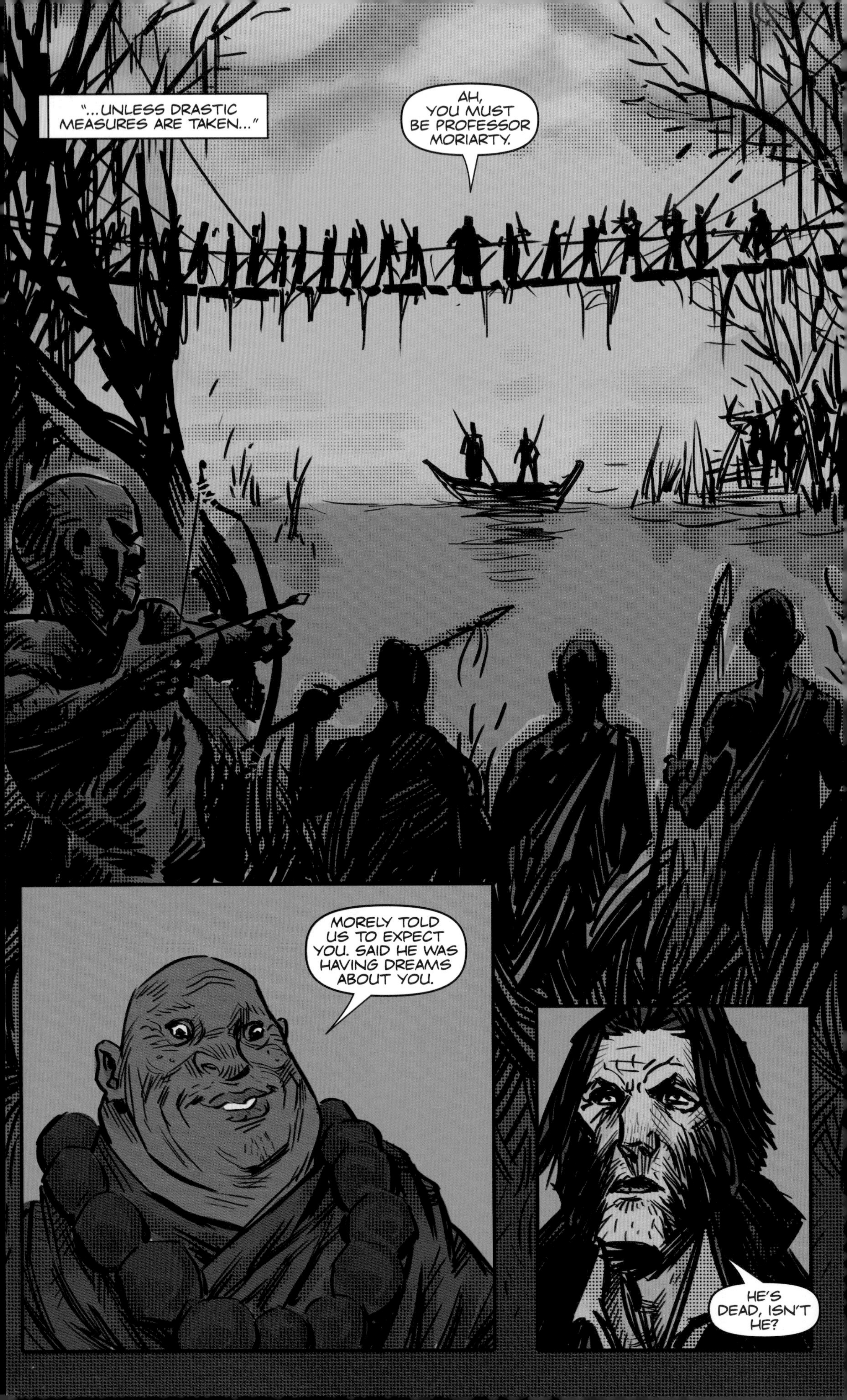
"...UNLESS DRASTIC MEASURES ARE TAKEN..."
AH, YOU MUST BE PROFESSOR MORIARTY.
MORELY TOLD US TO EXPECT YOU. SAID HE WAS HAVING DREAMS ABOUT YOU.
HE'S DEAD, ISN'T HE?

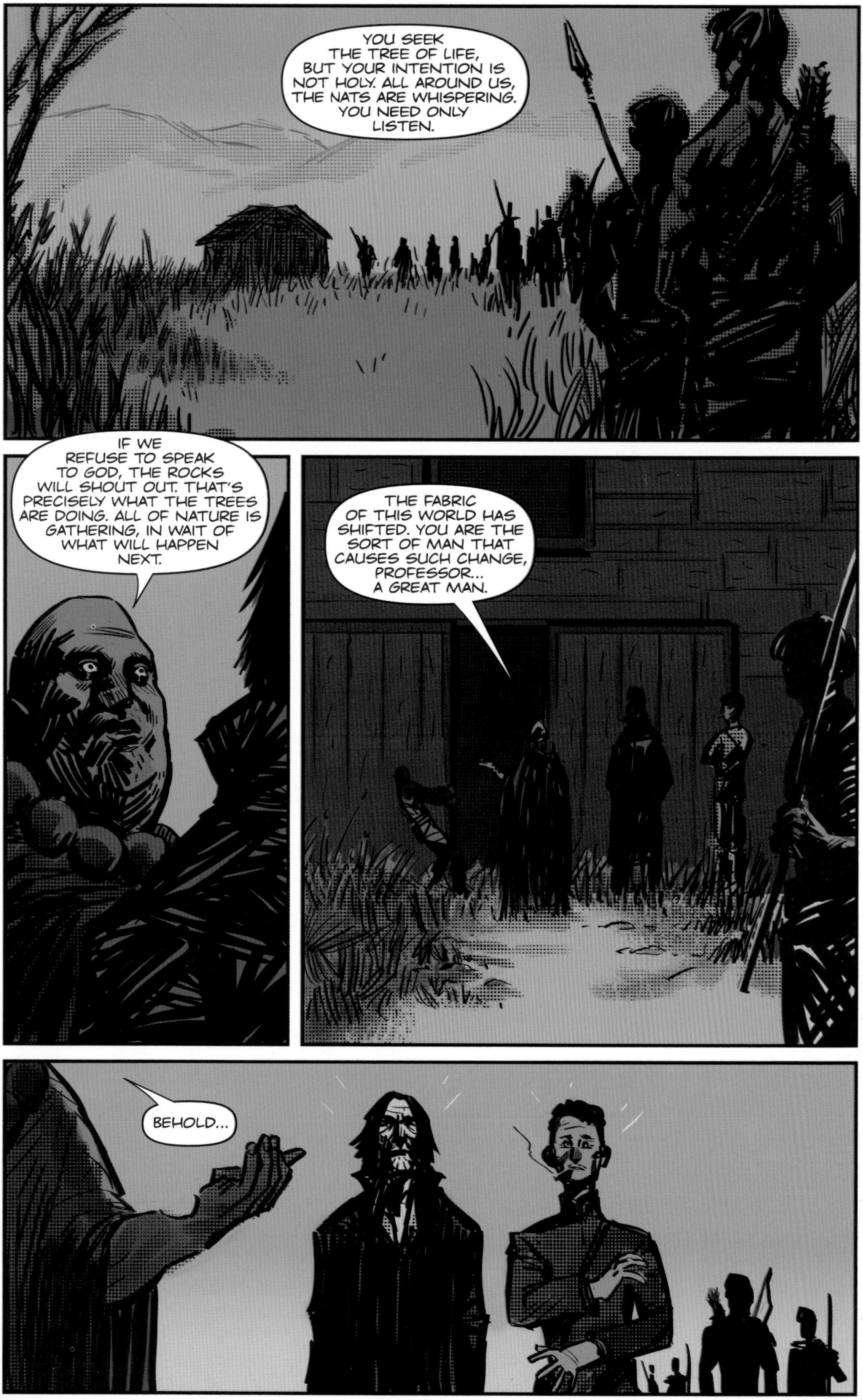
YOU SEEK THE TREE OF LIFE, BUT YOUR INTENTION IS NOT HOLY. ALL AROUND US, THE NATS ARE WHISPERING. YOU NEED ONLY LISTEN.
IF WE REFUSE TO SPEAK TO GOD, THE ROCKS WILL SHOUT OUT. THAT'S PRECISELY WHAT THE TREES ARE DOING. ALL OF NATURE IS GATHERING, IN WAIT OF WHAT WILL HAPPEN NEXT.
THE FABRIC OF THIS WORLD HAS SHIFTED. YOU ARE THE SORT OF MAN THAT CAUSES SUCH CHANGE, PROFESSOR... A GREAT MAN.
BEHOLD...

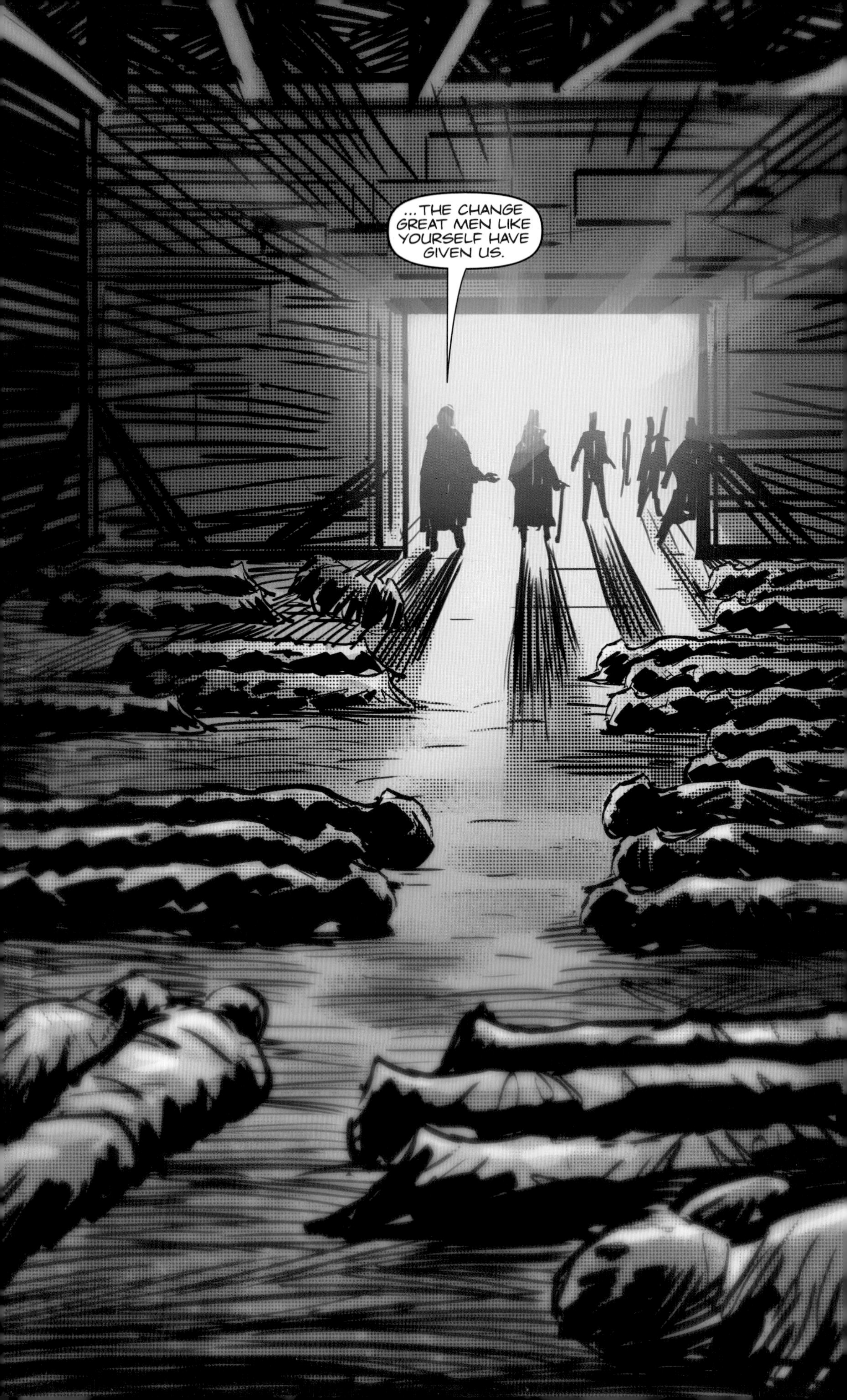
...THE CHANGE GREAT MEN LIKE YOURSELF HAVE GIVEN US.

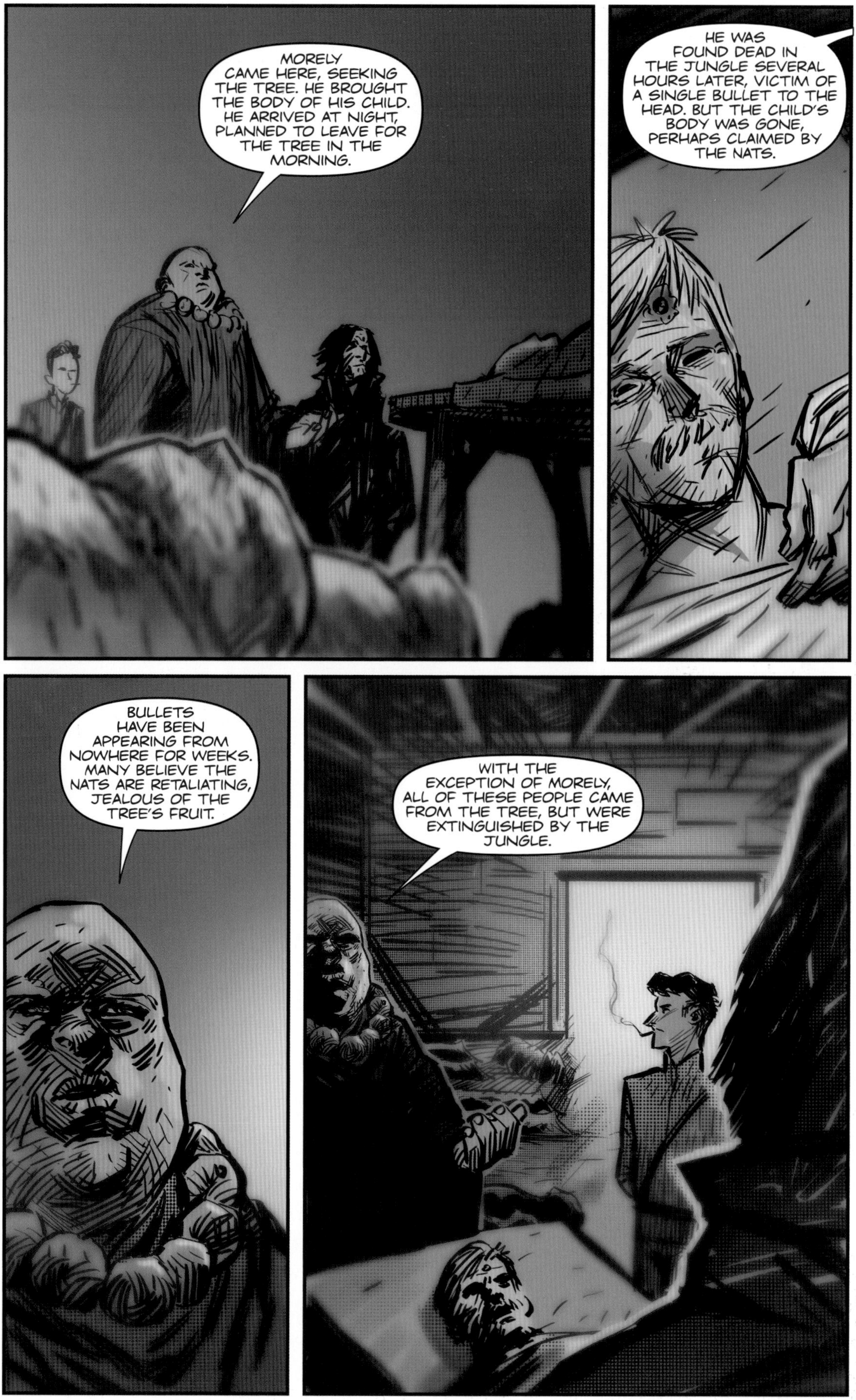
MORELY CAME HERE, SEEKING THE TREE. HE BROUGHT THE BODY OF HIS CHILD. HE ARRIVED AT NIGHT, PLANNED TO LEAVE FOR THE TREE IN THE MORNING.
HE WAS FOUND DEAD IN THE JUNGLE SEVERAL HOURS LATER, VICTIM OF A SINGLE BULLET TO THE HEAD. BUT THE CHILD'S BODY WAS GONE, PERHAPS CLAIMED BY THE NATS.
BULLETS HAVE BEEN APPEARING FROM NOWHERE FOR WEEKS. MANY BELIEVE THE NATS ARE RETALIATING, JEALOUS OF THE TREE'S FRUIT.
WITH THE EXCEPTION OF MORELY, ALL OF THESE PEOPLE CAME FROM THE TREE, BUT WERE EXTINGUISHED BY THE JUNGLE.

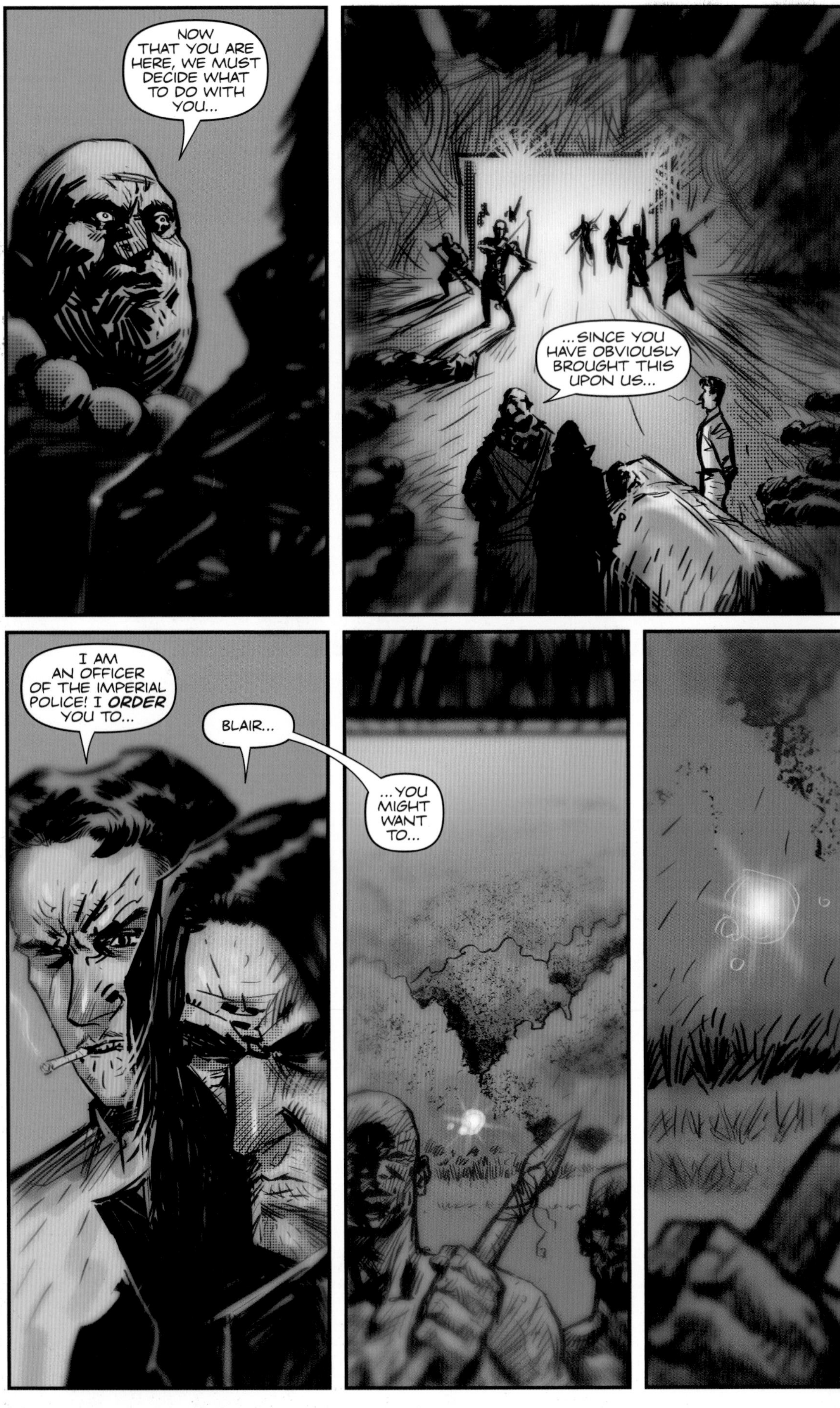
NOW THAT YOU ARE HERE, WE MUST DECIDE WHAT TO DO WITH YOU...
...SINCE YOU HAVE OBVIOUSLY BROUGHT THIS UPON US...
I AM AN OFFICER OF THE IMPERIAL POLICE! I ORDER YOU TO...
BLAIR...
...YOU MIGHT WANT TO...

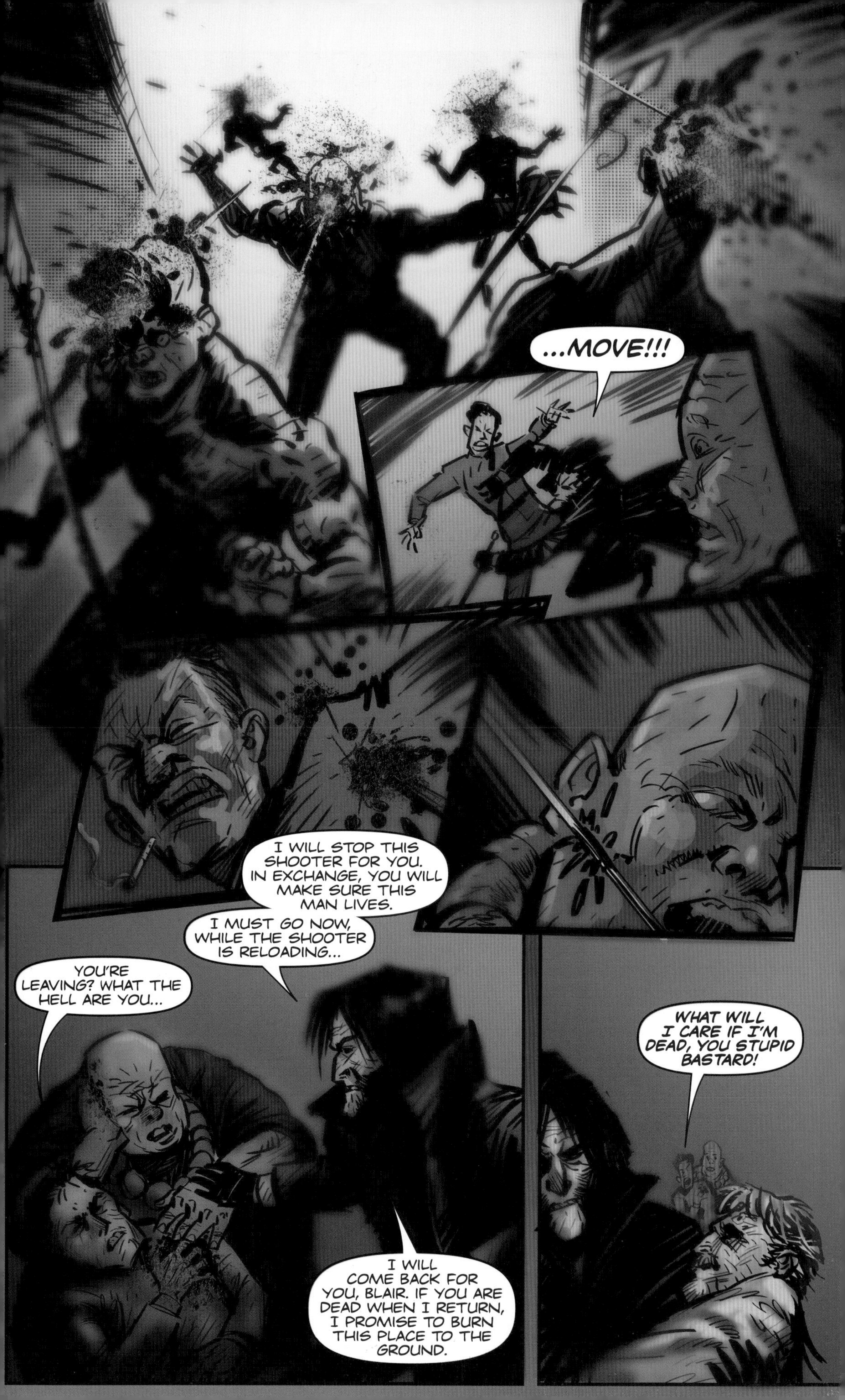
...MOVE!!!
I WILL STOP THIS SHOOTER FOR YOU. IN EXCHANGE, YOU WILL MAKE SURE THIS MAN LIVES.
I MUST GO NOW, WHILE THE SHOOTER IS RELOADING...
YOU'RE LEAVING? WHAT THE HELL ARE YOU...
I WILL COME BACK FOR YOU, BLAIR. IF YOU ARE DEAD WHEN I RETURN, I PROMISE TO BURN THIS PLACE TO THE GROUND.
WHAT WILL I CARE IF I'M DEAD, YOU STUPID BASTARD!

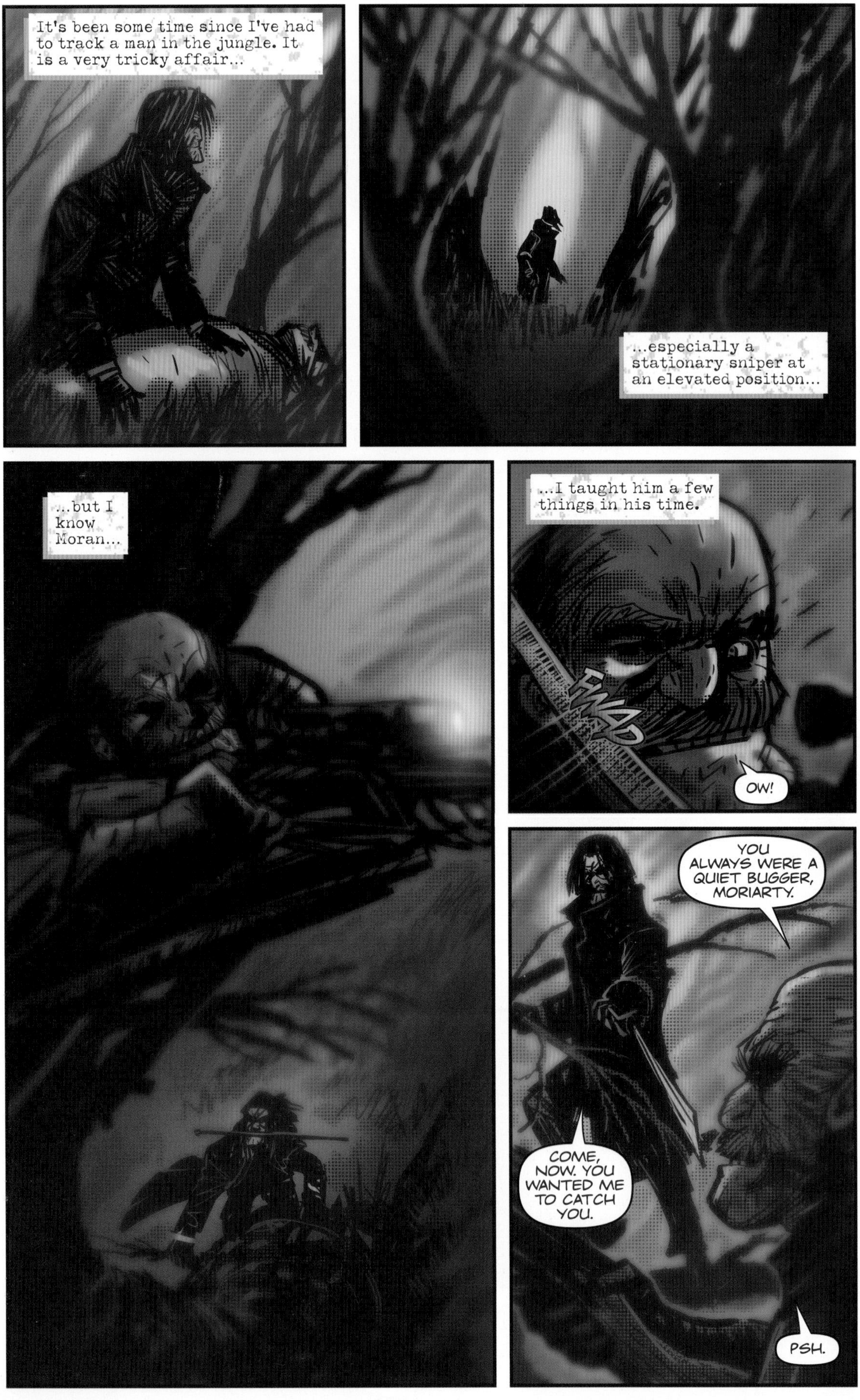
It's been some time since I've had to track a man in the jungle. It is a very tricky affair...
...especially a stationary sniper at an elevated position...
...but I know Moran...
...I taught him a few things in his time.
OW!
YOU ALWAYS WERE A QUIET BUGGER, MORIARTY.
COME, NOW. YOU WANTED ME TO CATCH YOU.
PSH.

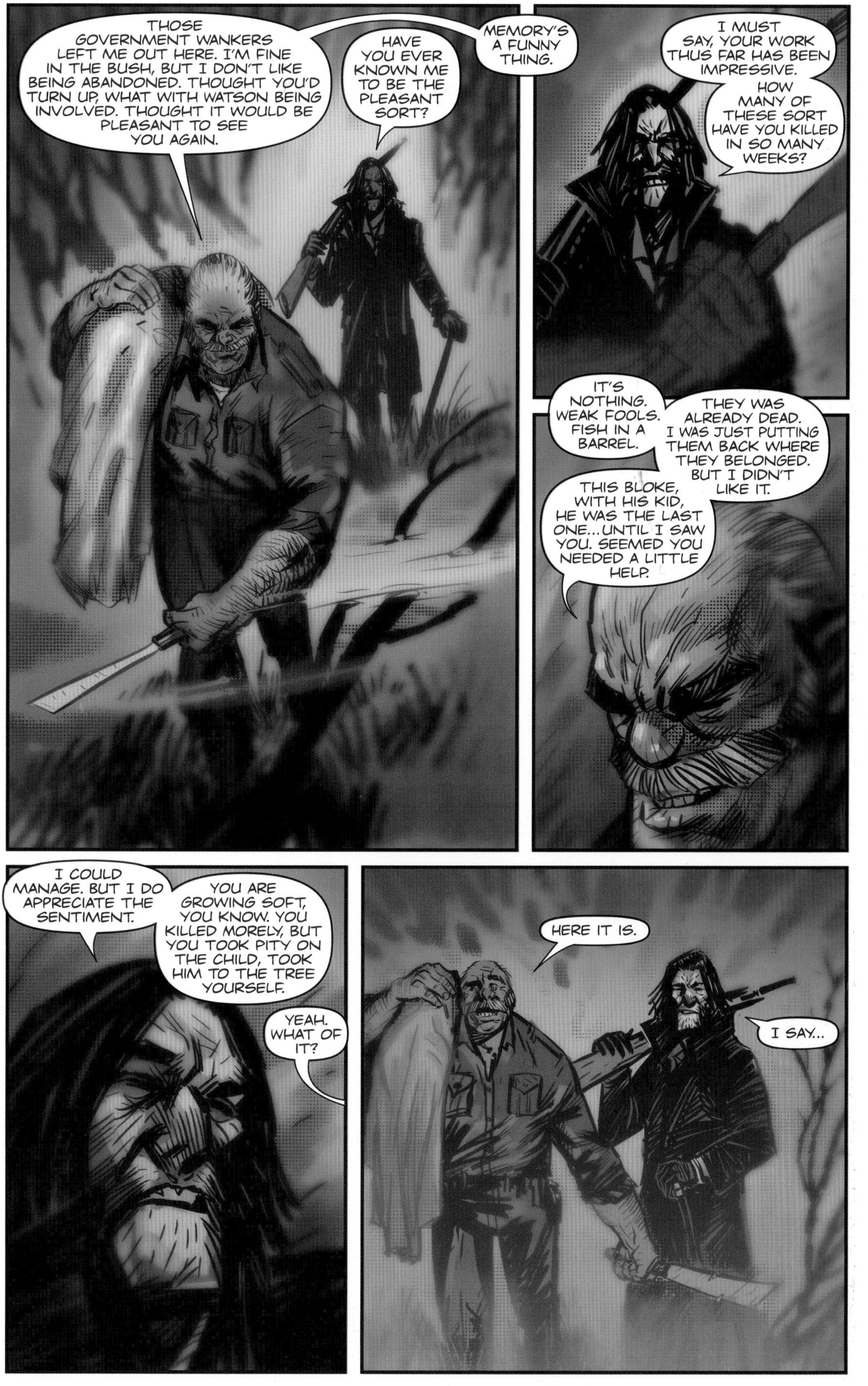
THOSE GOVERNMENT WANKERS LEFT ME OUT HERE. I'M FINE IN THE BUSH, BUT I DON'T LIKE BEING ABANDONED. THOUGHT YOU'D TURN UP, WHAT WITH WATSON BEING INVOLVED. THOUGHT IT WOULD BE PLEASANT TO SEE YOU AGAIN.
HAVE YOU EVER KNOWN ME TO BE THE PLEASANT SORT?
MEMORY'S A FUNNY THING.
I MUST SAY, YOUR WORK THUS FAR HAS BEEN IMPRESSIVE.
HOW MANY OF THESE SORT HAVE YOU KILLED IN SO MANY WEEKS?
IT'S NOTHING. WEAK FOOLS. FISH IN A BARREL.
THEY WAS ALREADY DEAD. I WAS JUST PUTTING THEM BACK WHERE THEY BELONGED. BUT I DIDN'T LIKE IT.
THIS BLOKE, WITH HIS KID, HE WAS THE LAST ONE...UNTIL I SAW YOU. SEEMED YOU NEEDED A LITTLE HELP.
I COULD MANAGE. BUT I DO APPRECIATE THE SENTIMENT.
YOU ARE GROWING SOFT, YOU KNOW. YOU KILLED MORELY, BUT YOU TOOK PITY ON THE CHILD, TOOK HIM TO THE TREE YOURSELF.
YEAH. WHAT OF IT?
HERE IT IS.
I SAY...

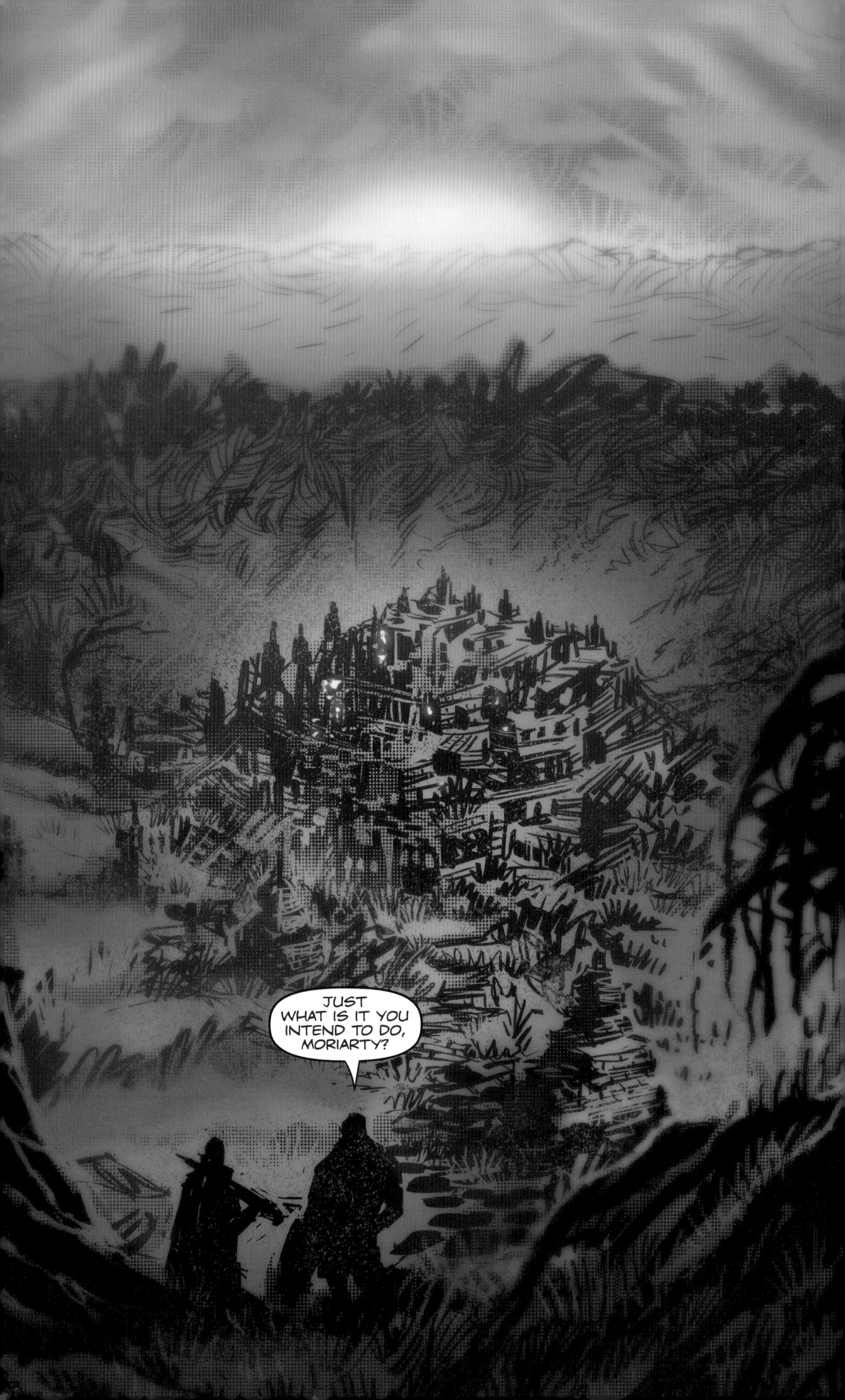
JUST WHAT IS IT YOU INTEND TO DO, MORIARTY?

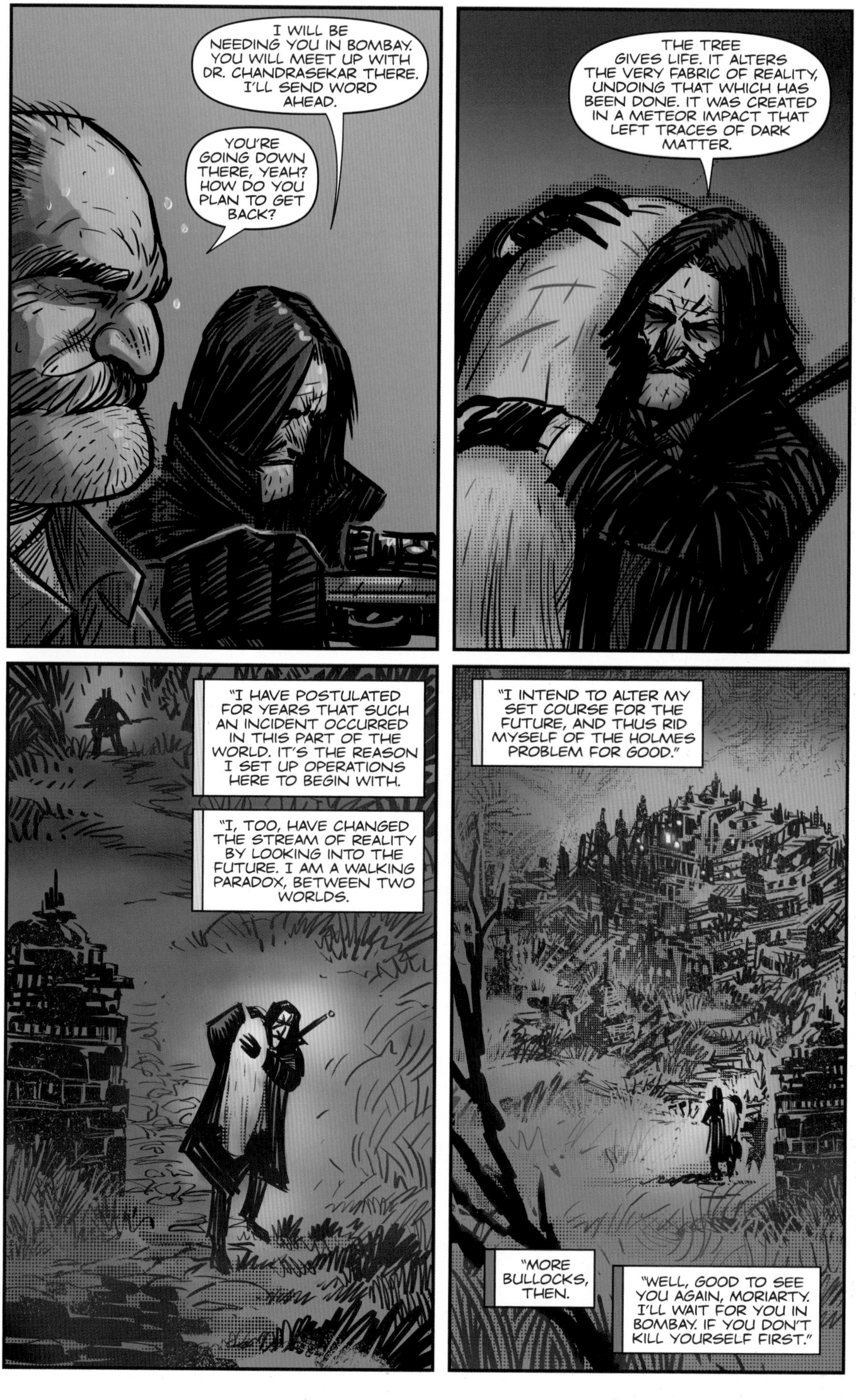

I WILL BE NEEDING YOU IN BOMBAY. YOU WILL MEET UP WITH DR. CHANDRASEKAR THERE. I'LL SEND WORD AHEAD.
YOU'RE GOING DOWN THERE, YEAH? HOW DO YOU PLAN TO GET BACK?
THE TREE GIVES LIFE. IT ALTERS THE VERY FABRIC OF REALITY, UNDOING THAT WHICH HAS BEEN DONE. IT WAS CREATED IN A METEOR IMPACT THAT LEFT TRACES OF DARK MATTER.
"I HAVE POSTULATED FOR YEARS THAT SUCH AN INCIDENT OCCURRED IN THIS PART OF THE WORLD. IT'S THE REASON I SET UP OPERATIONS HERE TO BEGIN WITH.
"I, TOO, HAVE CHANGED THE STREAM OF REALITY BY LOOKING INTO THE FUTURE. I AM A WALKING PARADOX, BETWEEN TWO WORLDS.
"I INTEND TO ALTER MY SET COURSE FOR THE FUTURE, AND THUS RID MYSELF OF THE HOLMES PROBLEM FOR GOOD."
"MORE BULLOCKS, THEN.
"WELL, GOOD TO SEE YOU AGAIN, MORIARTY. I'LL WAIT FOR YOU IN BOMBAY. IF YOU DON'T KILL YOURSELF FIRST."

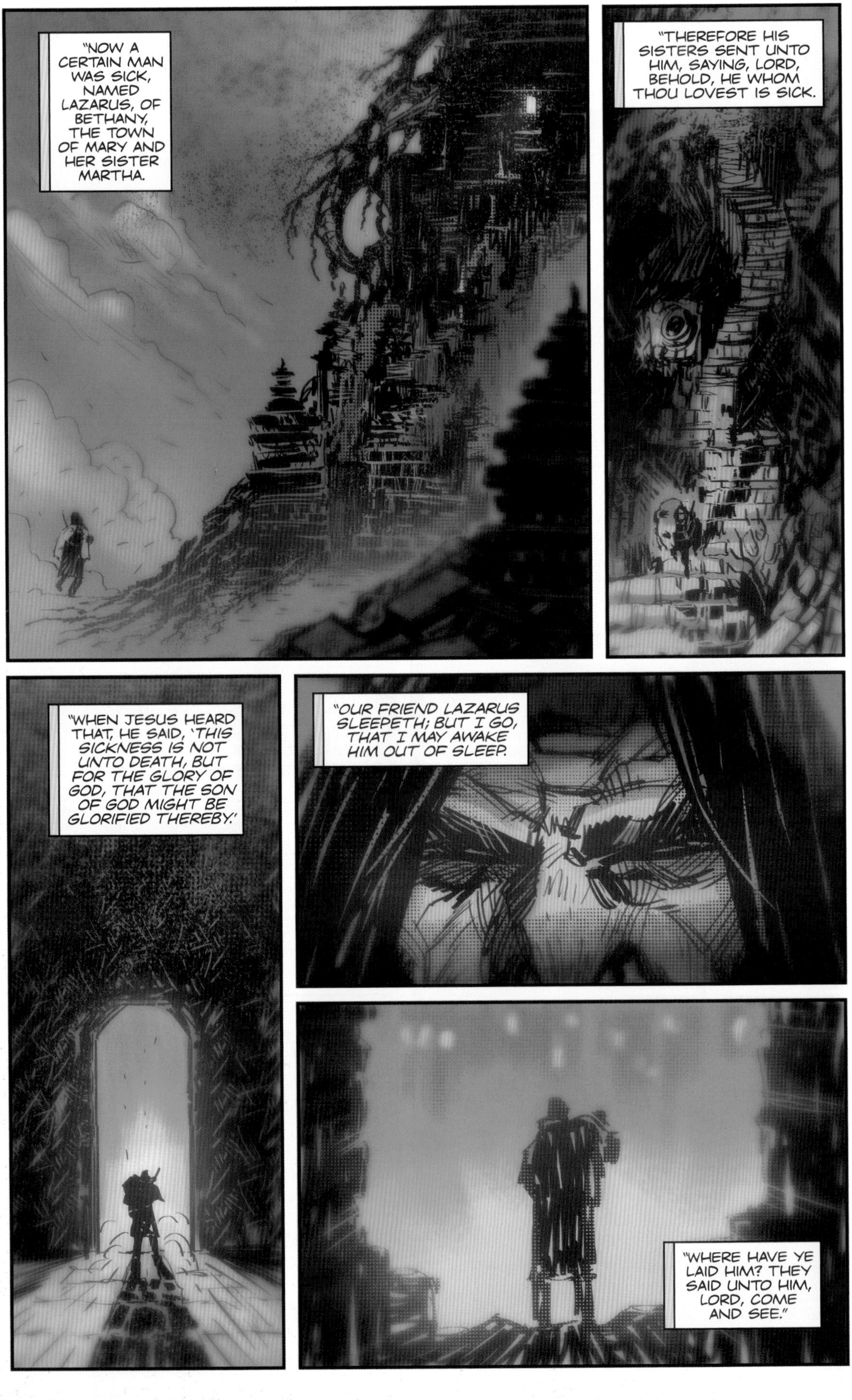
"NOW A CERTAIN MAN WAS SICK, NAMED LAZARUS, OF BETHANY, THE TOWN OF MARY AND HER SISTER MARTHA.
"THEREFORE HIS SISTERS SENT UNTO HIM, SAYING, LORD, BEHOLD, HE WHOM THOU LOVEST IS SICK.
"WHEN JESUS HEARD THAT, HE SAID, 'THIS SICKNESS IS NOT UNTO DEATH, BUT FOR THE GLORY OF GOD, THAT THE SON OF GOD MIGHT BE GLORIFIED THEREBY.'
"OUR FRIEND LAZARUS SLEEPETH; BUT I GO, THAT I MAY AWAKE HIM OUT OF SLEEP.
"WHERE HAVE YE LAID HIM? THEY SAID UNTO HIM, LORD, COME AND SEE."

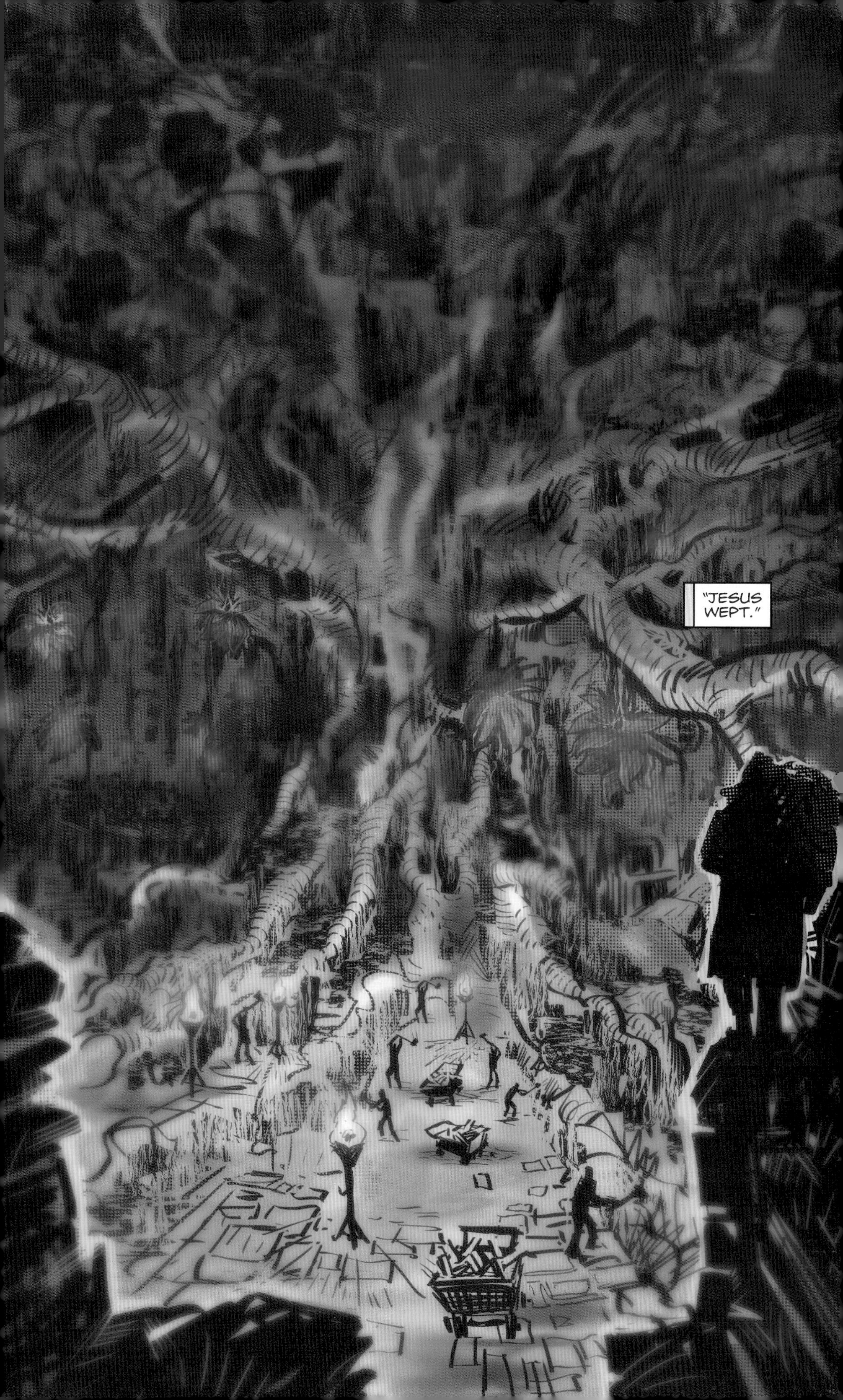
"JESUS WEPT."

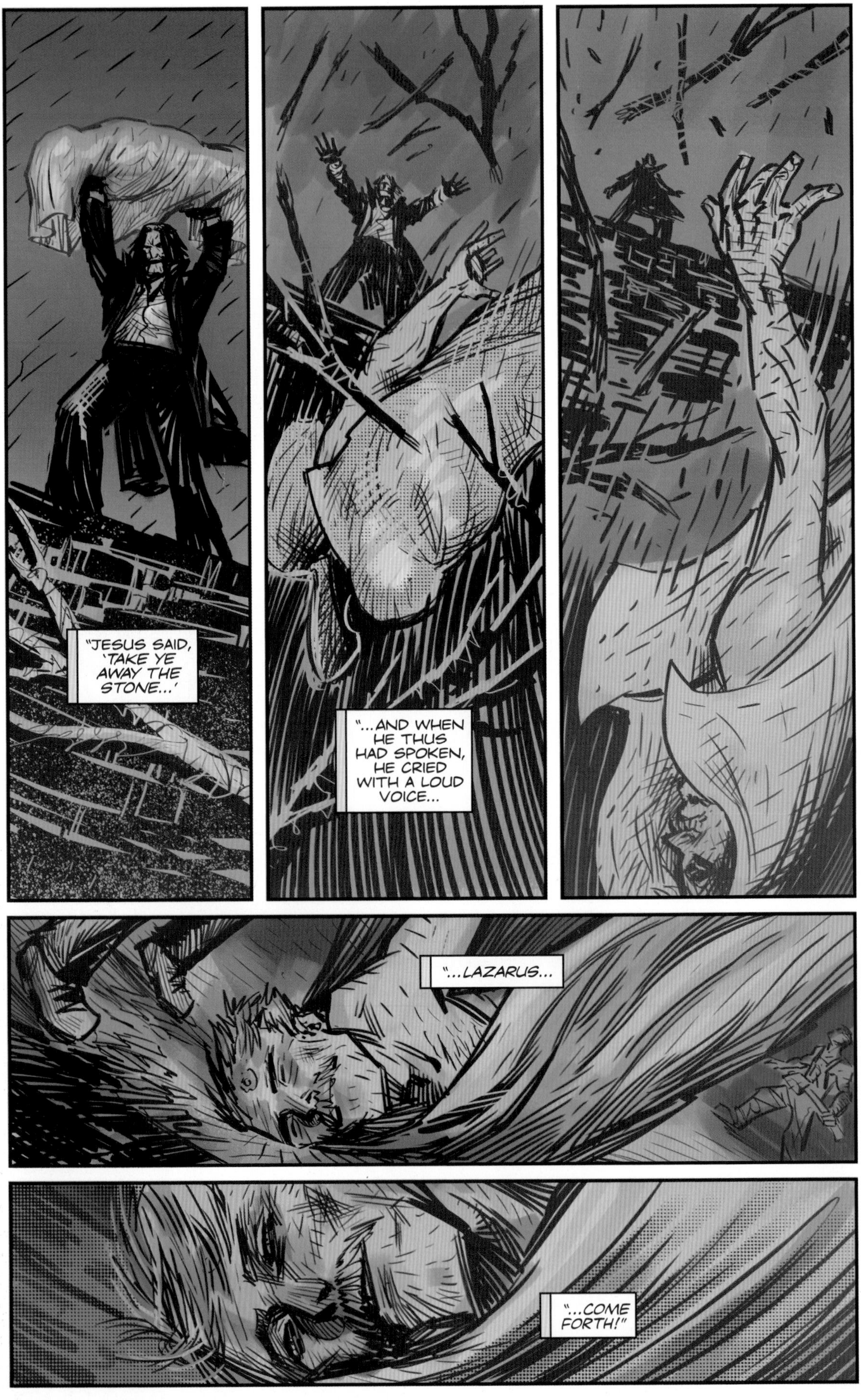
"JESUS SAID, 'TAKE YE AWAY THE STONE...'
"...AND WHEN HE THUS HAD SPOKEN, HE CRIED WITH A LOUD VOICE...
"...LAZARUS...
"...COME FORTH!"

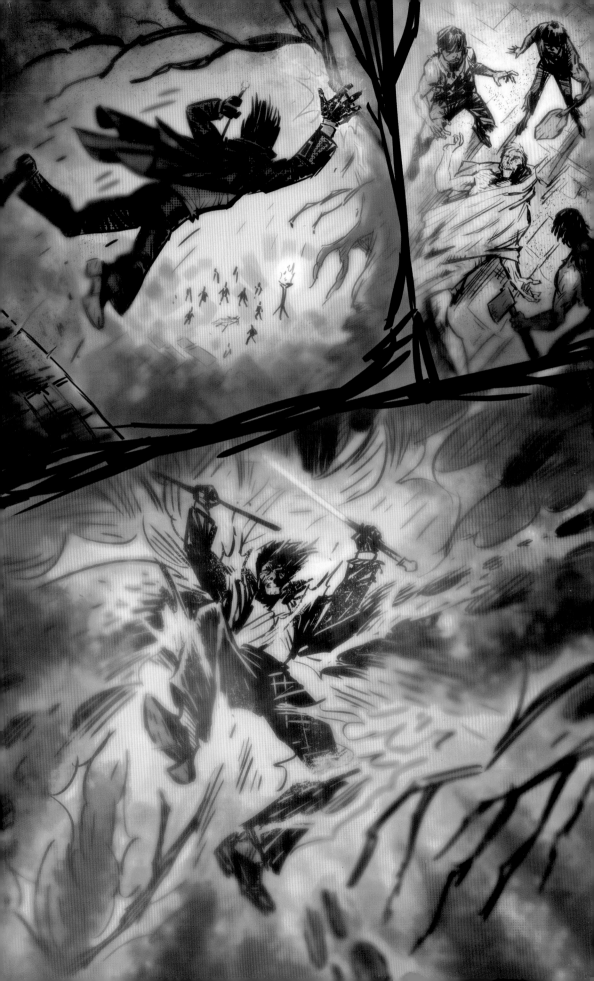

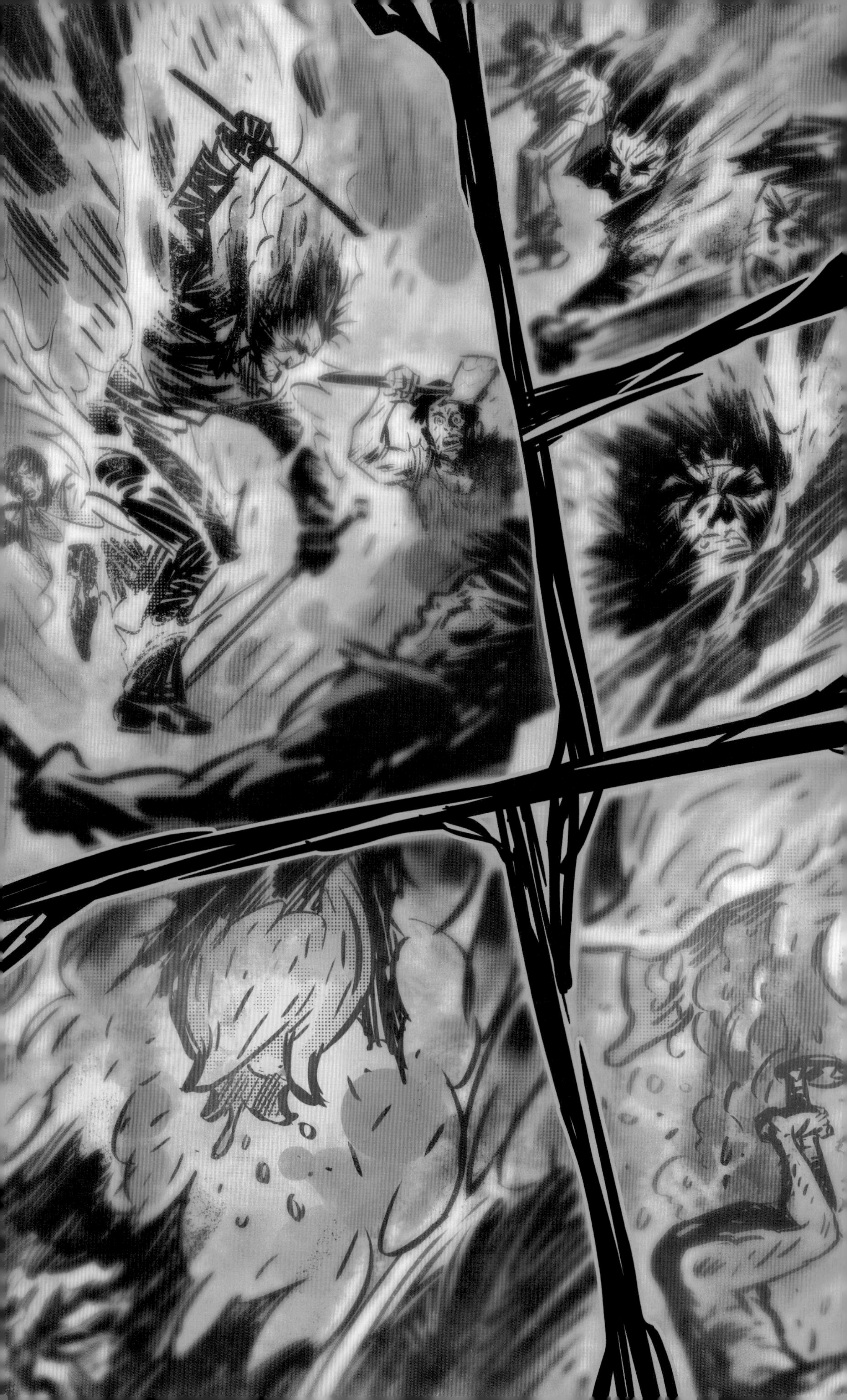

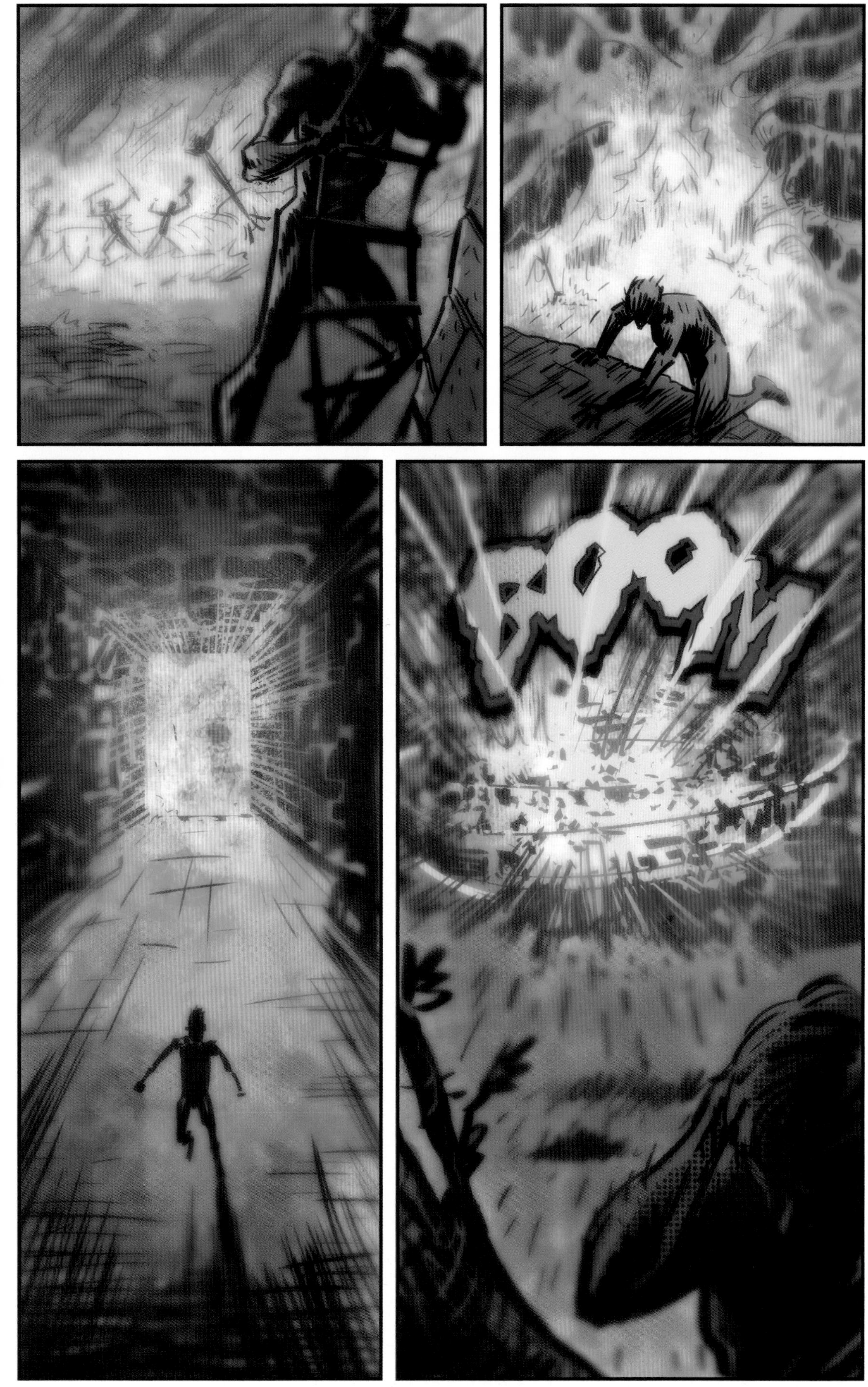
BOOM

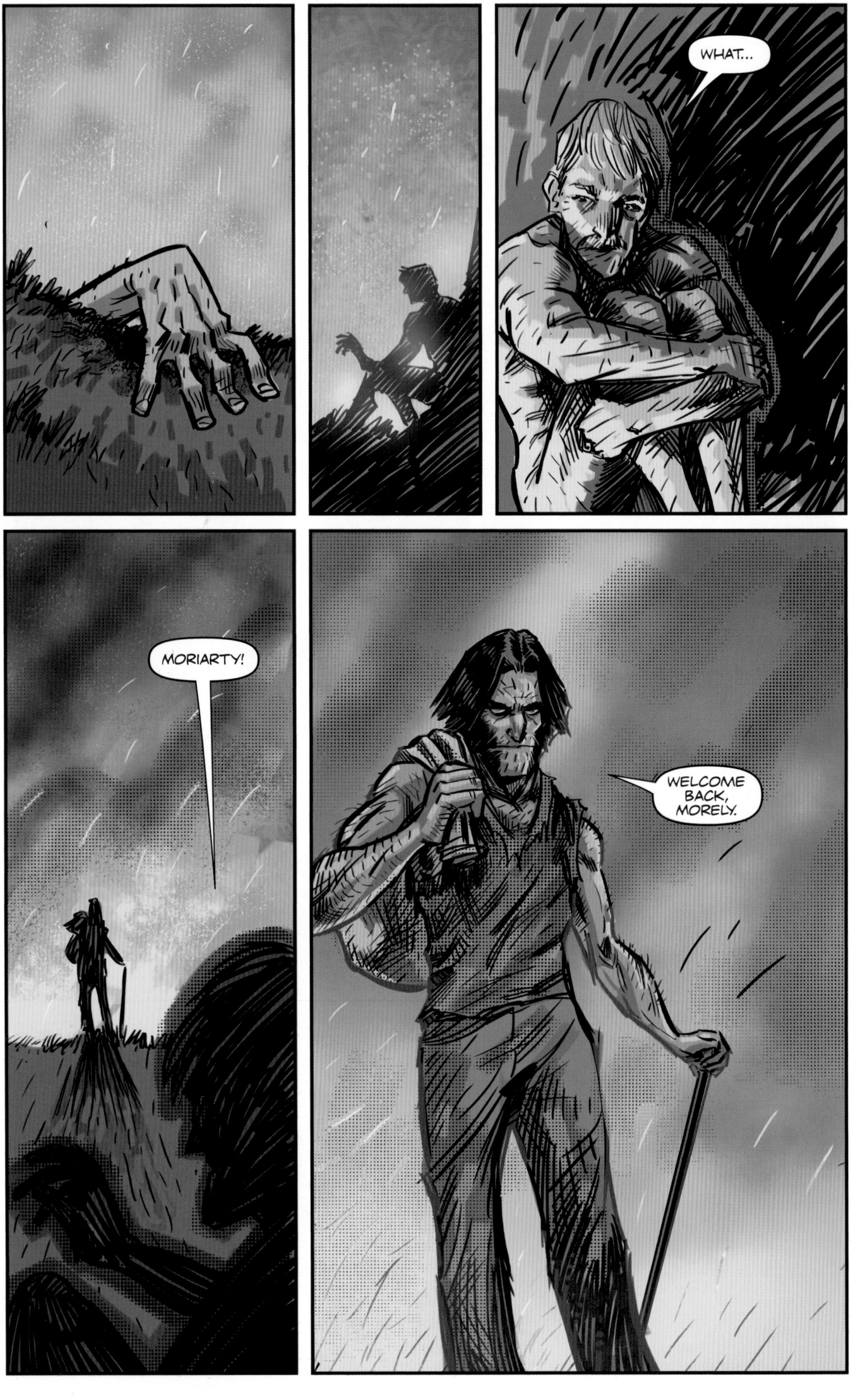
WHAT...
MORIARTY!
WELCOME BACK, MORELY.

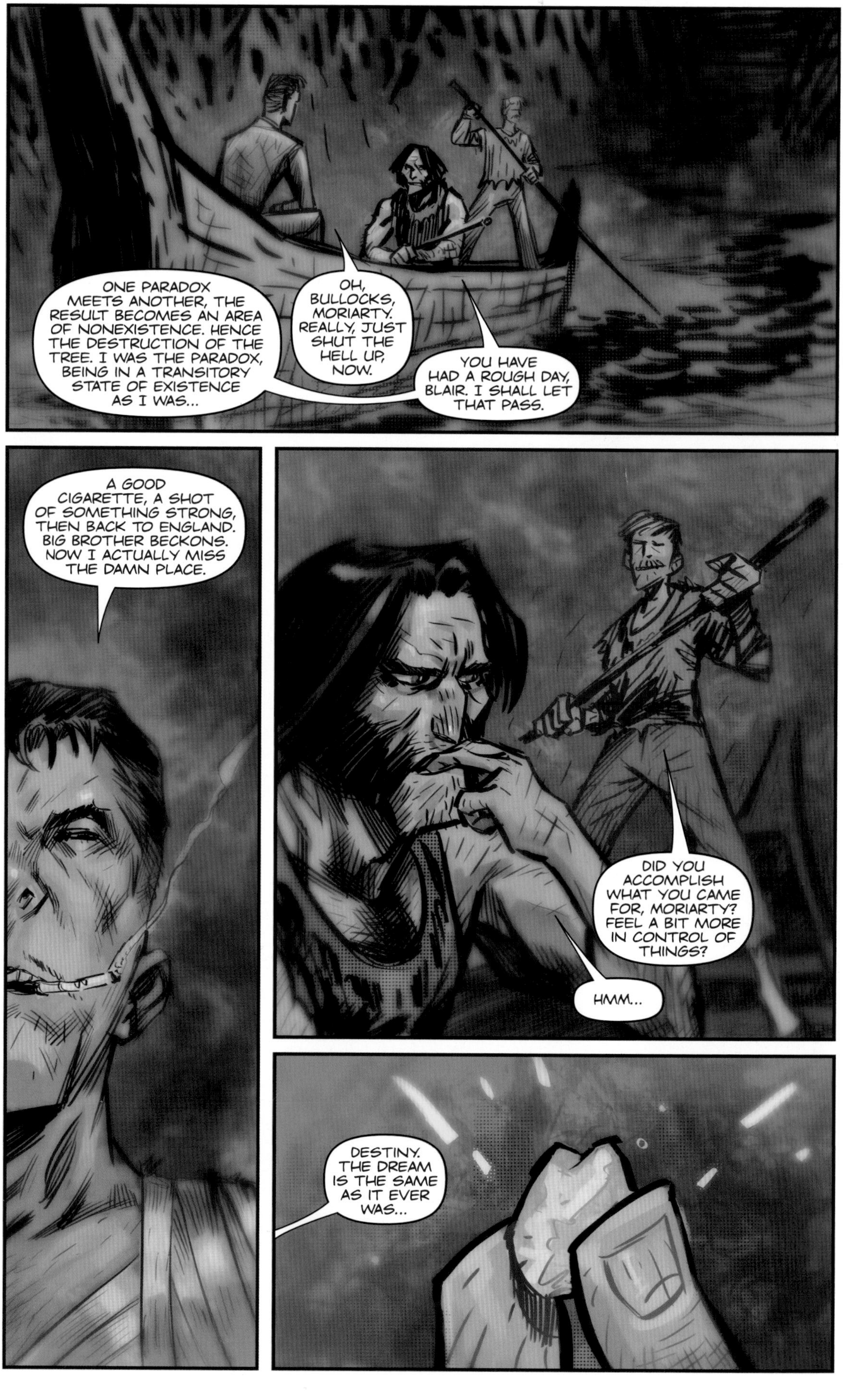
ONE PARADOX MEETS ANOTHER, THE RESULT BECOMES AN AREA OF NONEXISTENCE. HENCE THE DESTRUCTION OF THE TREE. I WAS THE PARADOX, BEING IN A TRANSITORY STATE OF EXISTENCE AS I WAS...
OH, BULLOCKS, MORIARTY. REALLY, JUST SHUT THE HELL UP, NOW.
YOU HAVE HAD A ROUGH DAY, BLAIR. I SHALL LET THAT PASS.
A GOOD CIGARETTE, A SHOT OF SOMETHING STRONG, THEN BACK TO ENGLAND. BIG BROTHER BECKONS. NOW I ACTUALLY MISS THE DAMN PLACE.
DID YOU ACCOMPLISH WHAT YOU CAME FOR, MORIARTY? FEEL A BIT MORE IN CONTROL OF THINGS?
HMM...
DESTINY. THE DREAM IS THE SAME AS IT EVER WAS...

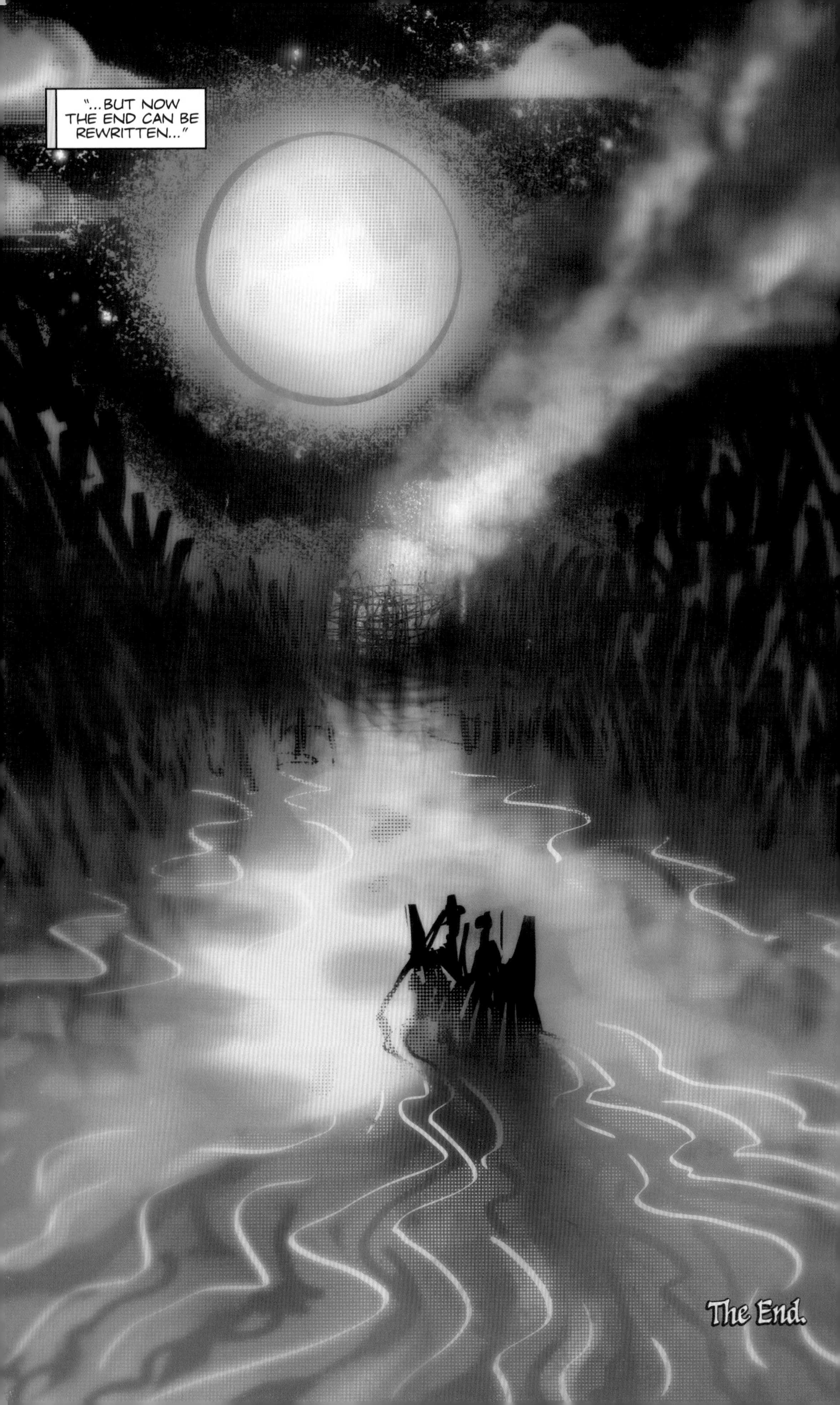
"...BUT NOW THE END CAN BE REWRITTEN..."
The End.

STEP BY STEP IPAD SPEED PAINTING BY
ANTHONY "ARTOFANT" DIECIDUE

YUP, I LIKE TO START WITH THE EYES OFTEN.

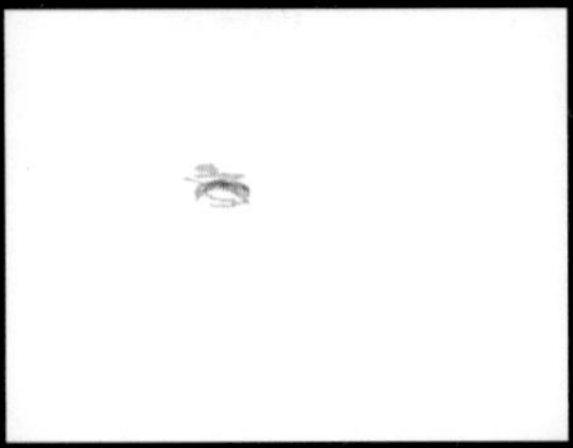

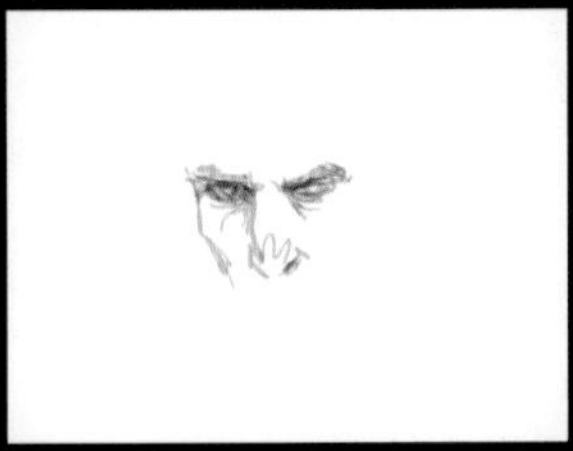

I WORK MY WAY DOWN THE FACE.

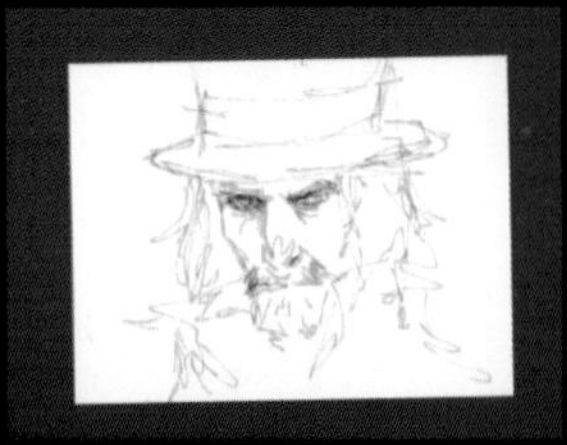

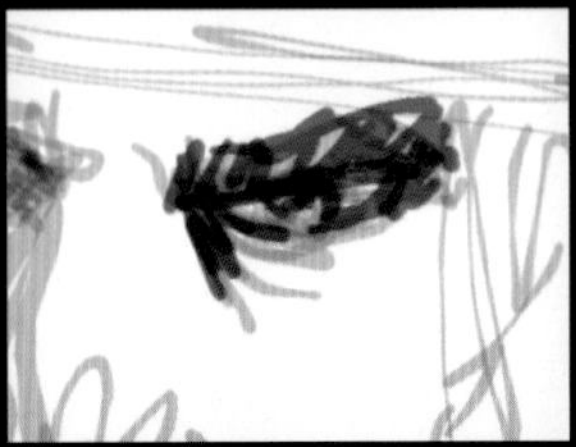

I GET IN CLOSE FOR EYE DETAILS.

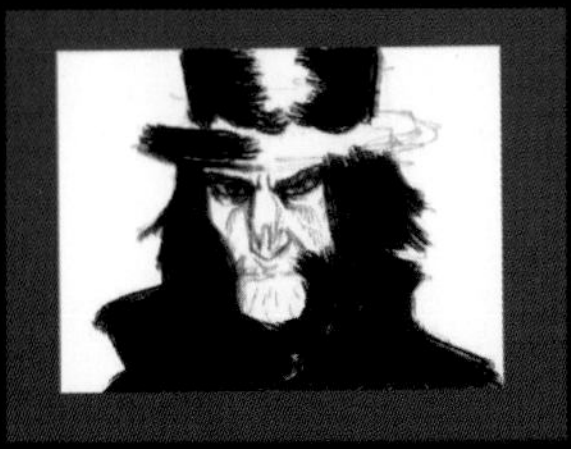

SPOTTING BLACKS.

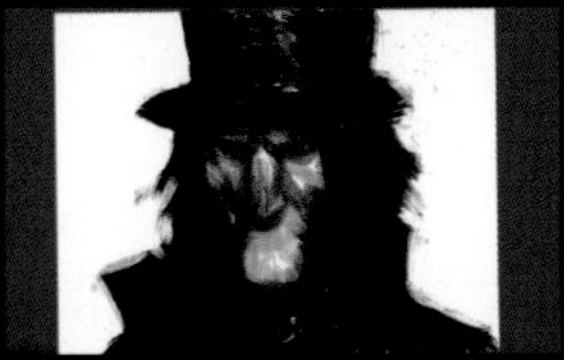

GETTING GREY...

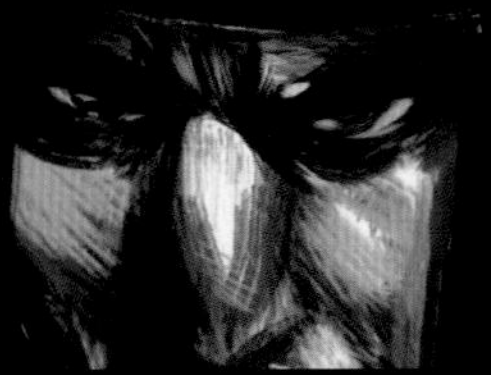

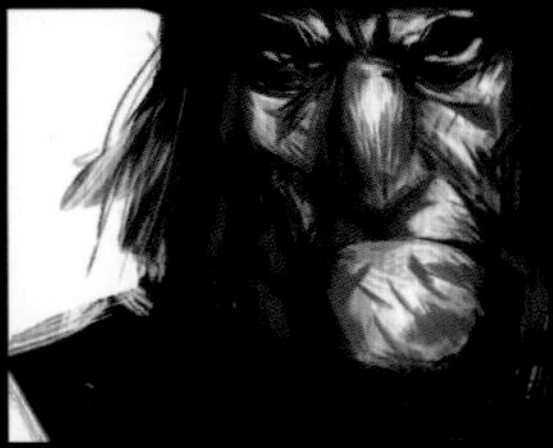

SLOPPY GREYS.

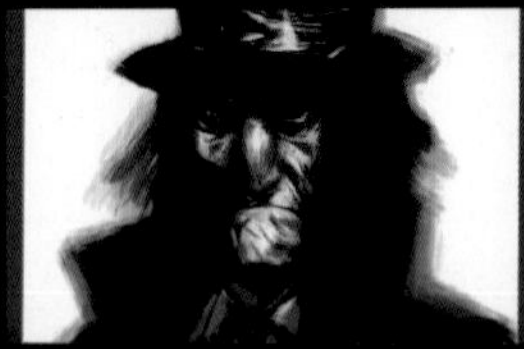

SOFTENING EDGES TO DIRECT FOCUS.

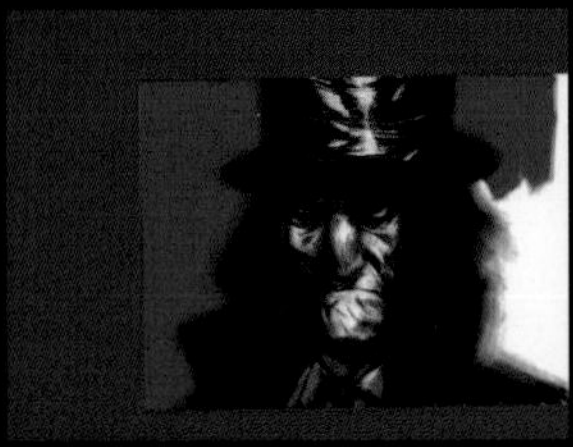

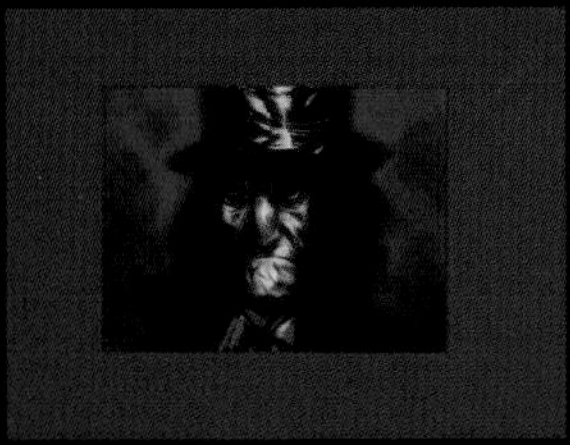

RED TO MAKE THINGS *POP!*

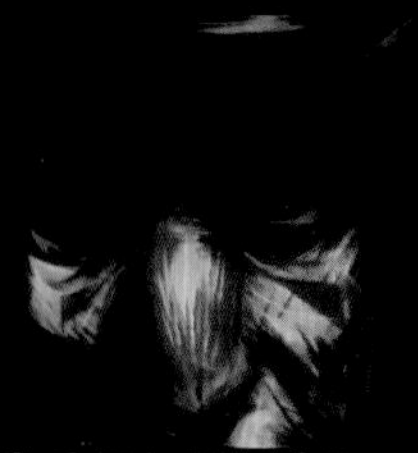

FLESH TONES AND DETAILS.

A DIM LIGHT IN THE EYES.

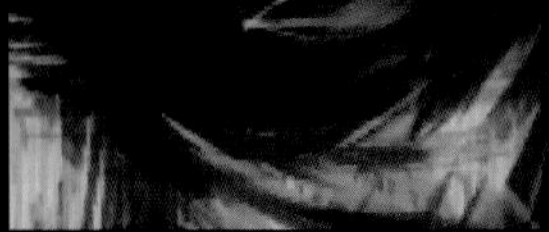

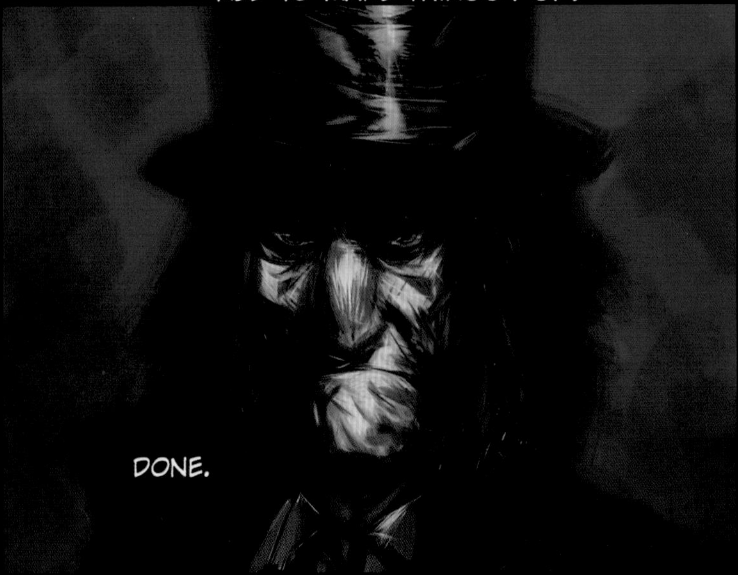

DONE.

COMMISSION PIN-UP
(FOR A VERY PATIENT FAN)

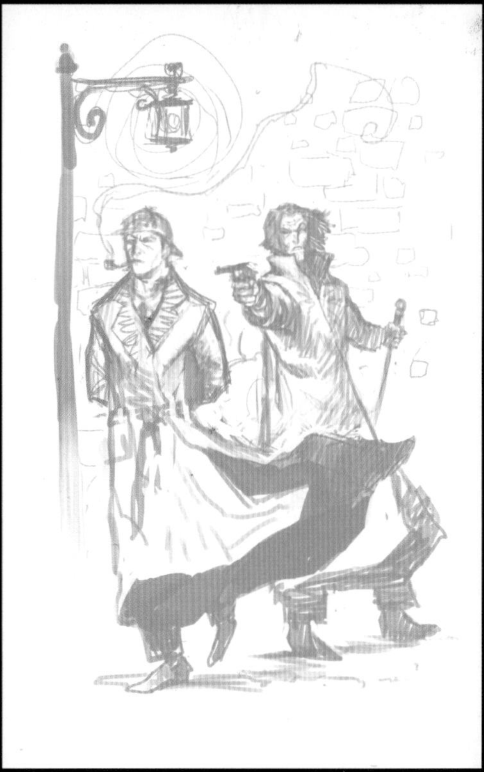

EARLY SKETCH WITH PHOTOSHOP. I DIDN'T THINK SHOOTING HOLMES IN THE BACK WAS M'S STYLE.

THIS WORKED MUCH BETTER! BUT I WASN'T FEELING THE INKS.

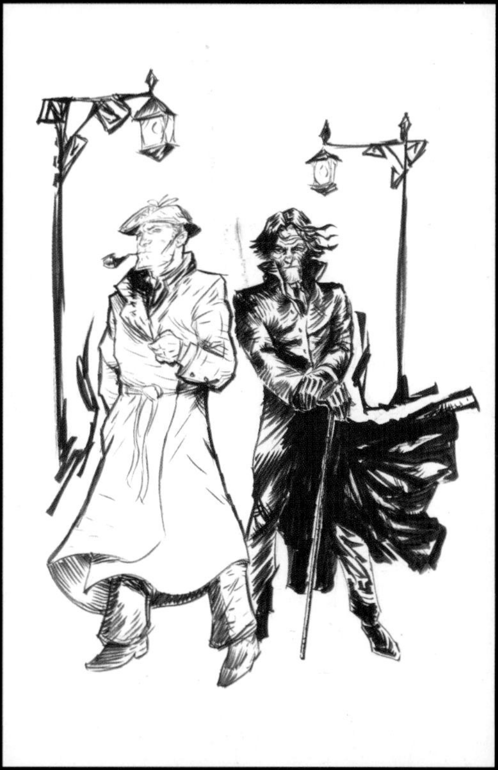

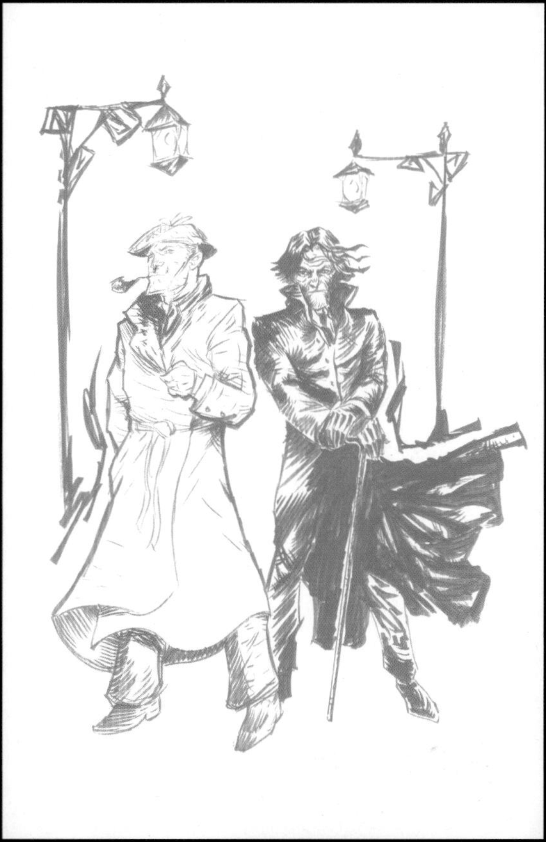

I SCANNED IN THE INKS, CHANGED THE COLOR AND PRINTED IT OUT.

THEN I RE-INKED AND USED COPICS, WATERCOLOR AND COLORED PENCIL TO FINISH IT UP!

CHECK OUT THE FINAL VERSION IN THE GALLERY SECTION. HOPE YOU DIGGIT!

A FEW INK AND WATERCOLOR COMMISSIONS OF SOME CHARACTERS FROM *MORIARTY: THE DARK CHAMBER.*

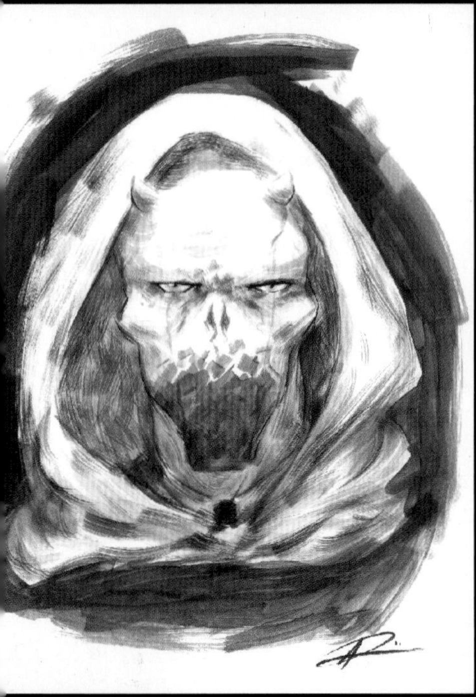

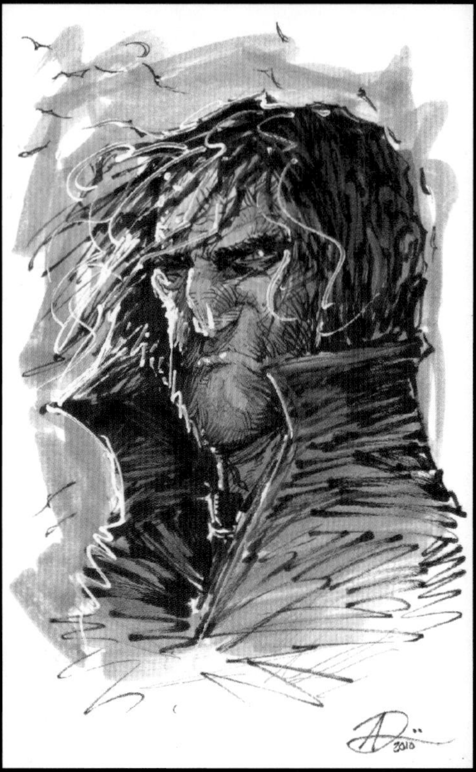

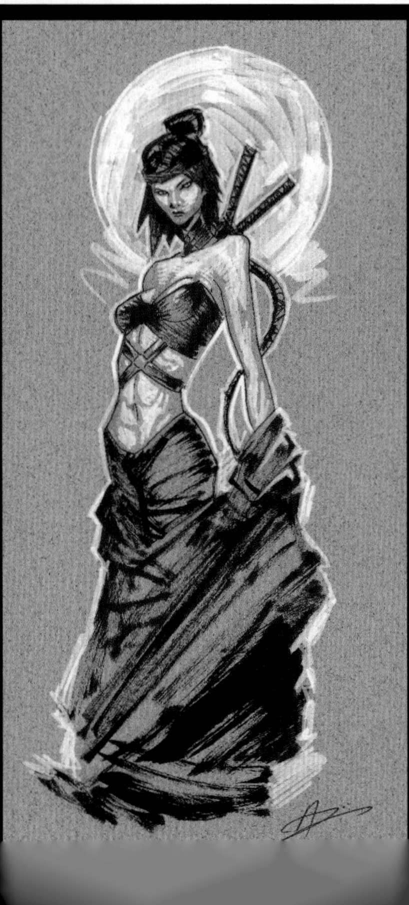

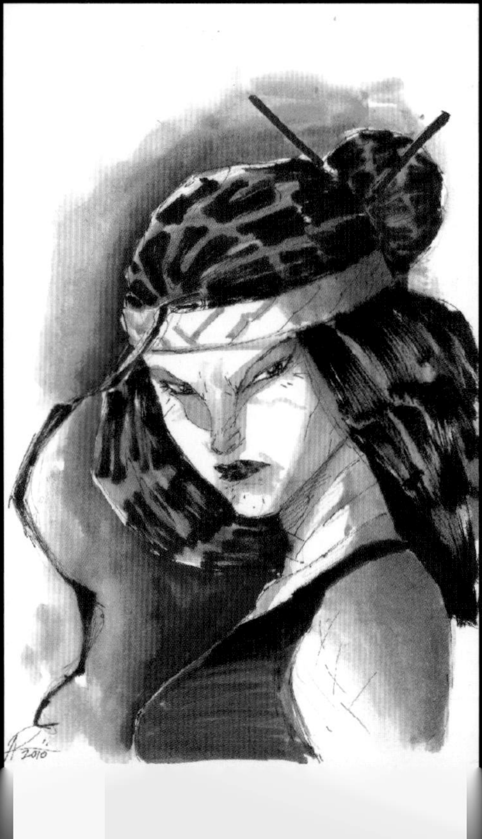

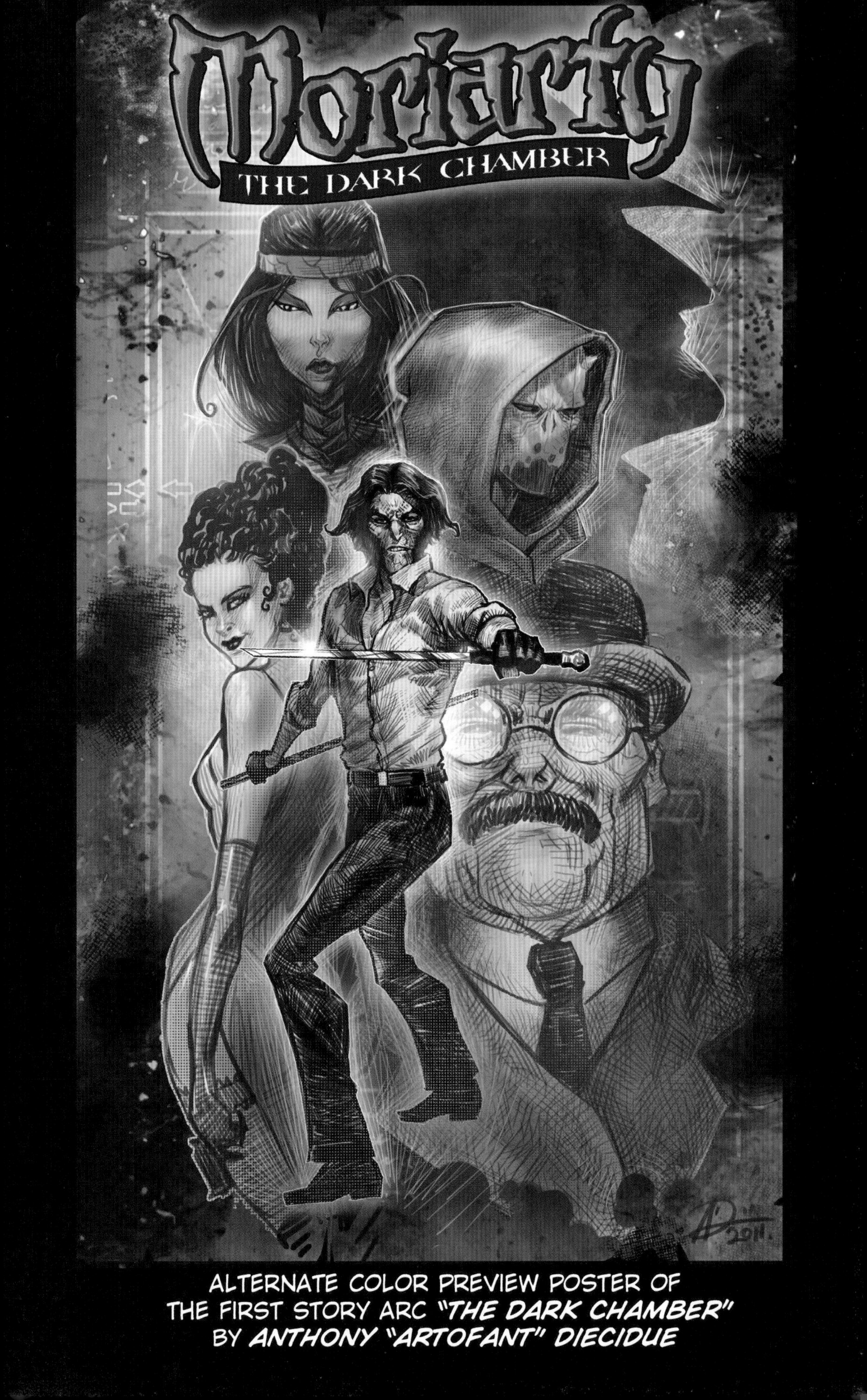
Moriarty
THE DARK CHAMBER

ALTERNATE COLOR PREVIEW POSTER OF
THE FIRST STORY ARC *"THE DARK CHAMBER"*
BY ***ANTHONY "ARTOFANT" DIECIDUE***

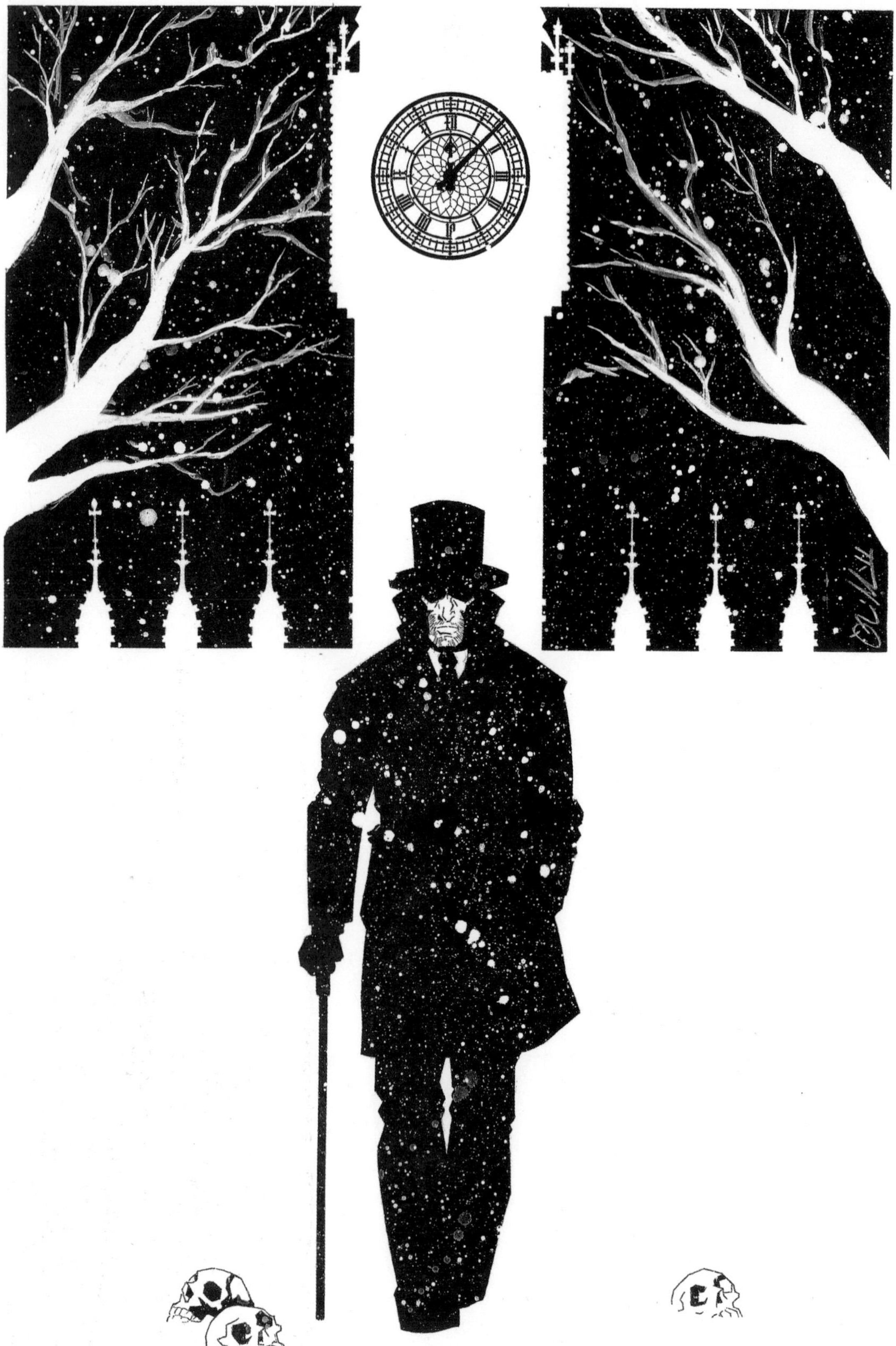

Pinup by Bill O'Neill

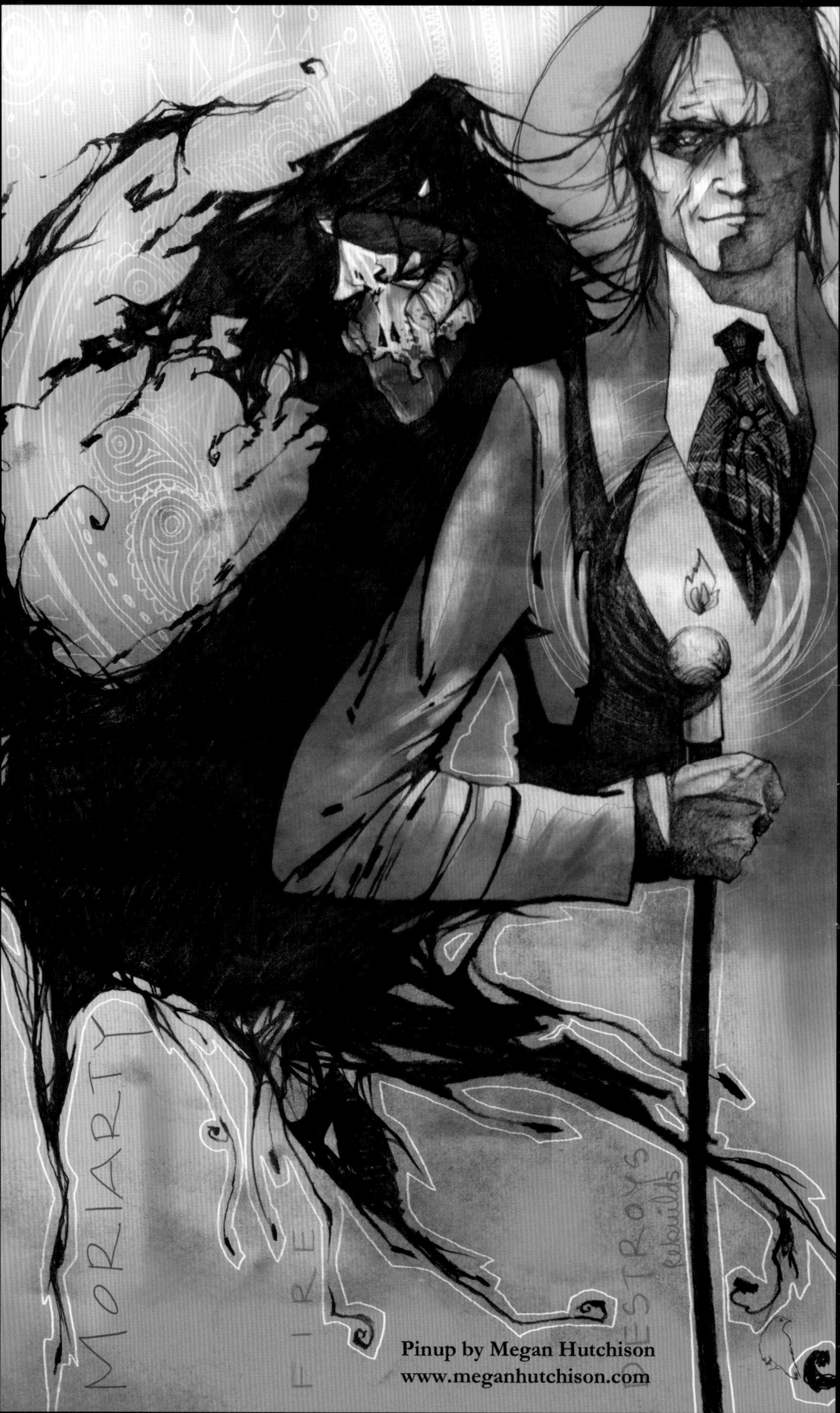
MORIARTY
FIRE
DESTROYS
rebuilds

Pinup by Megan Hutchison
www.meganhutchison.com

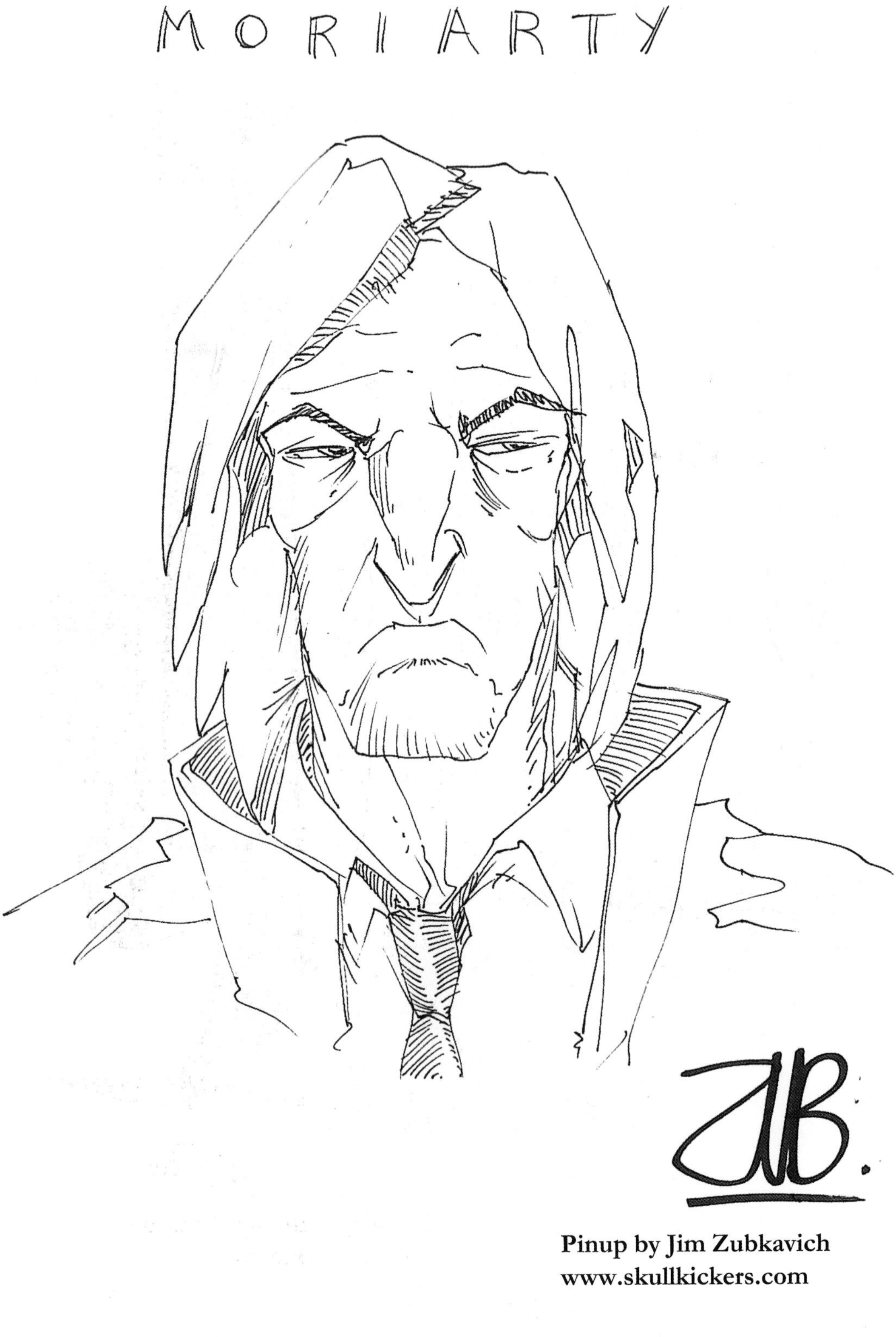
MORIARTY

Pinup by Jim Zubkavich
www.skullkickers.com

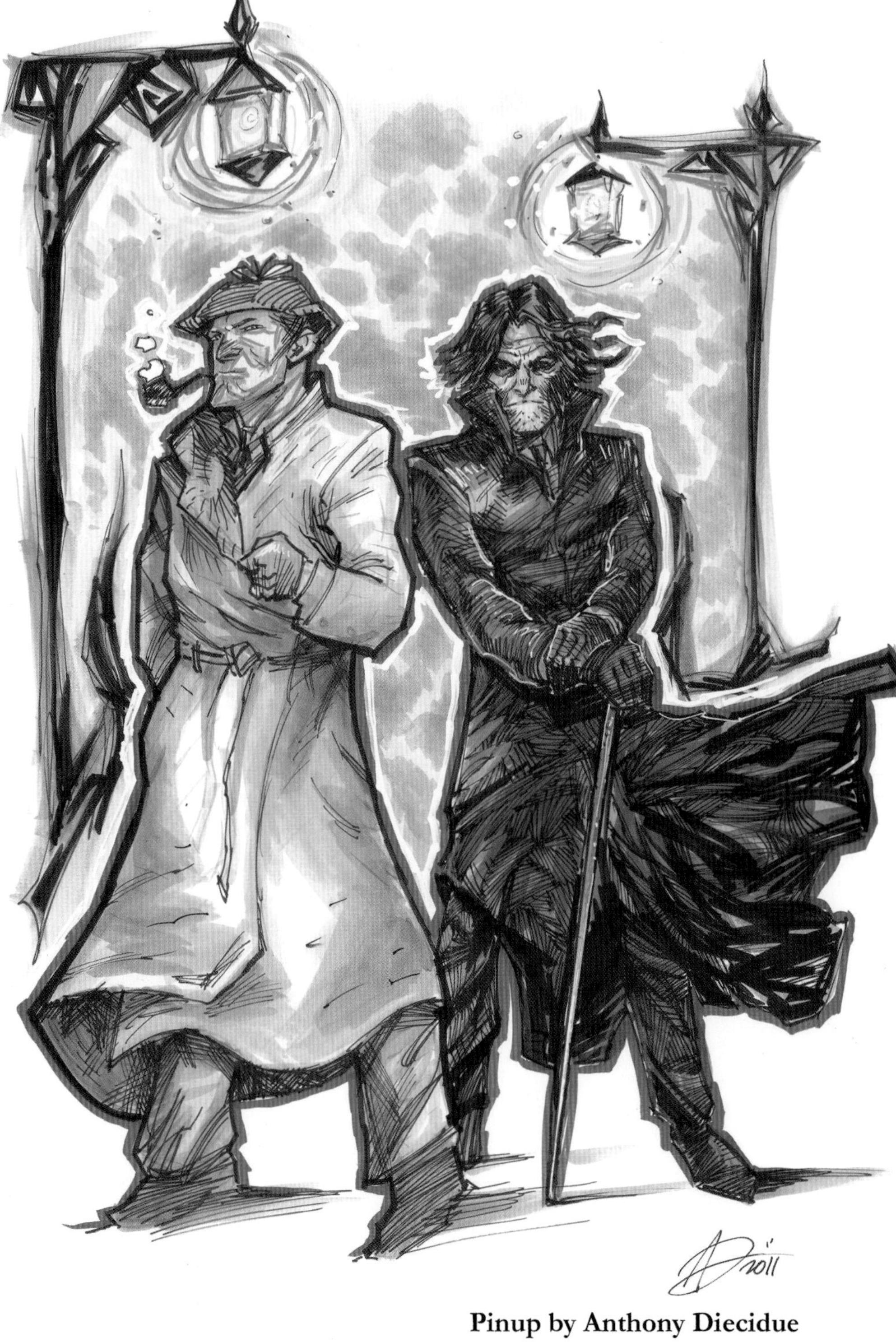

Pinup by Anthony Diecidue
www.artofant.com

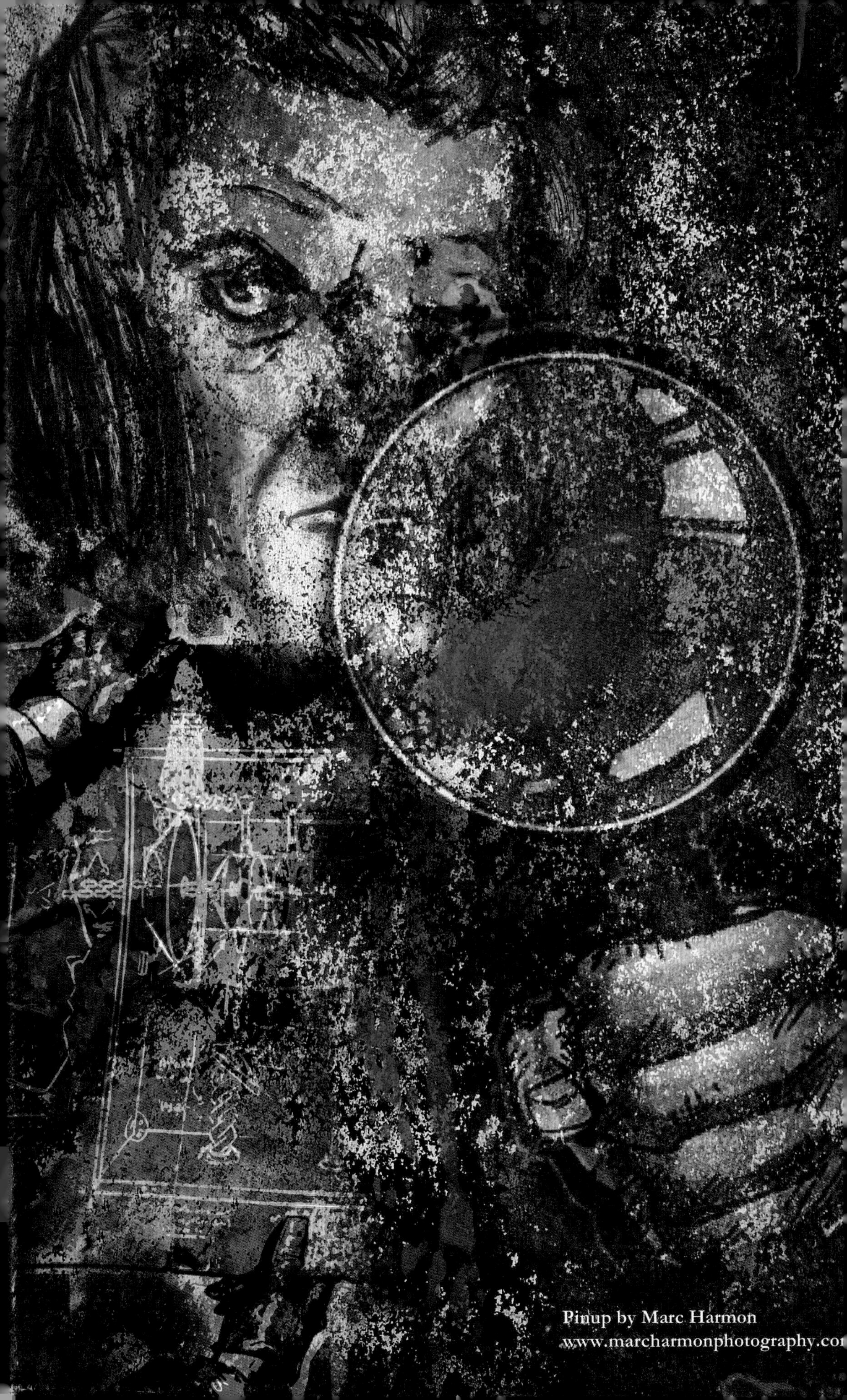

Pinup by Marc Harmon
www.marcharmonphotography.co